THE GOC

THE
GOOD
ENEMY

Taken from the original war diaries of

JAMES LESLIE
HUTCHINSON

(Transcribed by Richard Hutchinson)

Typeset in Galliard
Design, typesetting and publishing by
UK Book Publishing www.ukbookpublishing.com

ISBN: 978-1-913179-94-6

CONTENTS

PHOTOGRAPHS AND ILLUSTRATIONS

PREFACE

During my father's service in the Royal Air Force, from 1940 to 1945, he penned a diary recording his daily experiences.

Voyaging from Gourock on the River Clyde to Port Suez in Egypt via Freetown, Sierra Leone, and Durban, South Africa, he was stationed as a wireless operator in the Egyptian desert, transferred to duties in Cyprus and returned to the Egyptian desert for a second posting where he was captured by Rommel's army.

The remainder of World War II was spent in Prisoner of War camps in Brindisi and Modena in Italy, followed by confinements in Muhlberg and Chemnitz in Germany as a result of the take-over of Italy by the Germans in 'Operation Achse'.

The diaries, documents, photographs, medals and press cuttings had been in the safe keeping of my mother who bequeathed these to me upon her death in 2012 in the hope that I would transcribe the memoirs for publication. My father had intended to have them published, and indeed he started to re-write them, however my mother said that he abandoned this early on since the memories were too painful to recount.

My father's death was sudden and devastating. He was with his life-long friend, Peter Squires (whom he met on active service), whilst walking to the local football pitches to watch me play when he suffered a fatal heart attack.

He was a placid, thoughtful, caring, measured man who we all relied on for advise and support. Mine, my sister's and my mother's lives have been permanently affected by his passing. He was without doubt the nicest human being I have ever had the good fortune to know, and more, to be able to say he was my Dad.

I have taken a long time to summon the courage to read through his war diaries, no one likes to read about the hardship and suffering endured by a loved one, however I was encouraged by my wife to do so, I was also curious to know the details of this episode in my father's life which he would not disclose or recount whilst he was alive. Perhaps he was protecting us from the unpleasant details, or maybe they were too painful for him to re-live. I do know from reading the daily accounts, especially those after his release, that there were lasting psychological effects as a result of his experiences.

As you may expect, some of the daily accounts are repetitive and monotonous – just imagine what it must have been like having to live through them. There was a good deal of focus on where the next meal would come from and if it would be sufficient to maintain the degree of nutrition required to be able to complete a day's hard labour. We take for granted our 'daily bread', my father was 11 stones in weight leaving for duty, my mother told me that he was a little over six stones when he returned from service overseas.

My mother managed to gain some details by conversing with my father's friends and left me a letter, of which I knew nothing before her death, this included some information not noted in the diaries.

"Very little food and drink. A few times sections of prisoners had to dig their own graves with a firing squad behind, guns were fired. All were surprised that they were still alive, had to fill in the graves and return to camp. This happened more than once, all thought there would be a time when their name would be up. Red Cross parcels were sent out to them, many never arrived as the guards confiscated them. Some of the duties they were put on don't bare mentioning".

The following account has been transcribed in my father's own words, not mine. I have the original diaries which survived the rigours of the war

and are, in the main, perfectly legible with the exception of a few days –
I think these sections may have endured some of the weather my father
had to, and are illegible now.

For clarity I have included some route maps and pinpointed some
of the places mentioned in the diaries, also included are a selection of
photographs.

This book is a tribute to, and is dedicated to the memory of, a truly
wonderful man who endured so much when so young but complained
so little and who made everyone's life all the better for knowing him. I'll
never forget you, thanks for being my Dad, rest in peace my friend and
father.

Your loving son,
Richard.

James Leslie Hutchinson

AC1 1303999

Prisoner of War
Intrepid Against All
Adversity

1939–1945
War Medal

1939–1945
Star

Africa
Star

ENGLAND

1940

JULY 17

Joined RAF at Blackpool July 17th for training as wireless operator. Failed medical for air crew through eyesight. Plenty of drill and morse reception (4 hrs of each per day). Managed to get home every other weekend.

OCTOBER 11

Went to Compton Basset, Wilts, for more intensive training. Terribly dismal camp, eight and a half hours morse and technical instruction each day. Saturday half day, Sunday free. Hitchhiked to Bath for a few weekends, otherwise a very miserable time was had by all. Had two months infra-red treatment for my feet which gave me more trouble than somewhat.

DECEMBER 24

Passed out as a wireless operator, my pal, Leslie Jordan, failed and so has to do a fortnight's further training.

DECEMBER 27

Was sent on leave for the first time since joining up, 14 days embarkation leave as we are almost certain to be sent to Egypt. Weighed just over 11 stone on leaving Compton, having got rather fat and sluggish.

1941

WEDS JANUARY 1

Went with Harry to Bill Bulcock's and played records all evening, the volume all but bringing the house down about our ears.

SAT JANUARY 4

Went to a party at Bill Bulcock's and had quite a gay evening. Slept at Aunty Janey's.

SUN JANUARY 5

Harold came over from Manchester. Slept the night at Harry's.

MON JANUARY 6

Went to see Aunty Sally and in the evening to the Odeon with Alice and Harry.

TUES JANUARY 7

In the morning went to Communion with mother. Played billiards with Harry in the afternoon. Went to Victoria at night with Jean and Harry to see "Die Fleidermaus".

WEDS JANUARY 8

Went to Aunty Alice's and then to Evelyn's. Granville was at home on embarkation leave.

THURS JANUARY 9

Harry came in the evening and we had gramophone recital.

FRID JANUARY 10

Reported to RAF Wilmslow. Usual dismal camp, damp barracks.

SAT JANUARY 11

Was issued with tropical kit. Got a pile of junk to carry around now. Two kit bags, pack with two blankets and ground sheet attached, side pack, gas mask etc.

SUN JANUARY 12

Confined to camp for stretcher bearer duties.

MON JANUARY 13

On coal fatigues.

TUES JANUARY 14

Dodged fatigues and played table tennis in the N.A.F.F.I. At night went to free concert in Wilmslow. Not so good.

WEDS JANUARY 15

Rumours of 80 home postings. I think it is a load of bullsh' personally.

Thurs January 16

80 names called out to join a draft at West Drayton. My name was next to the last.

Frid January 17

Saw the list of postings for West Drayton. My name was with these more as reserves.

Sat January 18

Arrived at West Drayton. Not a bad place apart from the fact that there was a small pile of snow in the middle of the bedroom. Went to cinema in west Drayton at night. Robert Taylor, Vivien Leigh in "Waterloo Bridge".

Sun January 19

Can't get any gen at this place. Our corporal says we won't get any more leave. Looks as though we've had it.

Mon January 20

Appears that we are going to be on wireless mobile units. Went to a show in camp in the evening. A portrayal of Dicken's characters. Very enjoyable.

Tues January 21

Given a lecture on our job i.e. Wireless Intelligence Screen. We will be sent out on posts of six men each to screen aerodromes etc. sending wireless plots of enemy air or ground activity to Fighter H.Q.

WEDS JANUARY 22

Went to cinema in West Drayton. "Way of All Flesh". Not bad.

THURS JANUARY 23

Again went to cinema. "Foreign Correspondent". Herbert Marshall, George Sanders, Joel Melsea. Very good.

FRID JANUARY 24

Optimism increases regarding leave.

SAT JANUARY 25

Had a morse test in the morning. Went to Hebridge in the evening and saw "Pastor Hall" at the Odeon.

SUN JANUARY 26

Got our passes for 4 days embarkation leave.

MON JANUARY 27

Started the journey for home at 11.30 a.m. and arrived at 10.30 p.m. to the surprise of everyone. Mother was writing to me.

TUES JANUARY 28

In the afternoon went for walk with Harry around Heasandford and in the evening played Billiards with him at home. Afterwards went to Harry's house for supper.

WEDS JANUARY 29

Took Mother for a short walk in the afternoon. Took Auntie Jane to Tivoli at night. "Night Train to Munich"

THURS JANUARY 30

Went to Harry's for tea. Harold came over from Whitefield.

FRID JANUARY 31

Saw Harold off on the 8.50 a.m. train. After playing some of my favourite gramophone records I departed by the 7.40 p.m. Alice and Harry seeing me off.

SAT FEB 1

Arrived at West Drayton at 8.15 a.m. I was late but nothing was said. Arrived in with Bernard Scholfield. Bernard, Pete, Willie and myself went to cinema in Hebridge in the evening.

SUN FEB 2

Two lists of men leaving on Monday and Tuesday. I am in the left overs.

MON FEB 3

The first party containing Peter and Bernard left today.

TUES FEB 4

Was going to go to cinema tonight but decided to see off my friends in no.2 party. They were ready to leave, the roll was called and my name came at the end of the list. One of the originals had fallen ill and I had been added to the list, Sergeant Black omitting to tell me. I packed hurriedly and we departed by train for post unknown.

RAF Service Book

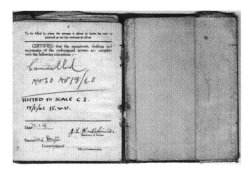

GOUROCK TO FREETOWN

(1ST LEG – 22 DAYS)

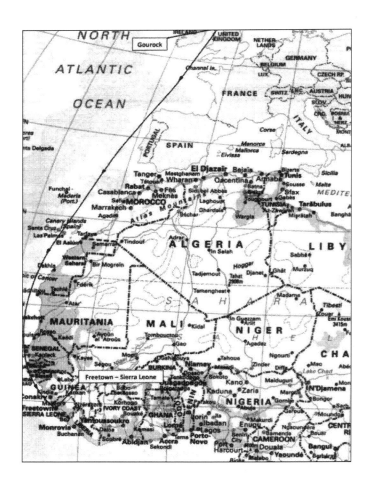

WEDS FEB 5

Journey was broken at Newcastle
where we got a cup of tea. We arrived
at Gourock where it was cold and
raining. After much delay and hanging
about we were conveyed by steamer
to the "Rangitata". Eventually, frozen
and wet through, we got on board.

RMS Rangitata

My mess deck is fourth deck down,
the bottom in fact; 126 of us are crowded in this small room where
we eat and sleep. There is not enough room for everyone to sleep in
hammocks and I slept on the floor. The atmosphere was terrible at
night.

THURS FEB 6

Conditions on board are just about murder. We are herded together like
pigs and the food distribution is terribly disorganised, the mess orderlies
have to queue hours for food, tea etc. The officers have sumptuous
lounges and are waited on hand and foot, getting unbelievable luxuries.
Fighting for democracy!!!

FRID FEB 7

There are 80 R.A.F. on board together with over 2,000 R.A's and
marines and French Colonial troops.

SAT FEB 8

Steamed out of port 10.30 p.m. Very uncomfortable sleeping on the
deck due to rolling of the ship and vibration of the engine.

Sun Feb 9

Was violently sick after dinner, due to either the fatty pork, the rough
sea or the stale musty smell on the mess deck.

Mon Feb 10

Was sick again in the morning, the smell of sweat, vomit and foul air
down below is enough to make a dog sick. Badly sea-sick chaps are
sprawled all over the passages and mess decks. Was on canteen fatigue
all morning, carrying boxes of minerals etc. from the hold up to the
top deck. Stayed on deck most of the day, couldn't face the smell down
below at night so Peter and I tried to sleep on deck using chairs to
shelter from the gale. Very cold and didn't get much sleep, but still
preferable to the mess deck.

Tues Feb 11

I was on canteen fatigues again. I only went down to our mess deck
for tea.

Weds Feb 12

Felt very well again today. Sea rough, cruisers and destroyers bouncing
about like corks. I did 4 2hr spells of sentry duty, wearing M.P.
armbands.

Thurs Feb 13

P.T. and rifle drill under a marine sergeant. Very smart chap.

FRID FEB 14

P.T. and rifle drill again. Weather bitter cold, slept in hammock down below. Wake up feeling drugged and inert.

SAT FEB 15

Vigorous P.T. in the morning, afternoon free. H.M.S. Rodney joined the convoy which consists of about 40 boats, troop carriers and cargo boats.

SUN FEB 16

Attended the ship's Church service in the morning.

MON FEB 17

We have an inspection parade every morning, generally carried out by that young fool P.O. Henley. Aircraft carrier and two cruisers joined the convoy. I feel very fit now.

TUES FEB 18

Our aircraft carrier is the Ark Royal which the Germans claim to have sunk on many occasions.

WEDS FEB 19

Today the Rodney left us and we were joined by the Renown.

HMS Ark Royal

HMS Rodney

HMS Renown

THURS FEB 20

Very nice day today. Very warm below. Our mess orderly, Ted Wilmott, sweats copiously and some of it, alas, goes into the food.

FRID FEB 21

Weather still good. More rifle dill. Wrote letters. All night flashes of light can be seen in the wake of the ship due to the electrical disturbances in the water. Very intriguing.

SAT FEB 22

My regular fatigue is deck sweeping, which is done five times a day. Not as bad as being mess orderly whose work is never done.

SUN FEB 23

Horrible smell of cat piss on the mess deck on awakening. Not a pleasant start to the day at all. Went to the Church service.

MON FEB 24

We were given a lecture by Free French officer on desert conditions, scorpions and all that. At dinnertime the orderly officer pronounced the meat as 'quite definitely bad' – the M.O. suggested a puree.

TUES FEB 25

Saw shoals of flying fish in the morning; glistening in the sun they make quite a spectacle. Bayonet drill in the afternoon.

Weds Feb 26

Weather is so warm that we changed into tropical kit. Listened to news for the first time. Anthony Eden in Turkey.

Thurs Feb 27

Played deck hockey in afternoon and scored three goals. Very warm work.

Frid Feb 28

Weather very warm and meals very unsuitable e.g. breakfast – minced meat, dinner – corned beef, tea – brown curried stew. Sickening.

Sun March 2

Came in sight of land this morning. Quite a thrill. It appeared, at first, as a high, dark rugged outline. The view on entering the harbour was very impressive; the port, Freetown, consisting of small dwelling places which seemed to be inset in the folding hills of very green vegetation. Before entering the harbour we were met by small naval craft but on becoming stationary we were surrounded by natives in long narrow skiffs, some containing fruit, a lively barter for which, taking place. The natives amuse me exceedingly; their English is quite adequate for their needs and their ability to swear effectively is more than adequate. They are very merry and those wearing bowler hats or trilbies definitely consider themselves infinitely superior to the others. Their skill in diving for pennies is only exceeded by their skill in diving for sixpences. One of the natives called Charlie claims to be an Englishman, he paddles around the ship all day exchanging amusing banter with us, and just to prove that he is a superior type, he throws oranges on deck in return for the pennies for which he dives. In the evening it is quite enchanting to see the twinkling lights from the mainland and what appear to be mysterious fairy lights floating on the surface of the water, but which in fact are motor boats visiting the different ships.

MON MARCH 3

We were forbidden to buy fruit today due to the lads bartering kippers, corned beef and other ship's stores to the natives yesterday.

TUE MARCH 4

Trading resumed. I got 13 oranges for 6d and 6 bananas for 3d. Prices going up. Only officers are allowed to visit the mainland.

WEDS MARCH 5

Natives are a source of constant amusement; they are however very cute businessmen.

THURS MARCH 6

Was admonished by P.O. Henley for having what he termed as a hefty growth. Bought more bananas.

FRID MARCH 7

Managed to get 15 bananas for 6d today. There are only two names used between us and the natives; we call them Charlie and Sam, and they reciprocate by calling us Sam or Charlie.

DEPART FREETOWN BOUND FOR DURBAN, SOUTH AFRICA

(2ND LEG – 18 DAYS)

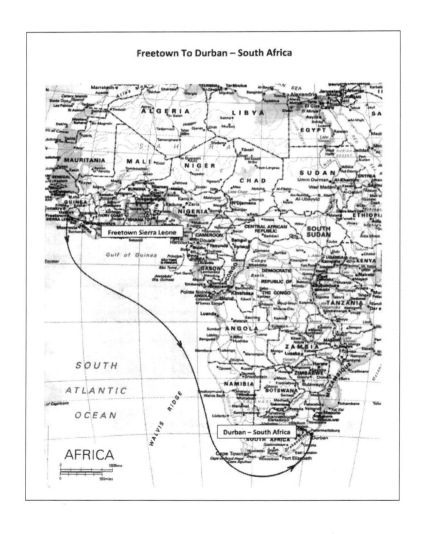

SAT MARCH 8

We steamed out of Freetown harbour at dinnertime. The natives followed us as far as they could in their skiffs waving goodbye. Sorry to see the last of them.

SUN MARCH 9

Went to the ship's service. It was very hot at night and I couldn't sleep.

MON MARCH 10

Sergeant king chose Peter and myself for police duties. He has got his knife into us possibly because we take few pains to conceal our dislike for him. I was on duty 8 a.m. – 12.30 p.m. and 8 p.m. – 12. p.m.

TUE MARCH 11

Police duty 12 a.m. – 4 p.m. meals are very haphazard on this job. If you happen to be a little late off duty there is very little left to eat.

WED MARCH 12

On duty 12 p.m. – 4 a.m. and 4 p.m. – 8 p.m. On night duty we get a cup of cocoa which invariably puts us to sleep. The corporal of the guard is pretty decent and wakens us all up just before the orderly officer comes around. We were given a very crude lecture on precautions against V.D. today by a medical orderly.

Thurs March 13

Crossed the Equator today. I managed to dodge the ducking ceremony by the skin of my teeth. The officers were given specially sever attention. I was mess orderly today; terrible job; consists of queuing up for food for an hour or so, dishing it out to the twenty chaps on the table, washing up, cleaning table and walls and sweeping up.

Frid March 14

My 21st birthday. Opened Mother's letter with card – a very nice idea. I was on police duty in the hold 8 a.m. – 12.30 p.m. and 8 p.m. – 12 p.m.. Very warm down here and abounding with flies.

Dear Leslie,

Today is a great day in your life, for it is now that you reach full manhood. You have, from the first day of your birth, been a great joy to your Mother and Dad. We also hope that we too have given that duty, each in our own way, smiling, yes, I say smiling through, helping others to do the same, a word of comfort here and a kindly act there, all united in one great effort for world peace and goodness, then of course happiness will follow. Now, Dear Les, there will be a present on the piano. Happiness which is the right of every true son. Distance will make our love the stronger, and the day will come, when we all join together once again, and with Music and laughter, make merry in the dear old way. We will in the meantime, all do ours and we will say from our hearts, 'God bless you now and for ever'

Many Happy Returns.

Your loving Mother & Dad.

March 14th
1941
Dear Leslie —
To day is a great day
in your life, for it is
now that you reach
full manhood.
You have, from the first
day of your birth, been
a great joy to your
Mother & dad.
We also, hope that we
too, have given that

Page 1

duty, each in our own
way, smiling, yes, I say
smiling through; helping
others to do the same,
a word of comfort here,
& a kindly act there,
all united in one great
effort for world peace,
& goodness, then of course,
happiness will follow.
Now, Dear Les, there will
be a present or the like. Piano

Page 2

happiness which is the
right of every true son
Distance will make
our love the stronger,
& the day will come,
when we all join
together once again,
& with Music & laughter,
make merry in the
dear old way.
We will in the
meantime, all do our

Page 3

We will say from
our hearts —
" God bless you
now, & for ever "
—

Many Happy Returns.
Your loving Mother &
dad .

Page 4

Sat March 15

Passed into the 4th round of the draughts competition by beating Ted Lewis the Wolverhampton loud mouth. On guard 12.30 – 4 p.m. This police job is doing me a lot of no good, due to lack of sleep.

Sun March 16

On duty 12 p.m. – 4 a.m. and 4 p.m. – 8 p.m. Weather is getting a bit cooler.

Mon March 17

On duty 4 – 8 a.m. and 8 – 12 p.m. Played draughts with Peter and won 5 games out of 7.

Tues March 18

On duty 8 a.m. – 12.30 p.m. My razor broke, someone pinched my toffee and lifebelt. Day of misfortune.

Wed March 19

On duty 12.30 – 4 p.m. Some ships left our convoy to go into Capetown.

Thurs March 20

On duty 12 p.m. – 4 a.m. outside Free French quarters; they brought me a cup of tea. Had a talk with one of them who was very favourably impressed with English hospitals. On duty again 4 – 8 p.m.

FRID MARCH 21

On duty 4 a.m. – 8 a.m. Passed into the semi-final of the draughts competition, winning in two straight games.

SAT MARCH 22

On duty 8 a.m. – 12.30 p.m. and 8 p.m. – 12 p.m. Weather quite cold. Wrote letters.

SUN MARCH 23

Got into final of the draughts competition, but was then beaten by Ken Shutt. Very good games. Received tin of 50 Gold Flake which I let Peter have.

MON MARCH 24

On guard Free French quarters and they supplied me with the usual cup of tea.

TUES MARCH 25

Sighted land late tonight.

WEDS MARCH 26

We were rudely awakened at 4 a.m. and told to pack our kit ready to leave the boat. On entering the harbour Durban presented a magnificent sight, the white high buildings gave a suggestion of New York. After standing by with our kit for hours, we eventually disembarked and travelled by train to Clairwood camp. People were waving and smiling at us throughout the journey. Very pleasant to see some nice girls pleasingly dressed in bright summer clothes. Clairwood camp consists of bell tents, open air showers and a comfortable NAAFI canteen. Went into Durban by train in the evening and had a good meal and a walk round.

THURS MARCH 27

Went into Durban in the afternoon with Peter. The people are only too anxious to be kind. We asked a chap the whereabouts of the Metro and he took us there in his car and we then booked for the night show. We then enquired of another gentleman the whereabouts of the army canteen, he immediately invited us to his house where his wife made us more than welcome. We had a delightful dinner in contrast to the ship's food. Beer, steak and kidney pie, potatoes, kidney beans and pumpkin. Blancmange with loganberries and cream, buttered scones and cups of tea. After leaving their flat we were waiting for the bus when a man stopped his car and took us to the Metro. A special welcome song was played on the cinema aspan, the film was "Comrade X" with Clark Gable.

FRI MARCH 28

Peter and myself went to Mr. & Mrs. Parr's again for tea and we took Willie McNeish with us at the request of Mrs. Parr who comes from Scotland. We stayed till late.

SAT MARCH 29

The three of us went for walk on the beach and then went to the Parr's for tea. Mr. Parr has been in S. Africa since 1902. I don't like the way the blacks are looked down on in this country.

SUN MARCH 30

We were given a lift into Durban and went to the Parr's. Mr. Parr took us in his car to Howard University from where there is a wonderful view on the interior.

A Moment of Relaxation – Dad in Durban

DEPART DURBAN BOUND FOR PORT SUEZ, EGYPT

(3RD LEG – 21 DAYS)

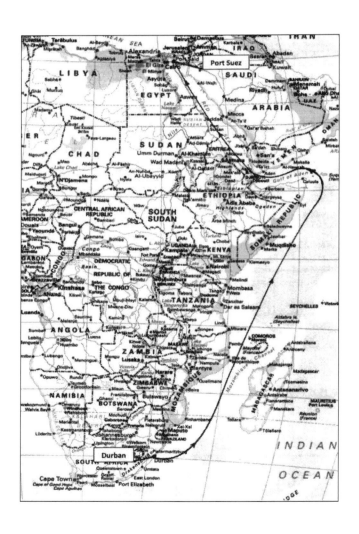

Mon March 31

Marched out of Clairwood camp with full kit and in the afternoon we boarded the Elizabethville which is not so big as the Rangitata. A very dirty ship but we have more room than on the previous ship. Before coming on board we were promised the night in Durban, but only the officers were allowed to go ashore.

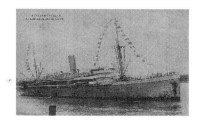

Elisabethville

Tues Apr 1

Left port in the morning. Lot of cleaning up to do. Woman signalled goodbye in semaphore. Man shouted Good luck on railway carriage.

Wed Apr 2

I had an attack of diarrhoea; M.O. gave me a dose of castor oil and I was O.K. before night.

Thurs Apr 3

There is a wireless loudspeaker on deck – a very poor one. Heard Greig's piano concerto today.

Frid Apr 4

On sentry duty, 2 hrs on 4 hrs off. Heard Cesar Frank's variations. Benghasi captured by the Germans.

SAT APR 5

Marine sergeant gave us boxing lessons. Heard Tschaikowsky's Pathetique symphony.

SUN APR 6

Germany invades Yugoslavia and Greece. Weather is exceedingly hot now.

MON APR 7

Washing day. We are allowed a bucket of hot water each. Beethoven's choral symphony was on, but the reproduction was terrible.

TUES APR 8

Was mess orderly today. What a job. Beety's 7th symphony. Rained heavily in the afternoon, providing a nice shower bath for us.

WED APR 9

Most of us sleep on deck now. A heavy thunderstorm woke us up early this morning and chased us all down below with our hammocks.

THURS APR 10

Germans capture Salonika. Things don't seem to be going so well for us.

FRID APR 11

Wrote letters

SAT APR 12

Our ship dropped behind today and the marines had rifle and Lewis gun practice at floating targets. Two officers gave an exhibition bout of boxing. Very funny.

SUN APR 13

Cruiser passed close to each ship in turn.

MON APR 14

Germans capture Belgrade. I did a lot of washing today.

TUES APR 15

Lecture from P.O. Henley on motor engines and generators. Very amusing to watch the perspiration gradually soak through his shirt. Played draughts in afternoon.

WED APR 16

Land in sight today. Various lighthouses could be seen at night. Played draughts with Peter beating him 3 – 1.

THURS APR 17

Sighted a few more small islands today. Germans reported to be on the borders of Egypt and advancing quickly in Greece.

FRID APR 18

Heard Mendelsohn's violin concerto. Sounded like Heifety.

SAT APR 19

Saw more islands today. Very high land, dark and forbidding.

SUN APR 20

Big defensive actions in Greece. Land very close on both sides now. Very cold at night.

MON APR 21

Arrived at Port Suez, weighing anchor early morning. The view of land is blank and desolate, no vegetation whatsoever being visible.

TUES APR 22

Arrangements to disembark cancelled but we docked at tea time.

FIRST POSTING –
EGYPTIAN DESERT

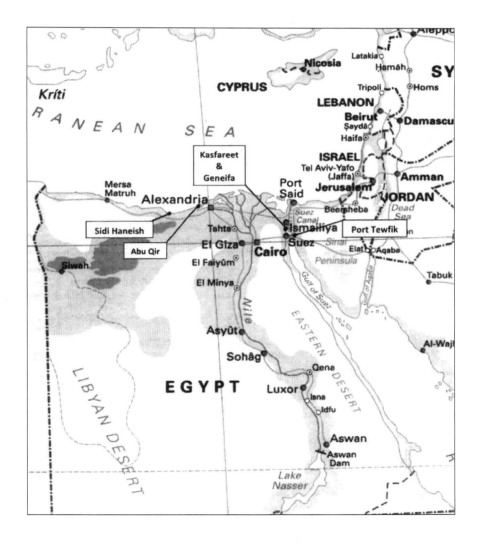

WED APR 23

Disembarked and travelled by train to RAF camp at Geneifa. The camp is just a mass of E.P.I. tents, there are millions of flies and everyone seems to carry fly switches with them. Italian prison camp very near – they seem to be quite cheerful.

THURS APR 24

Marched with full kit to another camp Kasfareet, about two miles away. All this kit is getting to be a ruddy nuisance. Flies don't give you a minute's peace – blast 'em.

FRID APR 25

We are quite near to the Suez Canal. Johnny George, Willie McNeish, Peter and myself have managed to get a tent to ourselves.

SAT APR 26

We went down to the canal road and got a lift on an army convoy into Ismailia. Had a good meal and were entertained at the table by conjuror of amazing ability. We were pestered to death by scroungers.

SUN APR 27

On fatigues at stores. Sand storm blew up.

MON APR 28

We had to move to another tent in the morning. I had a shower. We went to the cinema at night; the cinema being a big tent open at the

top; you have to wait till it goes dark before the show starts. Film was
"Submarine Patrol" – rotten. Sound was terrible.

TUES APR 29

March and infantry instruction in the morning. Lecture on hygiene in
afternoon.

WED APR 30

Had to change tents for the sixth time since arriving here. Went bathing
in the Suez in the afternoon. Very salty.

THURS MAY 1

On cookhouse fatigues with Italian prisoners. They did most of the
work. Went bathing in the Suez in the evening.

FRI MAY 2

Lecture in the morning. Route march to the Suez in the afternoon.
Cinema at night. I organised a draught league in the tent.

SAT MAY 3

We were going on weekend leave this morning, but before we could
get away Johnny George and myself were told to standby for moving.
Left Geneifa at 5 p.m. by train Bernard Scholfield and George Badham
were left in the front portion of the train which went to Cairo, Johnny
George and myself just managed to scramble out while the train was in
motion.

SUN MAY 4

Arrived in Alexandria at 9.30 a.m. and caught the Western Desert train at 11 a.m. Arrived at Sidi Hameish station at 8 p.m. Travelled by lorry to Bagoush where the 42 of us were allocated 2 E.P.I tents. Bit of a crush.

Dad, Willie McNeish, Peter Squires.

Near Suez canal from Kasfareet (Middle East Pool)

Left to Right – Willie, Dave, Peter, Nobby, Dad

Front – Egyptian with scrounged cigarette.

MON MAY 5

We were attached to Air Advance H.Q. I was detailed with some more chaps to bury 6 air crew who had crashed in Blenheims. I helped to dig the graves and after a short service we dropped the bodies in and filled in the graves. Very casual affair.

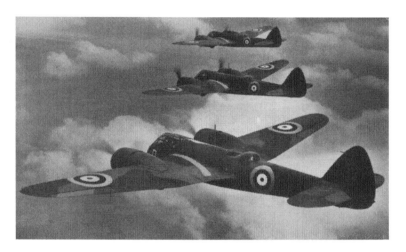

RMS Bristol Blenheim

TUES MAY 6

Whilst on pay parade a Kamsin blew up and one of our tents caught fire everything therein being destroyed within five minutes. This scorching wind increased in intensity and ripped the fly sheet of our tent; later brought the tent down. We crawled outside and for a short period the storm was of a dull red blinding sand and we couldn't see an inch in front of us. When it eventually abated we could see that every tent in sight was flat to the ground. Reconstruction work in the evening.

WED MAY 7

Filled sand bags for dugout in the morning. Re-erected tents in the afternoon. Late at night we had to put up a wireless mast that had been brought down.

THURS MAY 8

Excavated in the dugout all morning. In the afternoon we anchored our tent to big boulders and then went for a swim in a beautiful little cove where the water is calm and clear. The sand is white and the water appears to be pale blue in the shallows, deepening to a rich blue out to sea. I actually managed to swim ten strokes today.

FRI MAY 9

Another terrific sandstorm and Kamsin blew up. 127° in the shade. Went for a swim in the afternoon until it abated.

SAT MAY 10

Another Kamsin sprung up chasing us from our work to the tents. These winds are hellish, they are like the blast from a furnace. Only drink at the NAFFI tent is beer at 4 Piastres (10d). Shared a tin of plums with Nobby Clark – 9 Piastres.

SUN MAY 11

A nice day. Went for a swim after we knocked off work at 4 p.m. Played cricket in the evening.

MON MAY 12

Another day of digging after which we went for a swim. I didn't shape so well today.

TUES MAY 13

Sandstorm in the morning, clearing up in the afternoon. Dodged off work and went for a swim. Huge waves made swimming impossible. I was twice carried out of my depth and taken under but Garbull fortunately dragged me to safety.

WEDS MAY 14

Digging and sandbagging. Swimming in afternoon but sea rough again. Rudolph Hess reported to have given himself up, landing by parachute in Glasgow.

THURS MAY 15

Very cold today with a slight sandstorm. Cleared out officer's tent in the morning and had to watch a party of Wogs digging in the afternoon. It would be easier and quicker to do the work myself.

FRID MAY 16

Sea very rough; the breakers carry you right onto the beach. Good fun. Sallum recaptured from the Germans.

SAT MAY 17

Rumour has it that we are to return to Geneifa after having performed work that could have been done by Wogs.

SUN MAY 18

Work after which a swim.

MON MAY 19

Counter rumour that we may stay here. Sea very calm today, I am now able to swim about 20 yds.

TUES MAY 20

Did camouflage work on a wireless tender. Very pleasant in the sea today.

WEDS MAY 21

Erected aerials in the morning. Dug hole for officer's mess in afternoon. Extremely hot today. Good swim in the evening. Crete attacked by paratroops.

THURS MAY 22

Digging out for officers mess again. We remove to tents on the escarpment. With the aid of Hutson's primus stove we cooked a good meal of eggs and tomato purchased from a Wog. We cook in sawn off petrol cans.

FRID MAY 23

Extremely hot again. Received my first letters today. From Mother, Dad, Alice and Harold.

SAT MAY 24

A blasted sandstorm and Kamsin most of the day. Went for a swim in the evening.

SUN MAY 25

Cooler today. Did some sandbagging. Hood reported to have been sunk by Bismark.

HMS Hood

Bismarck

MON MAY 26

The cookhouse meals are terrible. In the evening I cooked 15 eggs with tomatoes and fried bread for the lads in our tent. There are five of us. In the words of the lads it was 'bloody good'. Fried everything in half a petrol tin having pinched the marge from the cookhouse.

TUES MAY 27

Dodged off work and had a good swim.

WEDS MAY 28

Bismark reported sunk by British naval and air forces. Another good swim in the afternoon.

THURS MAY 29

Battle still raging in Crete, looks as though Germans are getting on top.

FRI MAY 30

Dodged work once too often and got collared for spud peeling at night.

SAT MAY 31

Sandbagging in the morning but dodged away again in the afternoon for a swim. Fancy I could do a couple of lengths now.

SUN JUNE 1

We are going to re-join 15WOH tomorrow so we got the day off. Beautiful day for swimming.

MON JUNE 2

We missed the train by a couple of minutes so we had another good days swimming.

TUES JUNE 3

They got us up at 4.30 a.m. to catch the 8 o'clock train. Arrived in Alex at 5 p.m. and stayed in the city till 12 p.m. Amused ourselves by beating the Gypo merchants down to ⅓rd their original price. Grand YMCA in Alex.

WED JUNE 4

On the train journey our stupid Sgt. Dudley put two chaps whom he suspected to be spies in our custody. They turned out to be labourers from Cyprus. The poor blokes didn't know what was going on and looked scared stiff. I arrived back at Geneifa with a terrific growth of beard for we had no need or much facility to shave in the desert. Old Henley stared more than somewhat.

THURS JUNE 5

Bullshit supreme once again. Swimming in the Suez seemed very poor after the Med.

FRID JUNE 6

Putting up tents and camouflaging them with sand and water.

SAT JUNE 7

Two days leave. Hitch hiked to Cairo in 5 hrs via Ismalia. Put up at the Toc H.

Sun June 8

Visited the Pyramids and Sphinx. Only impressive by the size and the work put into them. Travelled up there on a camel. Had a swim at a bathing pool.

Peter and Dad, Sphinx and Pyramids

Mon June 9

Hitch hiked back to Geneifa in 3 hrs via Suez. Finished the journey in a Wing Commander car.

Tues June 10

Our wireless equipment arrived. Went to the cinema with Willie, Peter and Johnny.

Weds June 11

Reveille is at 5 a.m. every morning. Doesn't agree with me especially when the breakfast is not worth having. Trade Test, Morse and Tec.

Thurs June 12

Finished my Trade Test in the morning. I killed a tarantula spider that came out of Nobby Clark's mattress on to his arm. Damned big thing with an ugly beak.

FRID JUNE 13

Went for a shower to the other camp about two miles away, only to find that the water was off. Confound it!

SAT JUNE 14

Had a swim in the Suez in the afternoon. Weather very warm now.

SUN JUNE 15

Spent the day at Port Suez and Port Tewfik hitch hiking there and back. It took 8 lifts altogether. Port Suez is very scruffy and stinks. Port Tewfik is not bad in places.

MON JUNE 16

Volunteered to be tent orderly and dodged quite a lot of work, the others having to dispense equipment. Wrote a lot of letters. Lost my purse containing 15 ackers, RAF ivory broach, kit bag key and 3d bit.

TUES JUNE 17

New stone cinema opened today. Still open at the top. Sound very poor. Prices 3, 5 and 7 Piastres. 9_d, $1/-$, $1/6_d$.

WEDS JUNE 18

Went for a swim in Suez in evening. I got 61% in Trade Test. Should be AC1 now.

THURS JUNE 19

British nearing Damascus in Syria. Lot of importance attached to Russo – German tension. I don't think Russia will fight.

FRID JUNE 20

Went for a swim in the afternoon and Peter took photos. Cinema at night "Spy in Black" Conrad Veidt.

SAT JUNE 21

We went to Ismalia getting a lift in an armoured car. Could only get a lift half the way back so got on the Wop bus and had a row with the conductor about the fare. Only paid 3 Piastres.

SUN JUNE 22

Germany declares war on Russia. Everyone elated.

MON JUNE 23

Russians claim to have destroyed 300 German tanks and to have taken 5,000 prisoners.

TUES JUNE 24

Germans 75 miles inside Bessarabia.

WEDS JUNE 25

Russians claim to have brought down 382 planes since commencement of hostilities. I went to ENSA show at night. Not very good.

THURS JUNE 26

Tent orderly again today.

FRID JUNE 27

Russians appear to be holding out but no definite news is available.

SAT JUNE 28

Went for swim in Suez

SUN JUNE 29

Hitch hiked to Ismalia with Nobby Clark. Wop private car stopped for us and they wanted 5 ackers to take us to Ismalia. Not bloody likely. Had a sail in a yacht.

MON JUNE 30

We were told that our Trade Test results had been cancelled by Cairo H.Q. the miserable devils. Very annoying.

TUES JULY 1

Officers and NCO RAF played officers and NCO Army at football and defeated them 2-1. Very amusing game. Germans capture Ming on Russian front.

WED JULY 2

RA's defeated RAF at football 2-0.

THURS JULY 3

Went to free concert in the evening. Not very good. Weather very hot now; we never go out in the afternoon due to the heat.

FRI JULY 4

Long weekend. Hitch hiked with Peter and Willie to Port Said. Very nice in parts. Peter and Willie went to a dance at night but I went to a cinema and afterwards went into the English church in which someone was playing the organ.

Dad, Willie McNeish, Peter Squires

SAT JULY 5

Went for a swim at Port Fouad. In the evening saw Bette Davis and Charles Bryer in "All Two and Heaven Too".

SUN JULY 6

Hitch hiked back to camp and arrived in with but five minutes to spare.

MON JULY 7

Went to cinema at night. Garbo in "Marie Walewska". Sound was so poor that chaps threw stones in the loudspeaker – didn't improve it.

TUES JULY 8

Went for a swim in the Suez in the morning. Very calm. Can swim about 75 yds now.

WED JULY 9

American troops go to Iceland. Russians appear to be holding out fairly well against the Germans.

THURS JULY 10

RAF raids over Germany increasing in intensity. Armistice asked for by Vichy in Syria

FRI JULY 11

I was on guard duty at the machine gun post 7 – 11 p.m. Allan Docker brought me a plate of three fried eggs, two cakes and a pot of tea. Jolly good show I reckon.

SAT JULY 12

In the guard tent all day. Peace terms in Syria.

SUN JULY 13

On our unit there are 200 men, 8 sergeants and 8 officers. There are two shithouses with 8 seats each. The officers have one and now the sergeants have claimed the other, and we can go to hell if we like. Actually we have to walk about ½ mile to the main camp for a shit.

MON JULY 14

On fatigues again at the M.H. dispensing equipment. Expecting air raids.

TUES JULY 15

Fatigues at the M.H. again. In the afternoon Hutson and myself dropped off the fatigue lorry as it slowed down in front of the M.P.'s hut. We went for a walk and finished up at the C of E club and had tea and cakes.

WED JULY 16

Scrounged off fatigues again in the morning.

THURS JULY 17

Fatigues at M.H. in morning and afternoon. Hard work this weather.

FRID JULY 18

Set off for Cairo with Allan Docker and Willie McNeish. Arrived 12 a.m. and put up at the Toc H. Went to the Metropole at night.

SAT JULY 19

Willie a bit off colour. Went to Geyira and played tennis with Allan
who won 6-1. Had fruit salads with ice cream. Watched cricket match,
R. Tyldesley was playing. Went to Opera House at night. "Invisible
Stripes"

SUN JULY 20

Arrived back at camp 13.30 getting a lift all the way through for once.

MON JULY 21

Germans reported to have captured Smolenok.

TUES JULY 22

Fatigues at the M.H.

WED JULY 23

They've started giving us foot drills in the mornings. What a bind. I was
tent orderly.

THURS JULY 24

Foot drills in morning. Too hot to do anything in the afternoon.

FRI JULY 25

On guard at the machine gun post 9-11 p.m. and 3-5 a.m.

SAT JULY 26

Russians holding out. Japan takes over protection of French Indo China.

SUN JULY 27

We have to choose a partner to go out on a post with. Peter and myself are together. Nobby and Willie are HQ.

MON JULY 28

Went for long route march along Sweet Water Canal and in the desert.

TUES JULY 29

They are going to sort us out into posts and mix us with the R.A.'s, so in the evening we had a sing song which was very enjoyable thanks to a good supply of beer.

WED JULY 30

Changed tents today. 5 RA's to 3 R.A.F. Not a bad crowd we are with. I am on the last post in Section 1.

THURS JULY 31

Strong rumour that Section 1 are to move shortly. Several places mentioned but Cyprus is favourite. The C.O. is not coming with us. Good for him and us.

FRI AUG 1

Managed to get passes for tomorrow. Didn't expect them.

SAT AUG 2

Hitch hiked to Cairo via Ismalia; latter half of journey in a staff car.
Put up at British Forces Home. Went to Metro at night "Escape"
Robert Taylor and Norma Shearer.

SUN AUG 3

Wrote some letters at YMCA. Went to Metropole at night.

MON AUG 4

Set off for camp at 10 a.m. and arrived in camp at 1.45 p.m.

TUES AUG 5

Definite gen that we are leaving for Cyprus on the 13th. Changed my
red drain pipe slacks at the stores.

WED AUG 6

On Guard early morning. Did a big wash having got fed up with the
Wop service.

THURS AUG 7

Tent orderly. In the afternoon helped to pack wireless gear for the boat.

Fri Aug 8

Posted parcel of books home.

Sat Aug 9

Went to P.Suez and P. Tewfik today. Lovely swim in the afternoon – about 80 yds. Went to the Services Club, best cooked food I've had for a long time.

Sun Aug 10

Went to the NAAFI with Terry Byrne at night. Miserable grub at the NAAFI – cold and dear.

Mon Aug 11

Lecture from P.O. Brown on Cyprus. Usual V.D. Warnings. Big booze-up in one of the dining tents at night.

Tues Aug 12

Leaving tomorrow so wrote a lot of letters and airgrapho.

Wed Aug 13

Travelled by train to Port Said where we stayed the night at the transit camp which consists of insecurely fastened tents which are pitched in dirty fine grey sand which gets into everything. Went into the port in the evening and had a good meal and tin of beer canned in New York. Only food at the camp is bully beef and biscuits.

Dad and Peter at the
Transit Camp

THURS AUG 14

Air raid in the port during the night. Terrific barrage put up by the naval and ground defences, the camp being showered with shrapnel. Had to get up early but breakfast was late. We marched with full kit to the ferry, crossed it and waited on the quayside. We then returned all the way back to camp as, apparently, there was no boat for us. Usual mess up. Went to Britannia Club at night.

Port Said

Port Said – Harbour

DEPART FOR SECOND POSTING – CYPRUS

(13 HRS VOYAGE)

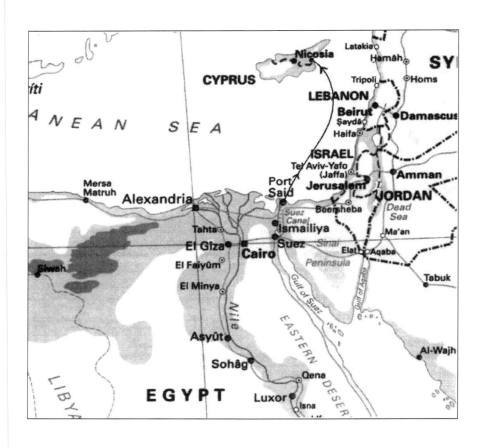

FRI AUG 15

Same as yesterday morning but this time
we got on board the Abdeil cruiser which
took us to Famagusta, Cyprus in 13 hours.
We then travelled by train through the
night to Nicosia the capital.

HMS Abdeil

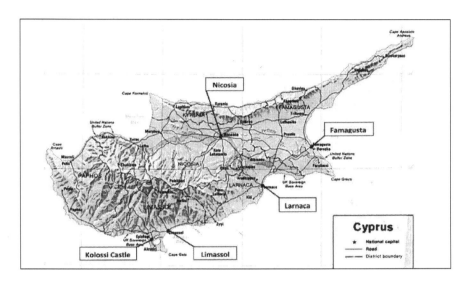

SAT AUG 16

Gharries transported us to our camp which
consists of a few trees under which we slept
for the remainder of the morning. Cyprus
consists of a barren plain stretching the
length of the island it is bounded on either
side by a high range of mountains. In
the afternoon we went in gharry over the

Gharry over Kyrenia range

Kyrenia range, The road winding up the mountain side is exceedingly treacherous, the acute bends overlooking very steep drops. We had a very pleasant swim in Kyrenia bay. We seem to be quite popular with the Cypriots.

SUN AUG 17

We sleep out in the open but still get plenty of army bullshit. O.C.'s parade every morning, marching to the cookhouse etc. Sorted out the wireless gear in the morning and afternoon and went into Nicosia at night. Not a bad little place. Beer is like cider, excellent wine at 2/- a bottle.

MON AUG 18

Sent a cable home. Went into Nicosia again at night. Went into a cabaret – a horrible dive full of dancing girls and low characters. Sleep very well at night in the open air.

TUES AUG 19

Went for a swim at Kyrenia. Very pleasant. Nicosia at night, drinking wine and eating nuts and raisins.

Bill Gardner and Dad – Kyrenia Bay

WED AUG 20

Eight of us are chosen to stay behind
here to keep in touch with Fighter H.Q.
the remainder going out on posts. Peter,
Derrick, Bill and myself are to stay here
as Screen H.Q.

Nicosia Wireless Tent

THURS AUG 21

Bill, Peter and myself joined the British Institute in Nicosia. There is
table tennis, billiards, reading room, library. I beat Peter 21-15, 21-16
and beat Bill 21-14, 21-14.

*British Institute –
Nicosia*

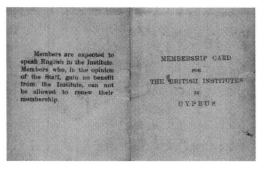

FRI AUG 22

At night we went to the "Gloria" a terribly low dive. Was glad to get out in one piece.

SAT AUG 23

Fixed up our wireless set today. The four of us went to the Kit Kat at night; we got rather squiffy due to Bill dosing our wine with 3 star brandy.

SUN AUG 24

Had an attack of sand fly fever today, we get bitten to death with them at night. Terrible headache and temperature. Took 3 aspirins at night.

MON AUG 25

Still ill all day, improved a little toward evening. Bill, Derrick and Peter are sharing my wireless watches.

TUES AUG 26

Head cleared a little today but I feel as weak as a kitten. Russians and British enter Iran.

WED AUG 27

Feeling a little better but legs are very weak. I have had little to eat since Sunday. Was on watch 12.30 – 4. Germans are attacking vigorously at Odessa.

THURS AUG 28

We get billeted in a garage with a concrete floor. It is alive with ants, mosquitos, sand flies, so we put up our mosquito nets. Played table tennis at British Institute in the evening.

Billet

FRI AUG 29

Did two four hour watches on the transmitter.

SAT AUG 30

On watch 4 hrs on the two receivers at Fighter Ops.

SUN AUG 31

Was on the transmitter 4 a.m. – 8 a.m. and 4 p.m. – 8 p.m. I was sick after dinner.

MON SEPT 1

Day off for Peter and myself. Played table tennis at the British Institute.

TUES SEPT 2

Was on the transmitter 4 a.m. – 8 a.m. and 4 p.m. – 8 p.m. P.O. Brown visited us. Our Accumulators are in a low condition as we have to rely on Fighter HQ for charging them.

WED SEPT 3

On watch at receivers in Fighter Ops. What a binding job. Intercepting post signals at last. Big battles for Leningrad and Odessa

THURS SEPT 4

Derek and Peter are recalled to our H.Q. at Limassol and replaced – repercussion of Brown's visit. Bill is still ill with sand fly fever and 7 of us are keeping 4 hr watches on 3 sets. Very hard work. Working 72 hrs a week.

Bill Gardner and Dad

FRI SEPT 5

Air raid at night but no damage done. Blast made the tent flap more than somewhat.

SAT SEPT 6

On watch 8 a.m. – 1 p.m. and 6 p.m. – 8 p.m.

SUN SEPT 7

On watch 12 p.m. – 8 a.m., 1 p.m. – 6 p.m. and 8 p.m. – 12 p.m. 17 hours watch in 24.

What a day. Bill is now out of hospital, which will make things a bit easier.

MON SEPT 8

Watch 8 a.m. – 1 p.m. and 20.00 hrs to 2 a.m. very hard work.

TUES SEPT 9

Watch 12 a.m. – 1 p.m. and 20.00 hrs to 2 a.m. Wheeler is sick now; that means more work; don't see how we can keep up with this.

WED SEPT 10

Woke up with a vile headache. Was on watch 1 – 6.25 p.m. at the end of which I had a terrible head; I only just made the billet. Blasted sand fly fever again. Cooney has got it as well.

THURS SEPT 11

Three reliefs sent from H.Q. and only just in time. Ate nothing today except aspirins.

FRI SEPT 12

Very weak today. Had a cup of tea at tiffin being my first drink since Wednesday. Staggered down to dinner and ate a few mashed spuds.

SAT SEPT 13

Felt a little better again today but legs still very weak.

SUN SEPT 14

A little better again. Had egg and chips at Peter's in the evening.

MON SEPT 15

Did an hour watch for Bill this morning. Went for a swim in the afternoon. Went into town in the evening, had a meal and collected some snaps (photographs).

Watch 01.00 hrs – 08.00hrs.

TUES SEPT 16

Watch 08.00 – 13.00 hrs. Brewed up in the watch tent.

WED SEPT 17

Watch 13.00 – 18.00 hrs. Went to the British Institute with Bill in the evening beat him at table tennis 8 games to 1. Beat a Cypriot 3-0.

THURS SEPT 18

Watch 08.00 – 13.00 hrs. Went into town with Alec and Henry and had a meal at the Vienna Café, later going to the Ambassadeur for coffee.

FRI SEPT 19

Watch 08.00 – 13.00 hrs. Went to British Institute with Bill and beat him 6-1 at table tennis.

SAT SEPT 20

Watches 08.00 – 13.00 hrs and 18.00 – 01.00 hrs. wrote letters.

SUN SEPT 21

Watch 13.00 – 18.00 hrs. Had supper in the watch tent. Germans enter Kiev.

MON SEPT 22

Watch 01.00 – 08.00 hrs and 18.00 hrs – 01.00 hrs. Took my washing to a new place. Two girls there, Georgia, ill in bed, and Zinovea. The mother made Turkish coffee for us.

TUES SEPT 23

Watch 08.00 – 13.00 hrs. had haircut in town at night. Haircutting is quite an art here.

WED SEPT 24

Watch 01.00 – 08.00 hrs and 13.00 – 18.00 hrs. Went to British Institute with Bill and beat him 4-3 at table tennis after being 3 games down. Had a meal of egg and chips, fruit salad and Vermouth.

THURS SEPT 25

Watch 08.00 – 13.00 hrs. Went to Peter's place for egg and chips. He's too dear 9 disasters (piasters) without bread.

FRI SEPT 26

Watch 01.00 – 08.00 and 13.00 – 18.00 hrs. Went into Nicosia where Bill and I had a good meal at the Imperial. Bill swiped a knife.

SAT SEPT 27

Watch 08.00 – 13.00 hrs and 18.00 – 01.00 hrs. Very cold in the evening now. Germans attacking in the Crimea.

SUN SEPT 28

Watch 13.00 – 18.00 hrs. Went to Peter's at night for egg and chips.

MON SEPT 29

Watch 01.00 – 08.00 hrs and 18.00 – 01.00 hrs. Went down to town in the morning and sent cables to Alice and Aunty Janey. Swimming in the afternoon at Kyrenia. Lovely day.

TUES SEPT 30

Watch 13.00 – 18.00 hrs. Cleaned my rifle for the first time since getting it.

WED OCT 1

Received 9 letters. Air raid at night whilst I was on watch – I felt the draught from the blast.

THURS OCT 2

Meant to go into town at night but had to wait for these two dopes
Sgt. Motherwell and Lt. Wright with the pay. They didn't turn up.
I had egg and chips at Peter's.

FRI OCT 3

Watch 01.00 – 08.00 hrs. I was violently sick during the watch vomiting
10 times before I returned to the billet at 6.30 a.m. I didn't eat
anything for the rest of the day.

SAT OCT 4

Did my morning watch 08.00 – 13.00 hrs but felt just about on my
knees.

SUN OCT 5

Watch 13.00 – 18.00 hrs. Air raid warning at night.

MON OCT 6

Watch 08.00 – 13.00 hrs and 18.00 – 01.00 hrs. Sent snaps home by air
mail.

TUES OCT 7

Watch 13.00 – 18.00 hrs.

Had to take over watch from Blackburn this morning 05.30 – 08.00.
He's got the shits bad.

WED OCT 8

Watch 01.00 – 08.00 hrs and 18.00 – 01.00 hrs. Went to town to do some shopping in the morning. Bought coffee, cocoa, tinned peas and brandy (2/- a bottle). P.O. Brown payed us a visit; Peter and Derrick are coming back to relieve the strain.

THURS OCT 9

Peter and Derrick arrived whilst I was on watch. Work ought to be easier now. They both remarked that I looked rather low and no wonder with the strain of work recently. Very cold today.

FRI OCT 10

All four of us (Bill, Peter, Derrick and I) went to town in the morning. On watch at night. I have got a very bad cold so took a nip of brandy before going to bed.

SAT OCT 11

Russian – German war at a very critical stage – big German push in central sector. Timochenko in difficulties.

SUN OCT 12

Went to town with Peter in the afternoon.

MON OCT 13

Took washing to Georgia's where I had coffee. Watch at night. Heavy static interference but managed to get a message through D.C.

TUES OCT 14

Received 5 letters. Went to cinema for first time since leaving Egypt. "Tower of London" very poor.

WED OCT 15

Went to town in the morning with Bill and had my photograph taken. Peter, Bill and I went to British Institute in the evening. I beat two Cypriots at table tennis.

THURS OCT 16

Timoshenko is in difficulties and Germans are attacking Moscow from three sides. Budenny seems all at sea in the south. Odessa falls.

FRI OCT 17

Vorishilov fighting back strongly in Leningrad sector. Japan is getting cocky now. The yellow devils.

SAT OCT 18

Went to gramophone recital of chamber music at British Institute in the evening. Very enjoyable.

SUN OCT 19

Germans claim to have annihilated Timoshenko's forces. Probably a slight overstatement. Position critical.

Mon Oct 20

Went to British Institute in the morning and played table tennis.
Went to watch tent at night and cooked supper of fried bread, eggs and
tomatoes on the primus.

Tues Oct 21

Went to Nicosia at night. Kiev has fallen to Germans – curse it. Fight
for Moscow very intensive, Germans within 30 miles at various points.

Wed Oct 22

In the evening I went to the wireless tent and cooked supper for Peter,
Derrick, Bill and myself. Fried eggs, tomatoes and bread. Absolutely
lush.

Thurs Oct 23

Collected my photos – not bad. Posted them by air mail to home.
Harry and Auntie Janey.

Fri Oct 24

Kharkov reported captured by Germans. Timoshenko now in charge
of southern armies. Zukov in charge of central armies. Varishilov and
Budenny training armies behind the lines.

Sat Oct 25

Russians getting the better of the battle in the Crimea. Our watch times
are 01.00 – 08.00, 08.00 – 13.30, 13.30 – 18.00 and 18.00 – 01.00.
We now do one on – two off which is not too bad.

Dad on Duty

SUN OCT 26

Set out for Church in the evening, thought it started at 8 p.m. but found that the service was over. Had egg sandwich and a beer instead.

MON OCT 27

Slight skirmish on Jap – Russian frontier.

TUES OCT 28

Went to a concert at British Institute – pretty poor. Kharkov falls to Germans – bad show.

WED OCT 29

Went to canteen at night with Peter and played table tennis. We managed to scrape enough ackers between us to buy a bottle of beer.

THURS OCT 30

Pay day. Good job too; I was just about broke.

FRI OCT 31

Went into town at night and had a big feed at the Imperial. Big German offensive in the Crimea.

NOV 1 SAT

Position in Crimea very grave. Germans 10 miles from Rostov.

NOV 2 SUN

Russians losing ground in the Crimea – very dangerous. Short cut to Caucasus involved.

NOV 3 MON

Went to British Institute and played table tennis – doubles with Bill and the two girls in black.

NOV 4 TUES

Went to dance at British Institute at night but didn't dance.
Had whiskey and ginger ale for my cold.

NOV 5 WED

The W.H. Screen HQ have come over to the island and are at Larnaca. A new Sqn. Leader Forrest and P.O. Rose. Sgt. King our old friend has come over – blast him. Had slap up meal at the Imperial.

NOV 6 THURS

British Institute in the morning and played table tennis with "Spitfire"; she plays quite well and is very amusing. She said "Do not be afraid of the Germans" and seemed quite reassured when I said I wouldn't.

NOV 7 FRI

Went to British Institute and played table tennis with "Spitfire" again. Great fun playing with her. Germans advancing in Crimea otherwise front fairly stable.

NOV 8 SAT

Went to the canteen at night with Peter. Beat him at table tennis 4-0 and played skittles. Had a bottle of beer.

NOV 9 SUN

On watch 1 – 8 a.m., therefore slept rest of the day.

NOV 10 MON

Russians appear to be holding out on the entire front. Navy sink convoy of ten ships in the Med.

NOV 11 TUES

I played in the first round of table tennis tournament at the British Institute. I beat a Cypriot 21-8, 21-14.

NOV 12 WED

I was beaten in the 2nd round of the tournament 21-18, 21-19.
Bad show – I played like a sap. Bill, Derrick and Peter all got knocked
out in the first round.

NOV 13 THURS

Germans are nearing Kerch and Sebastopol.

NOV 14 FRI

British Institute in the morning. 3 games of table tennis with "Spitfire"
otherwise known as Sofia or Sophulla. Let her win one, being big
hearted.

NOV 15 SAT

I was on watch 8 a.m. – 1 p.m. and was visited by P.O. Brown, P.O.
Rose, Sgt. Dudley and Mechanic Williams. They definitely set out to find
fault and as we are working under difficulties here, I used a lot of back
chat. I was on the defensive all the time. Ark Royal sunk in the Med.

NOV 16 SUN

Message came through that eight of us have to return to HQ at
Limassol. Curse it. Will miss the British Institute and "Spitfire".

NOV 17 MON

Journey by lorry to Kolossi Castle arriving there at 5.30 pm. We all had
to see P.O. Brown straight away for a telling off but before he could

start, we got stuck into him and stated our case and it is as well he was sitting down for we left him not a leg to stand on.

The trouble arose as follows;

H.Q. had ignored all our requests and told us to scrounge anything we were short of from 259 Wing who were not very obliging. As long as we could keep our sets working H.Q. were content to leave us alone. For the past month we had made repeated requests for H.T. batteries which were not forthcoming. When the new Pilot officer came to Larnaca he found that our note was weak and complained to Brown. Then came the visit at which time I had 5 old H.T. batteries in series and two six volt accumulators in parallel with 2, 2 volt accumulators for the generator. This was the only method by which we could keep the set working and Brown put the blame on us whereas it was the negligence of H.Q. In the end Brown admitted that we were blameless as regarding the working of the sets, but what he had really objected to was the dust on our set and table (in the open tent). Bill with some heat asked him to look at the HQ sets which fortunately for us were absolutely filthy.

Kolossi Castle near Limassol

NOV 18 TUES

Brown left the unit today and his followers nearly wept. They will have to creep around Rose now. Too many of these chaps curry favour with the Sgts. and officers, but we"ll have none of it. The eight of us are on our own against the lot. Had a row with Sgt. Parker about the fag ration; got 'em alright.

NOV 19 WED

Went into Limassol on lorry for baths. Sgt. Mothersalle refused to let Bill have one on account of the time, but Bill demanded his rights and got the bath.

NOV 20 THURS

Limassol is not a bad little town. Went to the Rex Cabaret And Violets Bar. There is a liberty gharry from Kolossi each night.

NOV 21 FRI

The big offensive (ours) has started in the Western Desert; about time we got something to shout about.

NOV 22 SAT

Bill and myself went into Limassol for the day. We went to a cinema at night – "12 Crowded hrs" I didn't get the hang of it.

NOV 23 SUN

Went for a walk in the plantations with Peter. Oranges, lemons and grapefruits for miles. Cypriot gave us oranges and grapefruit from the trees. Lovely.

Dad in the Farmer's Fields

Nov 24 Mon

Had a meal in Kolossi village. Meals in camp very poor. Ropy goat's meat, sandy spinach and potatoes. Issued with blues for the winter.

Nov 25 Tues

Went into Limassol in the afternoon. I was on the 12 p.m. – 8 a.m. shift so I cooked a lush supper of fried spuds, tomatoes and eggs.

Nov 26 Wed

In bed most of the day. Went into the village at night and had a feed of fried eggs, chips, tomatoes and fried bread.

Nov 27 Thurs

Had breakfast in the village. Walk in the afternoon on watch at night. Food in camp terrible, have to buy most of our grub.

Nov 28 Fri

Went to village café at night. It appears that we are going to get a Trade Test. About time too.

Nov 29 Sat

Went into Limassol in the afternoon. Went to cinema – poor. Meal at Violet's Bar – poor. Went to Rex cabaret – rough and noisy. What a boring day.

Nov 30 Sun

On the 12 p.m. – 8 a.m. shift. Cooked fried eggs, fried bread and cocoa. Slept till after tea. Had supper in the village.

Dec 1 Mon

Went long walk in afternoon. Watch at night. Tough fighting in Western desert.

Dec 2 Tues

Germans recapture Sidi Reyesh. Russians recapture Rostov. Germans closing in on Moscow. Far East situation delicate.

Dec 3 Wed

On watch in the morning. In the afternoon I went a walk with Peter and Bill, we raced match boxes in the stream for ackers. We must be getting childish but we enjoyed it.

Dec 4 Thurs

Went for a walk in the evening and had a feed in the village. Lull in the Western Desert fighting. Germans retreating in Rostov sector.

Dec 5 Fri

Rained all day, so we played Newmarket in the tent. I was on watch at night.

DEC 7 SUN

Japan declares war on U.S.A., Grt. Britain and Netherlands.
In an attempt to split up the three rebels, Peter and myself were
informed that we were to be posted to different posts, Bill remaining
here. We tackled P.O. Rose about it and he was very reasonable and got
volunteers for the posts.

DEC 8 MON

Japs attack Malay. Thailand surrenders. Honolulu, Singapore and Hong
Kong bombed. Damage to U.S. battle ships. U.S.A. losses heavy in
Honolulu. Japs hitting hard.

DEC 9 TUES

In raid on Manila U.S. Admiral of Eastern Fleet killed.

DEC 10 WED

Japs sink 'Prince of Wales' and 'Repulse', two of our best battleships, in
a combined air and submarine attack. What a blow. Germans appear to
have had it in Russia – for the winter at least.

HMS Prince of Wales   *HMS Repulse*

DEC 11 THURS

Jap battleship of 29,000 tons sunk. Germany and Italy declare war on U.S.A.

DEC 12 FRI

Had Trade Test board today. I did very well indeed. Morse – good, Procedure – good and Tech – good.

DEC 13 SAT

Went to Nicosia on a gharry to watch football match between 15 W.H. and 259 Wing. We lost 5-3. Russians attacking on all fronts. We are west of Tobruk in W.D.

SUN DEC 14

Japs are making it hot in Malaya.

MON DEC 15

Have passed the trade test and am now AC1. Hope there is no funny business this time.

TUES DEC 16

Russians recapture Klinn. Bill, Peter and myself went into Limassol in the morning as it is out of bounds in the evening.

Peter Squires, Bill Gardner and Dad

WED DEC 17

Russians retake Kalissia. We capture Derna airfield in Libya. I went for walk with Peter at night, having chai at Kostis'.

THURS DEC 18

Inoculated today. Arm very stiff towards evening. Went a walk with Bill and Peter in the afternoon.

FRI DEC 19

Rested most of day. Went walk at night.

SAT DEC 20

Hong Kong in grave danger. Germans on the run in Libya. Russians recapture Volokolamsk.

SUN DEC 21

Went for walk in afternoon. Hong Kong in state of siege. Benghasi next stop in the desert.

MON DEC 22

Went on dental parade and had a tooth filled; he nearly drilled through the back of my head. Walk at night.

TUES DEC 23

Went a walk with Peter in the afternoon. Sailed match boxes in the stream. Shades of childhood.

WED DEC 24

Went to Limassol at night. Saw "Lost Horizon" at cinema. Went to the Glorious V club to see the Christmas Eve celebration and had to pay 2/- for the doubtful privilege of buying drinks.

THURS DEC 25

On watch 18.00 hrs – 24.00 hrs. Cooked a good supper of fried steaks, eggs and fried bread. Butch, the cook, gave us the steaks. First thing he has ever given us.

FRI DEC 26

Unit Christmas feed at Violet's bar. Everybody got 'kettled' (drunk). Young Speller, the chump, passed out and I had to help him to the gharry.

SAT DEC 27

At 3 a.m. the tent nearly went up in a high wind. We all had to get out of bed and secure it what an aftermath.

SUN DEC 28

Japs take Hong Kong. On watch 12 p.m. – 8 a.m. Slept most of the day; got up for tea. Went a walk at night and then drank chai at Kostis'

MON DEC 29

Went walk in the afternoon. On watch at night. Fighting is now west of Beghasi. Russians capture Volokolamsk.

TUES DEC 30

Went into Limassol at night but there were no pictures showing. Had a feed at a services club and 2 bottles of milk stout – very nice.

WED DEC 31

Very impromptu Church service in the dining hall which is an old ruin. Things are very unsettled just now and it is strongly rumoured that we are going to leave the island. Hope we don't go to that lousy hole Egypt. Have enjoyed it here in Cyprus when at Nicosia but it has been pretty horrible since coming to Kolossi. Grub is terrible – goat's meat, spinach and cold spuds. Bully beef is a positive luxury. Weather is terrible just now, very rainy and windy and we are still living in tents. We are said to be going to Larnaca shortly, so I hope for some improvement.

SUMMARY AT THE END OF YEAR 1941.

Apparently we were originally destined for Crete where most of the Marines on the Rangitata were killed. "Tup three" the Sgt. who took us for rifle drill was killed – he was a grand chap. I saw Sgt. Pugsly the boxer in Alexandria when I returned from the desert; he had made his way back from Crete in an open boat with some other chaps. It took him several days.

I was glad to leave Egypt with it's scheming Wogs whose chief aim is to fleece the serviceman. Cyprus is a great contrast; most of the people seem nice and homely and CLEAN which is indeed a great contrast to the scruffy dirty Wogs.

Very disappointing getting moved from Nicosia where we were having a fine time thanks mainly to the British Institute where we came into contact with some interesting people eg. Loula – very cocky, self-assured yet very nice. Sophulla "Spitfire" full of life and 'joie de vivre'. Aliki and Agnes – the girls in black – very intelligent. Chances of getting back to Nicosia are very remote as Bill, Peter and myself are not very popular with the powers that be. Too many of the chaps here try to curry favour and we don't want any part of it.

1942

JAN 1 THURSDAY

Opened the New Year on watch at Kolossi Castle, the watch being from 01.00 – 08.00 hrs. A high wind raged outside and I was thankful insomuch that I hadn't to spend the night in the tent. I wrote four airgraphs. Slept most of the day and went for a walk at night.

JAN 4 SUNDAY

Should have been on watch 08.00 – 13.00 hrs but arrangements had been made for Bill, Peter and myself to go on the shooting range with a lot of the army chaps. We are about half way there when we are met by the preceding party who tell us that it is all cancelled. How like the W.H. nothing goes right first time. In the afternoon we go to Limassol to see our football team play a Cypriot XI. We lose 1-0 by an unlucky goal. Our team attacked most of the game and had hard cheese. Peters played a stormer at centre half. Peter and I went to Glorious V in the evening, we saw the film "The Women" very good.

JAN 5 MONDAY

On watch 00.01 – 08.00 hrs and again at 13.00 – 18.00 hrs. I had to do this latter watch due to yesterday's balls up.

JAN 6 TUESDAY

Went on the shooting range in the morning. 10 rounds at 100 yds in the lying position. I got 39 points (3 bulls – 15, 5 inners – 20, 1 magpie – 3, and 1 outer – 2). Peter only hit the target once 2 pts, and Bill got 17 points. Some of the army blokes put up a feeble show after the line they used to shoot to us. Quote "Your rifle is your best friend". They've been bullshitting with rifles for over two years and they can't shoot straight with the darned things.

Most of the R.A.'s have now transferred to the R.A.F. and are proud of their blues? The blasted hypocrites.

On watch at night 18.00 – 24.00 hrs.

JAN 7 WEDNESDAY

Sgt. Dudley called the three of us out of our beds (following our night watch) just to see if we had cleaned our rifles. The weak kneed shithouse. By jove we aren't popular here i.e. with the powers that be. P.O. Rose is a good chap but he is surrounded by ill advisers. When Cpl. Williams was in charge he tried to separate the three of us by sending Peter and myself on posts leaving Bill here, and we only averted that disaster by going direct to P.O. Rose. Was Williams marked. There is a big move coming off soon as HQ base and SHQ Larnaca are moving to Nicosia. There is bound to be a lot of gash operators and goodness knows what they'll do with them. If Dudley has anything to do with it I don't think we three will come off so well. On watch 13.00 – 18.00 hrs. Went a short walk at night.

JAN 8 THURS

On watch 08.00 – 13.00 hrs and had to get ready to go shooting again at 13.30. This time we shoot at kneeling and standing positions. I get

2 bulls and 6 inners. 34 pts. Not bad. I think the marker must have missed the other two shots. Having been a marker down at the butts I think that quite possible. Peter didn't hit the target at all. Bill got 24 pts. Kip down after tea as we are on night watch.

JAN 9 FRI

On watch 00.01 – 08.00 hrs. Have breakfast and then try to kip down but we are awakened at 11.00 a.m. for pay parade. Get paid and go back to bed but we keep getting interruptions. In the afternoon Bill, John Ilsley and myself go into Limassol. Bill is being confirmed at night and John goes to church with him. I wait for Peter and we go to a variety show. Not bad. Get back to Kolossi at 10.30.

JAN 10 SAT

Getting ready for the big move. Bill, Peter and myself have to get up and pull down aerials. Never seem to get a lie in these days. Went for a walk in the afternoon. On watch 18.00 – 24.00 hrs. I cooked fried eggs and fried bread – very good. Very warm during the day but windy at night.

War bulletin.
Russia front satisfactory. Libyan campaign O.K. Malaya – not so good. Phillipines – very grave.

JAN 11 SUNDAY

Had to get up at 7.30 to help load some kit to be moved to Nicosia. Played football a bit in the morning. Watch 13.00 – 18.00 hrs. Went to Kostis' at night and had a native dish, pig's head stewed in lemon, chips, and glass of Commanderia. Sgts. Motherselle and Parker came in later on and amused Peter and myself very much by their foolish crosstalk.

JAN 12 MONDAY

Told to prepare to leave for Nicosia tomorrow. Took AH set down after I had tuned it back to AZ frequency which we will use at Nicosia.

JAN 13 TUESDAY

Up at 7 a.m. helped to load three lorries full of stores and wireless gear and then travelled to Nicosia. On arriving at the camp near the aerodrome, Bill Peter and myself have to unload all the lorries practically on our own. Killing work. Afterwards we erected wireless set and got in

Dead Man's Gulch

touch with the posts on AZ frequency. They call this place Dead Man's Gulch. Very apt I reckon. Cross between Compton Bassett and M.E.P. Very derelict. Fortunately we are in huts for the first time since coming on the island. I lost one of my bed boards on the journey and had to sleep on two at night. Went into Nicosia, about 5 miles away, at night. Saw Loula at the British Institute and played ping pong beating Peter 21-19, 21-11.

JAN 14 WED

Dug a pit for the earth mat in the morning and got a seg on my hand due to picking. On watch in the afternoon. Went into Nicosia on the liberty wagon at night. Went to Papadopulous cinema. "Bridal Suite" Annabella and Robert Young. Good, could hear what was said for once. Went to the cabaret at the Ambassadeurs after, they have a floor show now – it is now the best class cabaret in Nicosia. Under cover of darkness I swiped a bedboard from stores. Sleeping on two, was too much like being a tight rope walker as the boards are only 1 ft broad.

JAN 15 THURS

Dodged fatigue column in the morning but got collared by Dudley in the afternoon. Had to help erect a tent and shift some blasted heavy boxes. On watch at night 17.00 – 24.00 hrs.

JAN 16 FRI

Peter and myself are cheesed off with fatigues so after breakfast we sneak out of camp and hitch into Nicosia. We take some washing to Georgia's and have a shave. Thence to British Institute where we play ping pong with the girls in black. Have a lush meal at the Imperial – cauliflower soup, steak, onions and chips, – apple pie and cream and coffee. 3/- the lot. Got back into camp by Cpl. Alderton's car without being noticed. Good show. Sgt. Dudley had been out all day so we weren't missed.

JAN 17 SATURDAY

On watch 05.00 – 08.00 after which Peter, Bill and myself treacled into Nicosia. Played ping pong in Institute. Had some exciting doubles with the girls in black. I beat a Cypriot 21-14, 23-20. Good games. After taking washing Bill went back to camp but Peter and I stayed in town. Went to pictures at night "Double Wedding" with Myrna Loy and Wm Powell at the Papadopoulos. Very funny.

JAN 18 SUNDAY

On watch 17.00 – 24.00. Weather very bad. Russian still advancing – nearing Kharkov. Halffaya falls. Japs still on the offensive in Malaya and Phillipines.

JAN 19 MONDAY

On watch 13.00 – 17.30. Went into Nicosia at night and saw "Abe Lincoln" with Henry Fonda at the Magic Palace. Pretty punk film. Went into the Ambassadeurs after and saw Derrick. Was treated to drinks by a Cypriot. Derrick's cabaret friend looked very pretty tonight wearing backless evening dress.

JAN 20 TUESDAY

On watch 08.00 – 13.00. Getting very good food here. Dinner was chips, onions and bully rissoles. What a difference to Kolossi grub. Bill, Peter and myself applied for leave this weekend.

JAN 21 WEDNESDAY

Went into Nicosia early morning on Alderton's gharry. Played ping pong at Institute. Spitfire turns up for the first time since our return. As perky as ever, I partner her in several doubles in which we are victorious (to Spitfire's great glee). The girls in black were there i.e. Agnes and Alice. Alice is the attractive one and they both work at the box office at the Magic Palace where we went in the evening. "You Can't Take It With You" being the film.

JAN 22 THURSDAY

Collected pair of gum boots from stores. The camp is now a mass of mud. On watch 17.00 – 24.00 hrs. Swiped two pairs of supports for my bedboards under cover of darkness. Wrote two A.L.C's – found it very hard going. Complete lack of inspiration.

JAN 23 FRIDAY

Got paid in the morning. I only get £1 as my allotment has come into force. Get £1 ration money. I borrowed £1 from John Ilsley and 10/- from Alec Blackburn as I am going on leave tomorrow. On watch 13.00 – 17.00. At night Peter and myself help Bill to eat some cream and fruit he got in a parcel.

JAN 24 SATURDAY

Got our papers and went with Alderton and Milchard into Nicosia. Go to Institute and play ping pong with Alice, Agnes and Sofia. After much discussion we persuade them to have their photographs taken. We had to promise not to show the photos to anyone – they were even chary about the photographs seeing them when developing. Bit thick. Went walk round the moat in afternoon. Finished up in 259 Wing canteen. Played ping pong – beat Pete 3-0, Bill 3-2. Went to Institute at night and finished up with cocoa at the Ambassadeur.

JAN 25 SUNDAY

Went to communion with Bill at 08.00 hrs, after which we all went to the A.P.O. and scrounged airgraphs. Walk in the afternoon and "Magic Palace" at night. "Holiday" with Cary Grant and Katherine Hepburn. Very good.

JAN 26 MONDAY

Ping pong with the three girls. We have long discussion and the girls miss their English lesson but in doing so get a better one from us. Went to Serimpi tea room in the afternoon. Tea and cake 1/- Institute at night and have some very keen games of ping pong. Beat Bill 2-1, Pete 3-0. Went to Papadopoulos at night "Vigil in the Night" Carole

Lombard, Brian Aherne. Very grim. Rather overdone. Cronin is inclined
to pile on the agony.

TUESDAY JAN 27

Ping pong in the morning at the Institute. I beat young Spitfire 2-1.
I generally let her win one game in three. Dinner as usual at the
Imperial. Jolly good grub. Derrick returns from Troudos and we all
have tea and cake at Serimpi's Tea Room. Institute at night. I beat Bill
2-1 in three very hectic games. Afterwards we chat to two young girls,
Rebecca and Cleopatra. Rebecca (16) speaks excellent English and we
have a very amusing conversation. We have dinner at the Imperial and
afterwards watch a cabaret at the Ambassadeur. Very poor turns.

War Commentry.
Japs 60 miles from Singapore. Threat to Australia via New Guinea.
Barham (31,000 tons) reported sunk. Considerable no. of Jap
transports sunk. Russians still advancing near Kharkov. Rommel fighting
back in Benghasi. American troops arrive in Ireland.

JAN 28 WEDNESDAY

Institute in the morning as per usual. After meal at the Imperial we go
walk on the outskirts of the town. We return to Institute where we see
Rebecca and Cleopatra. They spin yarns about some boys following
them the other night with obvious result that Peter and myself offer
to see them home. Quite some distance. Nearly got us lost. Rebecca
suggests corresponding with my sister.

JAN 29 THURSDAY

Institute in the morning. Spitfire challenges me to a chess dual. Gives
me a drubbing first game. Second game she takes my Queen early on

but I recover to final victory. Final to be played tomorrow. Walk in afternoon with John lsley who, thanks to us, is substituting for Derrick at UL8. At night we visit the Institute and I play chess with Bill. We finish the evening at the Papadopoulos, "Toy Wife", Louise Rainer, Melvin Douglas, Rbt Young. Not too good. Savors of Hakum. Russians still advancing. Rommel claims capture of Benghasi.

JAN 30 FRIDAY

Institute in the morning. After ping pong I beat young Spitfire in the deciding game of chess. Serimpi Tea Room in afternoon. Institute in evening; saw Rebecca and Cleopatra. Had an amusing talk with Cleo. Gave Alice's address to Rebecca. Saw "Mother's Making Eyes At Me" with that ham actor Tom Brown. What a 3rd rate hick effort.

JAN 31 SATURDAY

Played ping pong in the morning. Young Spitfire beat me at chess in about 1 min. Very quick thinker. Last day of leave today. Saw john at night and the four of us went to Papadopoulos only to find that there was a Turkish concert on. We proceeded to the American Bar and drank wine and brandy. Got really well plastered. Ride back to drome just about put the finishing touch to us. The three of us staggered through the camp and were sick as hell. Certainly preferable to coming back to this dismal joint stone sober.

War Resume

We withdraw to Singapore Island. Rommel retaken Benghasi.

FEB 1 SUNDAY

Very quiet day. Felt pretty feeble. The three of us are spare operators this week and therefore will do guards. Just as I expected.

FEB 2 MONDAY

John and myself on 24 hrs Lewis Gun guard. We clean six Lewis guns in the morning. NAAFI at night and have supper at John's expense. I am flat broke.

FEB 3 TUESDAY

Stayed in all day. Wrote few letters in afternoon. Had supper in the hut. Made toast and cocoa on primus and Bill supplied sardines and bloater paste from one of his parcels. Played whist, Pete and myself beat experts John and Bill gaining a valuable acker thereby.

FEB 4 WEDNESDAY

In all day. On aerodrome guard with John at night 3 to 7.30 looking after Hurricanes. Had some sharp words with Cpl. Ritchie at 3 a.m. about making tea. I made it nevertheless. Need it at that time.

War News

Rommel is now back to Derna.

FEB 5 THURSDAY

Tried to get some sleep in during the day. Not much good. John, Peter, Bill and myself went into Nicosia at night. Went to the Institute where I defeated Bill at chess. Went to Magic Palace where Aliki and Agnes are in the box office. They seemed pleased to see us and wanted to know when we'd be paying a morning visit to the Institute. The picture was "Only Angels Have Wings" Cary Grant and Joan Blondell. Seen it before. Pretty punk. Had coffee at Ambassadeur after.

FEB 6 FRIDAY

John and myself had to clean 20 rifles
in the morning. Bill and Pete are on
Lewis guns. Tippled down all afternoon
thus preventing us going out at night.
Played whist in the hut. John and myself
beat Bill and Pete. We made supper
afterwards. Cocoa toast and salmon, the
latter coming from one of Bill's
parcels.

Bill with Parcel Issue and Dad

FEB 7 SATURDAY

Day off. Left camp early morning and saw the girls in the Institute.
Sofulla wanted to know where we'd been all week. Went to football
match in afternoon. We (the W.H.) defeated 259 Wing 5-1. A good
revenge. Went to Magic Palace at night. "That Woman Again" Melvyn
Douglas. Very good. Went to Ambassadeur for French coffee etc.
Drunk officer came in got on a bike rode into our table and went arse
over tip. He sorted himself out and rode around the room. There
was a fight in the liberty gharry coming back. Crowded to hell. Very
unpleasant. Would rather walk the 5 miles than this palaver.

FEB 8 SUNDAY

Gave breakfast a miss had tea and cakes at the NAAFI at 10.30.
On wireless watch 17.00 – 23.59 hrs. I'm on AK band this week.

FEB 9 MONDAY

Stayed in bed again this morning. Breakfasts aren't worth bothering about these days especially when it involves ½ mile walk. On watch 13.00 – 17.00. Went into Nicosia at night Cpl. Alderton arranged a tournament for the W.H. table tennis team. Was defeated by Peke 21-8, 19-21, 18-21 but beat Fred Archer 21-18, 21-17. Went to Papadopoulos after. "Breakfast For Two" Poor show. Herbert Marshall and Barbara Stanwick. Saw Rebecca and Cleopatra at the Institute. Rebecca has written to Alice.

FEB 10 TUESDAY

On watch 08.00 – 13.00. stayed in the rest of the day. Very dull.

FEB 11 WEDNESDAY

Day off. Bill and myself had to ask permission of Sgt.King to go out in morning. Managed to obtain it after long argument. Saw Spitfire, Aliki and Agnes and had a chat. We have no bleedin' money (I'm in debt actually) so we have to get back to camp for tea. R.A. bloke gave us a lift to the drome. Come out again at night with Bill, Pete and John. Beat Bill once at chess and three times at draughts. Saw Rebecca and Cleo. Saw "Clouds Over Europe" at Magic Palace. Very good.

War Commentary

Japs on Singapore Island.

FEB 12 THURSDAY

On watch 00.01 – 08.00 hrs. Slept till dinner time. On watch 17.00 – 23.59.

Feb 13 Friday

Rifle inspection. I have to report at 6.30 to Sgt. King. On watch 13.00 – 17.00 hrs. Reporting to King didn't keep me in camp. The four of us managed to hitchhike to Nicosia. We see the ping pong tournament. 4 each side. I was No.5 for the W.H. We start to walk back to camp and an army lorry gives us a lift.

Saturday Feb 14

On watch 08.00 – 13.00. Go to Institute at night. Bill and myself have unfinished game of chess. Saw "Christmas Carol" at the Papadopoulos I enjoyed it very much.

War Commentry

The two German battleships Greiseman and Scharnhorst and cruiser Prince Eugen leave Brest for Helipoland. We attack with 600 aircraft. Lose 42 shooting down 18 German planes. No definite damage to ships reported. Weather unfavourable.

Scharnhorst   *Prinz Eugen*

SUNDAY FEB 15

Played whist in afternoon. Bill and myself beat John and Pete. At
night Bill, Pete and myself go to the English church in Nicosia. Very
enjoyable service. We have tea and cakes at the Imperial, Derrick having
joined us. We then see "The Gladiators", Joe E. Brown, at the Magic
Palace. We walk back to camp in just over 1 hr.
Singapore Surrender to the Japs.

MONDAY FEB 16

On watch 05.00 – 08.00 and 17.00 – 23.59. Played whist.

TUESDAY FEB 17

Air raid warning in the morning. We all assemble with tin hats and gas
masks, rifle and ammo. False alarm I reckon. On watch 13.00 – 17.00.
Went to NAAFI at night John and I had fritters for tea.

WEDNESDAY FEB 18

Watch 08.00 – 13.00. Pete's birthday luckily we are all four off tonight.
We call at the Institute where I beat John 3 times at draughts. I see
Rebecca and Cleopatra and have a chat. We then go to the Imperial and
have a big feed at Pete's expense. We paid for drinks and extras during
the evening meal. Bottle of sherry, cauliflower soup, cauliflower a la
Polonaise, paprika chicken, apricot pie and cream, coffee. We then go to
Papadopoulos see Laurel and Hardy in "Flying Deuces". Not so good.
Have coffee and cakes at the Ambassadeur and go back to camp in a taxi.

THURSDAY FEB 19

Off all day. Stayed in camp. Went to NAAFI at night and had tea and cakes. Was very depressed all day. Just about cheesed off to the limit. Slept in W/T cabin.

FRIDAY FEB 20

On watch 05.00 – 08.00. Pay parade 10.00 hrs. Got back pay for AC1 and forthwith payed off my debts of 24/-. Pete, Bill and self asked permission to go out in the morning. King refused – the sod. On watch 17.00 – 23.59.

SATURDAY FEB 21

Went to see football match in afternoon. 15W.H. & 259 Wing v. H.L.I. Bad spirit between 259 Wing and our men, lost a lead of 3 clear goals. Result 3-3. We have tea and cakes at Serimpi's then go to the Institute. Meal at Imperial then cinema Magic Palace. "I Am The Law" Ed.G.Robinson. Afterwards we went to Ambassadeurs for cocoa.

SUNDAY FEB 22

On aerodrome guard at night. No planes there just now. A couple of dummies are on the drome. Very well made jobs. Pete and myself do the 3 a.m. to 7.30 a.m. shift.

War

Japs progressing to Rangoon crossed the Slaween and Bliu. Allied air forces seem to be getting more organised in Far East. About time too. Russians still progressing. No news from desert.

MONDAY FEB 23

After our guard Pete and myself washed and sneaked over the gulch side and hitchhiked into Nicosia as we knew that we couldn't get permission from King.

Saw Spitfire, Aliki and Agnes at the Institute and arranged to see Spitfire in afternoon. Had haircut with the following additions, hot towels, face massage, cold cream and talc, moustache trimmed (nearly trimmed it away). Saw Sofia in afternoon and defeated her at chess and had an amusing conversation. Defeated Bill at chess. Saw Rebecca and Cleopatra later on. Cleo has got engaged, she's only 15. Had meal at Imperial then went to Papadopoulos. "Primrose Path" Ginger Rogers, Jack Melrea. Very good. Set off to walk back but were given lift in staff car. Still some decent officers about. PS Bill and John joined us in afternoon.

TUESDAY FEB 24TH

Didn't go out today. Played Newmarket at night. I won 11 fags. Swordfish aircraft operating from drome tonight. Searching for subs. Pete was on the flares.

WED FEB 25TH

I was to be on the flares tonight but operations were cancelled due to weather. We all four went to town and spent most of the time at the Institute. Beat Mac 2-1 at draughts. Saw Agnes, Rebecca and Cleo. Hot meal at the Imperial then walked back to camp.

Thurs Feb 26th

In all day. Finished off letter to Harold in afternoon. Played Newmarket at night and lost 17 fags.

War

Russians claim to have surrounded 16th German army. 96,000 men.

Friday Feb 27th

Meant to go out today but got nabbed for tonight's guard. On drome guard with Bill 18.00 – 22.30 hrs. Bombay on the drome also a "Wimpy" that had had an accident. Had cheese for supper. Dreamt like blazes (about Spitfire)

Saturday Feb 28

Manoeuvres are on. We have to carry rifle, ammo, gas masks, tin hat everywhere with us. No one allowed out of camp. One of our posts reported captured by imaginary paratroops. Drome captured. John, Bill, Pete and self play Newmarket at night. I lose 11 fags.

Card Games

SUNDAY MARCH 1

Sgt.King got Bill and myself on fatigue in afternoon. Cleaning billets
out and collecting squadron stores. Some Aussie airforce chaps arrive.
Great long shit-shooters. On drome guard at night with Bill
22.30 – 03.00 hrs. Wellington, Bombay, 3 hurricanes and Gladiator
on drome and 2 blokes guarding them. Got no sleep all night.

Japs invade Java after naval battle.

MONDAY MAR 2

Went out with Pete in afternoon. Saw Spitfire at the Institute. Tells us
that Aliki wants to know when we are coming in in the morning again.
At 17.30 I went to Yaxi's where I had ordered hot bath and boy was it
hot. Left me weak and sweating. Price 1/6. Returned to Institute where
John and Bill joined us. Saw Rebecca and Cleo. Played ping pong for
a short while. I beat Bill twice at chess. Meal at Imperial then we walk
back to camp, it being a lovely moonlit night.

TUESDAY MAR 3

On wireless watch 05.30 – 08.00. On watch also at 17.00 – 24.00. The
lads came to the WT cabin at night and we played Newmarket as I was
only standing by on the set. I lose 8 fags. Have toast, bully and cocoa
for supper.

WEDNESDAY MAR 4

On watch 13.00 – 18.00 hrs. Stayed in all day. Made toast and cocoa
for supper. It's mighty dull in the hut at nights.

THURS MAR 6

On watch 08.00 – 13.00. Pete and Bill are told to pack up to go
to 3VO Nicosia post tomorrow. Fancy I would have been chosen
if I hadn't been on watch. Pete and myself hitchhike to Nicosia in
afternoon. Saw Aliki and Agnes at Institute and had quite a chat. Aliki
was full of beans today. John and Bill turned up after tea and we all saw
"Three Smart Girls" with Deanna Durbin. Very good.

FRI MAR 6

After pay parade Pete and Bill pack their stuff into Cpl.Alderton's
gharry to go to 3VO. I decide to have the day out and get into the
gharry. We stop at the NAAFI and have tea. I am just about to get into
the gharry again when I see Sgt.King walking towards us. I re-enter the
NAAFI nonchalantly and go round the far side of the building and meet
the gharry further down the road. As we pass the guard room I lie flat
and Pete and Bill cover me with their overcoats. The Scarlet Pimpernel
touch. All difficulties surmounted I go to the Institute and Pete and Bill
carry on to their new billet. I have a couple of games of ping pong with
Loula and have a chat with Aliki, Agnes and Sofulla. They are upset at
my being separated from Bill and Pete. I tell Spitfire of my escape and
she says I must escape many times. I dine at the Imperial then go
and visit Pete and Bill at their billet. Very nice place.

I am playing for the table tennis team tonight against 259 Wing at the
Institute so in the late afternoon I practise with Derrick. I play Spitfire
at chess and after early shocks I gain the upper hand. Unfortunately the
game was unfinished as she had to go home before it was dark. I have
five gruelling games with a Turkish ping pong champion, he winning
3-2. Cleopatra and Rebecca turn up and I give Rebecca a Kolossi stamp
to send home to Alice. By the time of the tournament I am well nigh
exhausted and suffering from lack of sustenance. I made an awful mess

of my first game but I redeemed myself later when I earned the crowd's applause by defeating a former B'ham league player. Incidentally we lost, singles being 4-4 and the doubles match going to 259 Wing, the deciding game being won 22-20. At 9 o'clock we go to the Empire and have steak and potatoes starting with beer and finishing with coffee. My first food for 8 hrs. I was ready for it. Travelled back to camp in the liberty wagon the occupants of which were drunk and sprawling. Arrived back at midnight when I took my bed to the W/T room and sleep there. What a day.

SATURDAY MAR 7TH

On watch 05.30 – 08.00 and 17.00 – 24.00 hrs. John came to the drome at night and we made toast with sardines and cocoa.

SUNDAY MAR 8TH

Uneventful day. Went to NAAFI at night and had a beer. Had a mouse hunt in the hut. One casualty before the enemy retreated.

MONDAY MAR 9TH

Meant to dodge out of camp this afternoon. Got cleaned up and was just about to make my exit when Buckley comes in and tells me I am on drome guard tonight. Curse him. Was on 20.30 to 23.00 hrs and 03.30 to 05.30. What a bind. Wellington, 3 hurricanes and Gladiator on the drome.

TUESDAY MAR 10

Left camp on my own at 16.30, soon got a lift and was in Nicosia at 16.45. Went to Institute and saw Pete and Bill and Sofulla. Played ping pong for a while, then Peter and Bill went back to dinner at 259 Wing.

I played Sofulla at chess and beat her. Had a little talk then I went to
Serimpi's and had tea and cake. Saw Pete and Bill at Institute later on
and played table tennis. I left them and went to Magic Palace to see
"If I Were King" with Ronald Coleman. Afterwards I shared a taxi back
to camp with 5 more chaps. (6 Piastres each)

Rangoon lost, Java lost.

WEDNESDAY MAR 11

At 16.30 hrs I left camp and was fortunate to get a lift in the C.O.s
car. I went to the Institute and met Sophulla as pre-arranged. Had
quite an interesting chat. We afterwards played chess, myself being the
loser. Arranged to see her again Friday. Went to the piano recital at
the Institute. Price 1½ shillings. Very enjoyable. Had meal at Imperial
then went to Papadopoulos to see "Lady of The Tropics" Rbt. Taylor,
Heddy Lamar. Very good. I set off to walk back and had covered a
couple of miles before the C.O. picked me up in his car.

THURSDAY MARCH 12

On Lewis gun guard 24 hrs. Dodged off cleaning the guns. The lads
make a monopoly board and we play at night. John and myself make
toast on which we have the sardines that we snaffled from the W/T
rations not long ago. Washed that lot down with tea without milk.
Very good.

FRIDAY MAR 13

Played monopoly. Hitch hiked into Nicosia with Geoff Alderton. Went
to Institute. Pete and Bill were there and Sofulla. Played ping pong.
Went to pictures at night. "Society Smugglers" at Magic Palace. Very
poor. Liberty wagon was piled high with drunks so I arranged with
Geoff and 4 more blokes to go back by taxi.

SATURDAY MAR 14 BIRTHDAY

Went out in morning for first time in 3 weeks. Was in town at 10 a.m.
Visited Pete and Bill at their tent. Went to Institute and played table
tennis with Aliki, Agnes and Sofulla. Had discussion after. Had to be
back in camp at 2.30 p.m. for blood test. Indian gave me a lift. After
blood test John and myself went back into Nic and saw football match
259 Wing defeated W.H. 6-1. Had tea and cakes at Imperial then Pete,
Bill and self went to Institute. Sofulla was there. Played table tennis
and afterwards draughts. Had good meal at Imperial where I stood
the lads a bottle of sherry. Went to Papadopoulos to see "Swiss family
Robinson" not very good. Had coffee in Ambassadeurs then returned
to camp with John. Received telegram from home.

SUNDAY MARCH 15

Missed breakfast so had tea and cake at NAAFI. On guard at night.
On middle shift 10.30 p.m. to 3.00 a.m. with old Trudgeon. On
the drome were 2 Beaufighters, 4 Albacores, 1 Walrus, 2 Bombays,
1 Wellington, 1 Gladiator, 3 hurricanes. I get into the cockpit of one
of the Beaufighters.

Bristol Beaufighter   *Fairey Albacore*

Supermarine Walrus

Bristol Bombay

Vickers Wellington

Gloster Gladiator

Hawker Hurricane

MONDAY MARCH 16

Tried to get to sleep in the morning, couldn't for the row in the hut.
Played monopoly at night. I won. Had cheese toast and tea for supper.
Shaved off my moustache today.

TUESDAY MARCH 17

Went into town with John at night. Loula immediately noticed the missing moustache. Bill arrived later and we had tea at the Imperial. John and myself went to Papadopoulos to see "Rich Man Poor Girl" which was very enjoyable. Lew Ayres and Rbt.Young being outstanding. Had coffee at Ambassadeurs then retired to camp.

WEDNESDAY MARCH 18

Game of monopoly in morning. Watched half football match in afternoon. The W.H. beat the Heavy Ack-Ack Battery 11-1. Twigg scored 7. On guard at night. Middle shift again 10.30 p.m. to 3.00 a.m. with Sid Williams.

THURSDAY MARCH 19

Got permission from Sgt.King via Sgt.Black to go out in morning. Not very promising day but went out on Geoff's gharry. Bill and Pete were at the Institute with the three girls. We tell them the news that we are leaving the island in a fortnight. They give us photos and we return the compliment. Bill and Pete accompany me to the Imperial and we dine. Went to their billet afterwards and had dinner at 259 Wings expense. Went to Papadopoulos at night and saw "Five came Back" Chester Morris.

FRIDAY MARCH 20

Was on fatigue in morning. Filled two big lorries full of empty petrol tins and oil drums and went to station to dump them. The station would not have them, so we had to bring them back to camp. Typical W.H. procedure. At night John and myself hitched into Nicosia and met Pete. We went to gramophone recital at a house on the outskirts of the town. "Messiah" pt 1. Enjoyed it tremendously.

SATURDAY MARCH 21

Dodged out on my own in the morning, got a lift into town. Bill, Pete and the girls were already at the Institute and we played ping pong. Aliki's brother turned up and I beat him at table tennis 21-16. Bill and Pete went back to tiffin being on watch in afternoon. I then beat Loula in two straight games and gave Sofulla similar treatment. Had quite a chat with the three girls, then dined at the Imperial where I had a confab with the waiter whose home is in Athens. I waited until the rain stopped then set off walking back. I got a lift and got the bloke to drop me beyond the guard room. I dodged back to the hut over the hill and found that I hadn't been missed. On drome guard at night and was on last shift which should be 03.00 – 07.30. As it was I didn't get up till 06.30 as the guard commander was sleeping in an anti-room. Best guard I've done to date.

SUNDAY MARCH 22

Had a day in today. Bitterly cold all day even though the sun was out. Went to dinner in my overcoat. Still a lot of snow on Troodos.

MONDAY MARCH 23

Exchange parade in morning. Managed to change my boots shirt and tie. Bill and Pete came up to the camp in afternoon to exchange various articles. I went out with them in afternoon, getting permission from Sgt. King. Had tea and cake at Serimpi's (Mrs Cook's) then I went to Institute (Bill and Pete were on watch). I beat a Cypriot in 3 straight games of ping pong. John came down and we both went to Geep tent where we, the four of us, had supper of eggs, fried bread and one of Mrs Cook's cakes and cocoa.

TUESDAY MATCH 24

Dodged out of camp over by the M.T. place. Got lift on Indian lorry.
Saw the girls, Pete and Bill at Institute. Pete and Bill are on watch and
they go early. I played Sofulla at table tennis and beat her 4 games to 2.
I tell them that I am going on Thursday and they are very sorry. After
the usual chat I dine at the Imperial with McManus. I got my hair cut,
then go up to Pete's billet where I pick up tin and some olive oil. I set
off to walk back but get a lift early on which takes me into camp. On
guard at night. On middle shift 22.30 – 03.00 but didn't trouble to
leave watch but spent time reading and short kip.

WEDNESDAY MARCH 25

Was sneaking out of camp with Geoff Alderton when who should we
bump into but Sgt. King, so took the bull by the horns and asked
permission to go out. After a helluva argument he agrees under
condition I return at 14.00 hrs. I proceed to Institute where Pete is
with the girls. I play ping pong for a while being on top form beating
Pete 3 straight games. Say my goodbyes to the girls who wish me good
luck etc. They are sorry to see me go but not as sorry as I am to go,
as Egypt has no attraction for me. I return to camp as per schedule.
Go out again at night and meet Pete and Bill. We go to Magic Palace
and see "Music in my Heart" Pretty punk. Liberty gharry ran short of
petrol. Had to walk about half way.

THURSDAY MARCH 26

Went into town with John at 5 p.m. Had tea and cake at Serimpi's.
Bought some lace work to send home. Went to Institute probably for
last time and Bill and Pete turn up. We have feed at Imperial. Bottle of
sherry, oxtail soup, omelette and chips, coffee. John and myself walk
home (not exactly home).

FRIDAY MARCH 27

No signs of moving today. On guard at night 18.00 – 22.30. Spent an hour of the time in the NAAFI with beers and biscuits.

SATURDAY MARCH 28

Went out in afternoon and had tea and cake at Serimpi's. Met the lads at 7 p.m. at Institute where I give them both a sound drubbing at table tennis. We have tea at Imperial then set off to walk back but get a lift on army wagon.

SUNDAY MARCH 29

We clean our huts and prepare bed boards for 17 W.H. 80 of whom came in this afternoon. Went to Church service in camp and afterwards play monopoly in hut. I make about 15 slices of toast for the lads and scrounge tin of salmon and make tea also. Not bad.

MONDAY MARCH 30

We get definite news that we are leaving tomorrow, so I dodge over Gulch side and get on to the road where I soon get a hitch. I went to the Institute where I had my photo taken with a group. Aliki, Agni and Sofulla turn up and are surprised to see me. Bill and Pete turn up later and we play table tennis. The lads have to leave early as they are on watch. I have a talk with the girls then say 'goodbye' as I do not expect to see them again. I dine at Imperial where I spend my last 10 Piastres on egg and chips.

I see Mrs Cook of Serimpi's who invites me to her place. We have doughnuts and coffee and a chat. She has lived in Java 12 years and Singapore. I leave there and intend to walk up to the lads billet but meet Sofulla, Aliki, Agni and Loula and they drag me to the skating rink where we gass until 4 p.m. Sofulla, Aliki and myself then go to Institute where we play table tennis. Aliki leaves at about 5 p.m. and Sofulla beats me 2 games to 1 at ping pong. We then play chess three times myself being the victor 2-1. I also beat her at draughts. We talk quite some then I say 'Goodbye' for the 3rd and last time I think. She was quite touched up and ran up the street and out of sight amongst the crowd. I give Loula a walloping at ping pong then John arrives with several letters for me. Bill and Pete turn up with another letter and Harry's catalogue. I read my letters then have a talk to Rebecca and Cleopatra who did not know I was leaving. They wish me to write to them. We go to the Imperial and have sherries and coffee, Geoff Alderton joining us. We all go to Magic Palace and see "Golden Boy". I see the last of Aliki and Agni at the back of the "Magic" in between reels. We miss the liberty gharry but cadge a lift on an army lorry.

RETURN TO THE
WESTERN DESERT

TUESDAY MARCH 31

Reveille 04.00. Breakfast 05.00. Parade with full kit 05.30. We travel to
Nicosia station by gharries. Train departs 07.30. we arrive in Famagusta
early afternoon and after a bit of hanging about with pack on etc. we
get on to the boat which is crowded with Indians. Boat anchors outside
harbour and leaves at 18.00 hrs. We have to sleep as best we can on the
kit bags which are all over the deck.

WEDNESDAY APL 1

Was slightly sick this morning but it didn't put me off my grub.
Wearisome day, some pretty rotten stinks on deck. Beautiful full moon
at night, the reflection was as a path of solid gold through the sea.
Spent a bloody uncomfortable night, a kit bag sticking in the middle of
my back. Got up early and shaved.

THURSDAY APL 2

Boat docked at Port Said 09.00 hrs. Got our kit ready and hung about
for a few hrs. Eventually got onto barges and lay roasting in the sun for
an hour or so. Wogs visiting us in rowing boats trying to sell us oranges
etc. being without money they didn't bother me much. It was turned
14.00 hrs before we got on the quayside. We dragged ourselves and
the kit to the transit camp where we had to erect the walls of the EPI
tents. We were hungry, weary and near to collapse. We had a meal and a

wash, made a quick recovery and went into Port Said. I changed 5 bob which Geoff kindly lent me and sent a cable to Dad for his birthday. We then went to pictures. "Old Wyoming" with Wallace Beery. Very good. Cheapest seat 6½ piasters (1/4 $_d$ approx). Crossed the ferry to Port Fouad and went to Clover Club. Had some good chai and eggs on toast. Returned to camp and slept like a log.

FRIDAY APL 3

Up at 7 had breakfast. Parade with full kit at 8. Hung about till 9. Marched with full pack and rifle to ferry. Crossed ferry, marched to station. Piled in the train which didn't set off till 11.30. What a weary journey. Long waits at small stations. Wogs trying to sell their rubbish. I'd liked to have seen Pete's reactions to this lot. Arrived Cairo station at 18.00 hrs. Dragged our kit to awaiting lorries which took us to Helwan transit camp where we arrived about 19.00 hrs, tired, weak and hungry. We were allotted tents, 16 in some tents, John and myself were lucky to get into a tent where there were only twelve. We had a meal then went to NAAFI. Slept well at night. Dreamt like blazes.

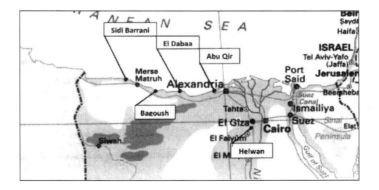

Saturday Apl 4

Got paid in afternoon. Good job too I'm broke. Actually I owe 16/- but creditors Pete and Geoff are still in Cyprus. Was pestered to death with flies in the afternoon. Went to NAAFI at night with John and wrote letters. Joined at a beer and had couple of egg sandwiches. Turned in early.

Sunday Apl 5

Played monopoly in morning. Tried to sleep in afternoon. The flies are hell. Went into Helwan immediately after dinner. Went to cinema. "Trade Winds" 4½ Piastres. Had tea and cakes at the Homestead club. Long walk back.

Monday Apl 6

Went to Cairo in afternoon by train. About ½ hrs run. Posted letter to Sofulla. Had tea at Empire club. Went to Metro at night. "Third Finger Left Hand" Melvyn Douglas and Myrna Loy. Very good. Had tea and sandwich at YMCA. Hell of a crush on the train back. Managed to get seats by a bit of sharp practice. Quite some walk from Helwan to our tents.

Tuesday Apl 7 Dad's birthday.

Another wearying day. Wrote four airgraphs in NAAFI at night.

Wednesday Apl 8

In morning went to main camp and had hot bath. Were not supposed to but nobody stopped us. Went to pictures at main camp at night.

Judy Garland and Mickey Rooney "Babes in Arms". Not very good.
Supposed to be on guard at 4 in the morning but failed to get up.
Air raid warning at night. Hope there's no enquiry.

THURSDAY APL 9

Failed to get up for breakfast so went to NAAFI. Played monopoly
in afternoon. Pictures at camp cinema at night. "First 100 yrs" Bob
Montgomery and Virginia Bruce. Not bad. Remainder of unit expected
in tonight but failed to arrive. Landed at Alex.

FRIDAY APL 10

Another dull day. NAAFI at night, wrote letter to Aliki.

SATURDAY AP 11

Played monopoly during day. Camp cinema at night. "Ice Follies of
1939" Joan Crawford Lew Ayres, James Stewart. Not bad. Remainder
of unit come in late at night but we don't get chance to see them.

SUNDAY AP 12

See Pete and Bill in morning. They bring note from Sofulla for me.
The four of us go to camp cinema at night. "Ninotchka" Greta Garbo
and Melvyn Douglas. Very good. Went to main camp NAAFI after.

MONDAY AP 13

John and myself got up for breakfast which consisted of some terrible
concoction. We took Pete and Bill tea. Very dull day. Wrote letters in
NAAFI at night. What a row there was. Was on guard 00.30 – 02.00
hrs on my own. Nothing much to it.

Tuesday Ap 14

Bill and Pete lend John and myself 5 bob each so we go to Cairo in afternoon. The walk to Helwan station nearly put us on our backs. Terribly hot. We arrived Cairo before four and had the usual trouble with boat blocks. We had a quiet hour in the Victoria reading rooms. Went to a few book shops. Dined in style at the Toc H. very good I scrounged extra cup of coffee. Had a draught beer at the Pole Nord then went to Diana Cinema to see Shaw's "Major Barbara" Wendy Hiller and Rex Harrison. Excellent. The return journey wasn't too bad. We had to make our beds in the dark as the lamp had run dry.

Wednesday Ap 15

Another dreary day. Meant to write letters in NAAFI at night but found it impossible as the joint was crowded.

Thursday Ap 16

Went to main camp for swim but the bath was empty this being the only drawback. We returned to the tent and the four of us played monopoly. I won. Went to Homestead, Helwan at night. Played Chinese Chequers then had a feed.

Friday Apl 17

Failed to arise for breakfast. Went to NAAFI. Went down to main camp in afternoon to write letters. What a trek! worried to death with flies in the writing room. Went to camp cinema at night. "Murder in Pictures" Sure was murder in pictures it was bloody awful. What a long day.

SATURDAY APL 18

Went to NAAFI this morning. Breakfast is never worth bothering with. Pete, Bill, John and myself went to main camp for swim in afternoon. Crowded but I can still swim a bit. Had some beer at NAAFI at night. Pete calls it appropriately "The Thieves Den".

SUNDAY APL 19

Had a walk to Japanese Gardens. Helwan in afternoon. Warm work. Gardens not bad, but I'm too cheesed off to appreciate anything in this country. Homestead at night and drank tea etc.

MONDAY APL 20

Set off on 48 hrs leave to Cairo – the four of us. Put up at Toc H. tried to book for Palestine Orchestra but couldn't get a seat. Went to see "Ziegfield Girl" at Metro, 2nd house, I had 1st house ticket so had to sit on steps. Very poor film.

TUESDAY APL 21

Went to Geyira Club in morning. Met Nobby Clark and Dave Abbott. Watched cricket match. Was sat at table having a spot of tea when who should come to the table but Walter McNiven who was billeted with me at Blackpool. He was in hospital blue. He came out 5 months after me went straight up the blue got badly burnt. Saw "Gondoliers" at night. Pretty amateurish. Was sick after tea. Too much rich food after the shit we get at the camp.

WEDNESDAY APL 22

Bought some books in morning. Went to Empire Services club for some grub. Bloody poor. Had a fracas with a boot black. Kicked him up the arse with the shoe he'd dirtied. Wrote letters at YMCA to Harold and posted it. Saw "Three Girls About Town" at night. Had some American beer at Pole Nord. Arrived back in camp about midnight.

THURSDAY APL 23

Our anniversary for service in Middle East. Played monopoly in Pete's tent in afternoon. Went To NAAFI at night and drank beer. Willie McNeish turned up in afternoon having got 48 hrs leave. Supped with us at NAAFI.

FIRDAY APL 24

John and myself got the job of checking our wireless equipment this morning. When I'd finished I went with Pete and Willie to Cairo. Spent afternoon in Victory club reading. Went to Metropole at night. "Affectionately Yours" Merle Oberon and Ralph Bellamy. Very good. Afterwards we went to the YMCA and drank tea. Willie saw us off on the train. Arrived in camp about midnight – nearly got lost. Not feeling very well tonight. A mass of aches and pains.

SATURDAY APL 25

Felt very bad today, aching all over. Helped load lorries morning and afternoon. The four of us went to Homestead at Helwan at night and drank chai etc. On our return to camp there was an air raid not far away. Ack-ack, searchlights etc.

SUNDAY APL 26

Leaving Helwan for Aboukir. Arose at 6 a.m. and had breakfast which wasn't very filling. Pulled some tents down before leaving. The convoy left at 9 a.m. Our lorry soon dropped out of convoy with engine trouble. We had to keep getting out to push. After four stops we got towed to Half Way house by an RAF chap who gave us cheese sandwiches. We had one cup of tea 10d and 1 cake 4d at Half Way House (our rations with the rest of the convoy). Taffy and Jack struggle with the engine till 7 p.m. and we manage to get to Aircraft Pool where we spend the night. Hot meal at NAAFI.

MONDAY APL 27TH

The lads repaired engine and after a bit of breakfast we set off. We reached Alex and then had to be towed to Aboukir by lorry that had been sent to look for us. Aboukir seems to be a damned sight better than Helwan. Went to camp cinema at night "Pagliacci" with Richard Tanber. Best camp cinema I've been in.

TUESDAY APL 28

F.F.I. in afternoon. Went to cinema at night. "Pot O'Gold" Show interrupted by air raid. Very heavy raid 10 to 20 miles away. Heavy ack ack barrage, flaming onions etc. Saw 2 kites brought down in flames and a 3rd was shot down which I didn't see. 1 ack ack, 2 fighters.

WEDNESDAY APL 30

Uninteresting day. John, Bill and self went to NAAFI for Tombola but it wasn't on. Pete was ill.

FRIDAY MAY 1

Had splitting headache all day. Four of us went to Alexandria and saw "49th Parallel' at Rio. Not bad.

SATURDAY MAY 2

Headache all day. Cleared a bit at night. Went to camp cinema "Henry VIII" Charles Laughton. Very good.

SUNDAY MAY 3

My headache resumes and I feel rotten generally. Went into Abu Qir village at night, nothing much there. Air raid 4 a.m., 3 kites brought down by night fighters.

MONDAY MAY 4

Feel worse today. I take some salts. Pete gives me a Cascara Segrada. Newton gives me 2 aspirins and 3 $MgSO_4$ tablets. I shit 4 times in evening and feel better for it. This camp is overrun with bugs, fleas, ants etc. Everybody is getting bitten rotten, myself included. Not half. Curse it.

TUES MAY 5

Feel bit better today. Uneventful day. NAAFI at night.

WED MAY 6

Head cleared today. Pete and myself go into Alex. See "Golden Fleecing" Lew Ayres. "Free and Easy" Ruth Huxley. Spend evening in Jewish club.

THURSDAY MAY 7

A day of letter writing at NAAFI. British invade Madagascar. I was talking about such a project yesterday.

FRIDAY MAY 8

Bill's birthday. We all go into Alex and see "And So Ends Our Night" with Frederich March, Margaret Sullivan – Remosque's "Flotsam". Quite good.

SATURDAY MAY 9

Writing at NAAFI in afternoon and evening. Checked our equipment in gharry in morning. Pete and I are on post. Big naval engagement in Pacific. Invasion of Australia stemmed.

SUNDAY MAY 10

Quiet day at NAAFI writing. Fleas and bugs still biting. Horrible.

MONDAY MAY 11

Cleaned the water tank in our gharry. Read at NAAFI in afternoon. Pictures at camp cinema. "Poison Pen" seen it before. Had a beer at NAAFI later at night.

TUESDAY MAY 12

Moving up desert tomorrow. Filled our water tanks in morning. Collected our rifles and ammo in afternoon. John, Pete, Bill and myself go into Alex. Had meal at Fleet Club. Dear place. Saw "The Little

Foxes" Bette Davis and Herbert Marshall at the Rio. Very good indeed.
Had a beer at the Jewish Club and caught 9.30 train back to camp.

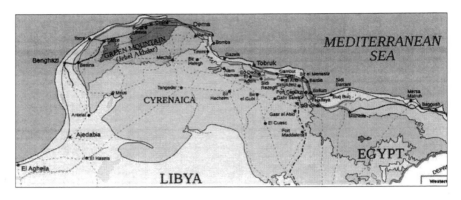

Western Desert

WEDNESDAY MAY 13

Up at 5 a.m. Left Abu Qir before 7 a.m. 6 men in back of our gharry
with kit (personal and post). Very uncomfortable. We stop at El Daba
and have meal at NAAFI – poor meal. "Muddle Easters" gave show
at NAAFI at night. Very good. We slept out in the open at night. No
room in gharry.

THURSDAY MAY 14

Left El Daba 8 a.m. arrived Bagensk 12 a.m. I was at this place a
year ago today. We have tiffin in transit camp after a long wait in sun.
Horrible. Have a rest in the afternoon. Pete and I go to canteen at
night and have couple of bottles of beer each. Enjoyable.

FRIDAY MAY 15

Set off about 9 reached Mersa Matruh before 12 picked up tents and petrol. Had scrappy tiffin of bully and biscuits and went straight to our future H.Q. near Sidi Barrani. It is by the sea. Searched for NAAFI at night in vain. Nearly got lost coming back. Germans starting big offensive in Crimea.

SATURDAY MAY 16

Spent morning putting tents up for HQ. In afternoon Pete and myself go about mile from HQ in gharry and test set. I did all tuning back etc. and shook Pete rigid. Rather a good job.

SUNDAY MAY 17

About ten posts going out today ours included. Our post is about 3 miles west of Sidi Barrani. We are near to A.M.E.S. post and are going to feed there. Got in touch with HQ in about 1 minute. I think Mr. Rose was rather pleased. There are a lot of crosses round the post – Italian soldiers and bags of shrapnel.

MONDAY MAY 18

I was on duty 06.00 – 11.00 and 16.00 – 20.00. We call HQ every 2 hrs. had 31 (aircraft) plots today. P.E. set started OK. I have got a slight dose of the shits. Food at the AMES is jolly good. Got the news on at night – Kerch falls but Timochenko is attacking near Kharkov.

TUESDAY MAY 19

Trouble with receiver. I changed limiter valve – OK now. 20 plots.

WEDNESDAY MAY 20

PE set fuses burnt out. Changed them. 36 plots today. Heavy raid on Mannheim by R.A.F. Sent message for fuses and limiter valve.

THURSDAY MAY 21

Visited by Williams and Sgt. Black. Williams repairs the fuses. 31 plots today.

FRIDAY MAY 22

(Beer ration 1 bottle a week).
Visited by Cpl. Holmes who takes both our primuses. No more nightly chai now. We got our football blown up and have a kick about had a bottle of beer at night.(weekly).

SATURDAY MAY 23

Went to watch football match at A.M.E.S. at night with Tom Tyler. 15 posts now on air. Not many of them on frequency. 53 plots.

SUNDAY MAY 24

P.O. Rose and naval officer visit us. We now have to plot naval craft. P.E. set failed to start.

MONDAY MAY 25

Ginge fettled P.E. set. Transmitter failed to start. I traced it down to break in arc leads which I fixed.

TUESDAY MAY 26

Went swimming in afternoon. Water oily and rough. Bottom rocky.
I cut my foot. Poor show. Welfare officer leaves us some books and fags.
Haven't been paid for three weeks and no mail. HQ tell us to draw
water from AMES, sure want us off their hands.

WEDNESDAY MAY 27

Jerry commences a push up the front. Between 7 & 8 p.m. about 100
fighters (chiefly Tomahawks) pass over us from the front. We commence
night plotting tonight. I do all night duty.

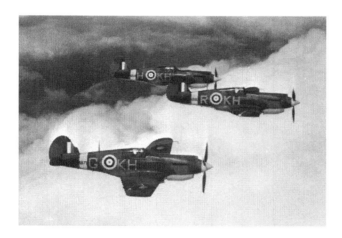

Curtiss Tomahawk

THURSDAY MAY 28

Did bit of writing in afternoon. Bomb dropped pretty close during
night.

FRIDAY MAY 29

Got paid today. Les Milchard visited us, brought our mail. Some bad news, Jock Lawson got drowned at HQ. Had a bottle of beer at night. I was on night shift again.

SATURDAY MAY 30

Bottle of beer at night. Uninteresting day.

SUNDAY MAY 31

Did lot of writing today. Tom says he saw lorries with Chinese going up the front. 1000 bombers over Cologne. On night duty. Bags of plots – curse it.

MONDAY JUNE 1

Plotted our first hostile bomber. Junkers 88. Did some writing at night. Had bottle of beer.

Junkers JU88

TUESDAY JUNE 2

Had terrific fight with P.E. (petrol electric) charging set and eventually won having to change the plug. I also changed petrol lead. 1036 bombers over Essen. 35 lost. Must have given Krupp's the works. Jerry's attack in the desert held. 200 tanks captured. On night duty.

WEDNESDAY JUNE 3

Very hot day. Quiet day. Gave the accs a good charge. Had bottle of beer at night.

THURSDAY JUNE 4

Uneventful day. On night duty. Very busy. Hostile bombers bombing aerodrome always pass right over our lorry's quite low. Big fire started at drome.

FRIDAY JUNE 5

Beer ration day. 1 bottle. Heidrich, Gestapo chief in Czechoslovakia killed. Good show.

SATURDAY JUNE 6

HQ now tell us to scrounge paraffin from AME. Looks as though they don't want to visit us although we are only 200 yds off main road. About time they brought our mail. I am getting good with PE set. I deal exclusively with the acc charging, also do my share of watches on the set. The Chinese that Tom saw turn out to be Ghurkas. On night duty.

Sunday June 7

Was cheesed off to buggery all day. HQ sent us paraffin and forgot to send the mail. The rats. Didn't know what to do with myself today. Cleaned the generator, armature and bushes and gave the accumulators (accs) their daily charge.

Monday June 8

Keep doing my P.T., just another day. On night duty. Enemy kites bombed drome on both sides of us, using flares. I manage to contact 9BX through heavy interference.

Tuesday June 9

Tom hitch hikes to HQ and brings back our mail. Good show. Went for short walk at night. Lots of Iti graves around base.

Wednesday June 10

One of the South Africans near us got injured with Italian land grenade. Two of our blokes at Bardia got injured similarly. Lots of them lying about – little red tin efforts. Went a long walk at night and inspected some of the Iti lorries that are burnt out all over the place. A lot of the graves have rat holes in them. On night duty.

Thursday June 11

Got 2 bottles of beer each night. Bags of stuff gone up the road since we've been here. Tanks, guns etc.

FRIDAY JUNE 12

One more day of eating, reading and sleeping. Rommel has broken through at Beir Hacheim and has started big push against Tobruk. On night duty.

SATURDAY JUNE 13

Managed to get some beer in for the night. Germans attacking in Kharkov sector.

SUNDAY JUNE 14

Rommel takes El Adem. Lot of our staff returning from front. On night watch.

MONDAY JUNE 15

An AMES post (from the front) plonk themselves right next to us. A damned nuisance, always on the scrounge.

TUES JUNE 16

Still heavy fighting up the front. Lot of stuff returning from front. On night duty.

WED JUNE 17

AMES trying to get an old GP set working. Then ask me to look at it. I mess about with it, no avail.

Thurs June 18

Message to all posts telling us to return to HQ. Had one last good meal at AMES then joined the never ending stream of traffic on the road. Arrived HQ 7 p.m. Got some beer.

Friday June 19

Had to shift our gharry again for the 3rd time. Done nothing but pack and repack so far. Butch (HQ cook) just dumped 14 days rations on us and we have to make our own meals, even though we haven't got primuses. Just like HQ.

Saturday June 21st

Tobruk falls. Germans at Bardis where one of our posts was. Didn't get away any too soon. Filled our water bowser tonight, leaving tomorrow after an unpleasant stay. The only shade at midday is under the lorry.

Monday June 22nd

Set off with map reference and eventually settled at a spot 30 miles east of Sidi Barrani. No sooner had we ripped our set up than HQ send us a message telling us they have given us the wrong map reference. We go about 10 miles further west and after much difficulty find suitable spots (for observation). The desert track gives me the heebies, you get thrown all over the place together with the stuff in the gharry. What a bind. Bumping about 10 hrs today to get a distance of 30 miles from HQ.

TUESDAY JUNE 23RD

Message to return to HQ at Mersa. Returned and got straffed by Jerry (planes) at night. Our lorry nearly got hit, tracer bullets crossing it on either side.

WEDNESDAY JUNE 24

We get sent to post we have just returned from. Rather exasperating. As we went up the desert road everything else seemed to be in retreat. Peter and myself were in favour of staying by the roadside and awaiting developments. Tyler insisted on going down to the coast some ten miles from the road. Together with a mania for carrying out orders to the letter he had the mad idea that a mobile canteen we had previously seen would still be down there. At night we got a message from HQ telling us to return to Bagoush. It was decided that we move out at dawn. Felt a bit uneasy, everything dead quiet, but had a good night's sleep in some beds we found at a deserted rest camp.

CAPTURED

THURSDAY JUNE 25

We drive up the road from coast and go slap into a Jerry Panzer division and get taken prisoner. German officer a very nice bloke. We get sent up to Barrani at night.

A.C.1 HUTCHINSON

A.C.1 Leslie Hutchinson, son of Mr. and Mrs. E. Hutchinson, of 295, Colne-road, Burnley, is officially reported missing on June 25th while serving with the R.A.F. in the Middle East.

Aged 22, he was employed by the Burnley Building Society before being called up two years ago. He went abroad in February last year, and served for a short time in Cyprus. His brother Harold, a member of the "Express" reporting staff in civil life, is serving in the Army.

FRIDAY JUNE 26

An Italian gives us some tinned carrots and fags and we give him some chai. We get shifted to Borsia at night and sleep in a wayside building.

SATURDAY JUNE 27

German soldiers lend us their fire and kettle to make chai. We go to Tobruk and then to Derna. Pretty grim at Derna.

SUNDAY JUNE 28

Day at Derna. Not so good.

MONDAY JUNE 29

Got moved to Benghasi. These gharry rides are sure tough.

TUES JUNE 30

Got bivowacks. Not much room. Rations ½ tin of bully, ½ loaf bread per day.

WED JULY 1

Had to close our bivowacks tighter together. Bit of a squeeze.

THURS JULY 2

Got a bit of lime juice and 5 cigs. What cigs!

FRID JULY 3

Lot of blokes with dysentery. One bloke collapsed in a shit trench.

SAT JULY 4

Rations increased 1 tin bully and 1 loaf. Get coffee and sugar and wood issue.

SUN JULY 5

2,000 of us sorted out to go to Italy. In a compound of our own now.

MON JULY 6

Mobile shower in camp.

TUES JULY 7

Used the shower today. Very grateful.

WED – SUN 8 – 12 JULY

Usual routine. One loaf, 1 tin bully, sugar and coffee regularly now. Bags of rumours floating about camp. Got first cooked meal tonight. Mouthfull of macaroni pea mash. Very grateful, ½ bully in lieu of the usual one.

MONDAY JULY 13

Half tin of bully and hot meal again.
Raid by Wimpy's. 1 shot down.

TUES JULY 14

No hot meal.

WED – SAT JULY 15 – 18

Monotony. Hot meal on Frid served after dark. On Sat in lieu of half tin bully I've got tin of sardines between 7 men. Just a taste.

SUN – TUES JULY 19 – 21

Rumours of leaving received.

LIBYA TO ITALY

BENGHASI TO TARRANTO
(2 DAY VOYAGE)

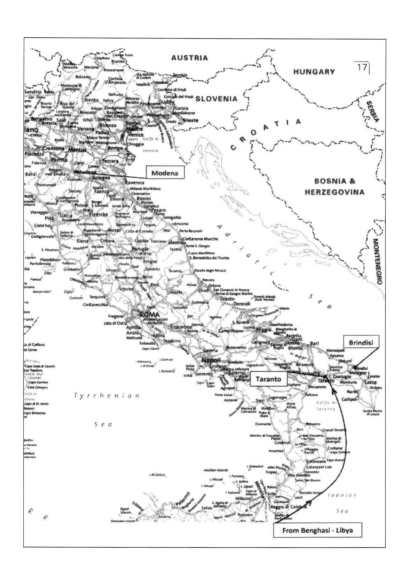

WED JULY 22

Reveille at 3 a.m. got rations at
gate and were on the boat at 9 a.m.
3,500 on board 5,000 ton ship. We
are down bottom hold. Did we get
any sleep at night? did we hell. Too
crushed for anything.

Ravello Napoli

THURS JULY 23

Allowed on deck thank goodness. Slept a little better at night but a
bloke sat on my head at 2 a.m. due to being on a slope.

FRI JULY 24

Sighted land and docked. Taranto. Slept on deck after shindy with
guards.

SAT JULY 25

Still on board. Bully and biscuit ration brought on board. Had a shower
with the shit-house hose pipe.

SUN JULY 26

Left boat at 6 a.m. and went by train to Brindisi. Marched to
fumigation camp 4 miles away. Some luck on ½ tin bully and 1 biscuit.
Got no grub at night.

Mon July 27

No grub till 4 p.m. Just about ravenous. Jack, Bill and Tom have been feeding on rations they had stocked 6 tins bully 6 biscuits. Did they give Pete and self any to last us out? Like hell. Esprit de corps? At night marching 15 kilometers to camp. Don't know how we managed it. In bivowacks at camp.

Tues July 28

Got two meals of hot macaroni and rice etc. (the usual stew). 1 loaf (small). Got 1 Red Cross parcel between 10 men. What a glorious surprise. 5 Gold Flake each and tinned goods. Carrots, marmalade etc.

Wed July 29

Same as yesterday. Got my ripped shirt changed by Italians. They have also given us dixie, spoon and blanket all of which I have been managing without up till now.

Thurs July 30

Did ½ hr on latrine digging.

Fri July 31

Parcels still turning up. Keep us going. Got Iti fag issue – 25 per week.

Sat Aug 1

Left Brindisi at 4 p.m. Marched 4 miles to station. Travelled all night on train.

SUN AUG 2

Off train about 7 a.m. Camp not far away. 25 men in bivowack.
Still with Pete but separated from Tom and co. – not sorry.

SUN AUG 3

Grub similar to Brindisi. 2 hot, ½ servings of rice and macaroni stew
a day. 1 small cob and little piece of cheese. Built fire in compound at
night, promise of double rations.

TUES AUG 4

Built rubbish compound. Got double dinner issue. Good. Roll call
parades 6.30 a.m. and 6.30 p.m. Took 2 hrs at night at attention most
of time, 5 blokes passed out. Reveille 5 o'clock 1st meal 11.30.

WED AUG 5

Grub here not as good as Brindisi – too thin. No parcels yet.

THURS AUG 6

Promise of fags keeps falling through. Stew is like soup these days.
lLittle rice and macaroni and bags of greens – mangled tops.

FRI AUG 7

Bit colder today. Nothing to read. No smokes. Hungry, weak. What a
life!

SATURDAY AUG 8

Fags turn up at night. The grub we get is little different to soup made bitter by greens.

SUN AUG 9

All talk here is of grub. No mention of women. The RSM's here are a big let down. Meals awful today.

MON AUG 10

Iti cook made the tea time sully, and did he drop a bollock. He left three dixies without rice and had to sort it all out at the finish.

TUES AUG 11

Staff sergeant put in klink for pinching another blokes bread. Been a good bit of that going on. Poor show.

WED AUG 12

Grub improving slightly. Pete a bit off colour, gave me his tea.

THURS AUG 13

Helped Pete to make cheese, onion and bread risole – passed afternoon on. This cheese is damned good but you only get a small piece with $\frac{1}{10}^{th}$ onion.

Friday Aug 14

Wrote postcard home. 1ˢᵗ since being prisoner. Made me sob. Got shirt, socks and vest comforts from Red Cross.

SAT AUG 15

Morning count up took about 2 hrs. Chiefly our RSM's to blame.
Fag issue.

SUN AUG 16

Tippled down at about 3 a.m. Parade took 1½ hrs in morning.
Got our first pay. 10 lire instead of 50. Caught about 20 crabs on shirt.

MON AUG 17

Went on outside work. Filling in ditches in the road. Got double grub.
Felt full for once.

TUES AUG 18

Big uproar about grub today. Very poor. Colonel gave us a lecture.

WED AUG 19

New system of grub. Cheese and bread tiffin. Double scilly at tea time.

THURS AUG 20

Got my sores (ankle) dressed.

FRI AUG 21

Got my beard sheared off. 8 weeks growth. Lads didn't know me.
Another 10 lire.

SAT AUG 22

This new grub system isn't so good. The double at night is hardly double and thinner. New rumours of continental invasion. Germans still supposed to be at El Arnein. Got my ankle dressed. Sores last for months here.

SUN AUG 23

Meat day. Not bad. Got 4 pieces in stew.

MON AUG 24

Rumours of Red Cross parcels again. Heavy shower in afternoon.

TUES AUG 25

On fatigue in morning. Building walls with piles of stones. Officer kept us at it 4 hrs without break. Rained in afternoon thank goodness.

WED AUG 26

Got bit of olive oil issued. Fried bread in it. Very good. Had my foot dressed again.

THURS AUG 27

Awful headache all day. Parcels arrive at last. Canadian. 1 between 8. Contents, tea, sugar, powdered milk, jam, bully, meatloaf, cheese, prunes, raisins, chocolates, salmon, butter, biscuits, sardines. Went through lot of my supply of aspros with no result. Couldn't sleep at night.

FRI AUG 28

Stopped in bed all day. Parcel between 6. Pity. I'm not fit now the parcels are here. Cup of tea and aspro last thing at night did some good. Rumours of leaving.

SAT AUG 29

Reveille 4 a.m. Got us all lined up outside the gate then the whole thing cancelled. Got parcel between 8.

ON TO MODENA
POW CAMP

SUN AUG 30

Moved off at 7 a.m. on train 11 a.m. rations 2 loaves, ½ tin of bully, cheese. Travelling all day and night.

MON AUG 31

Travelling till 6 p.m., 4 mile march to camp near Modena. Must have travelled over 400 miles.

PG73 Fossoli Di Carpi – Modena

TUES SEPT 1

Coffee at 7.30 a.m. Stew at night, 100% better than grub at Barri. Still in tents but camp much more organised. Got ½ apple with tiffin.

WED SEPT 2

Got de-bugged and shower in morning. I think everyone has crabs. Got our British Red Cross parcel between four, 10 Players each. We have now had 1 13/120 of a parcel.

THURS SEPT 3

Heavy downpour at night.

FRI SEPT 4

Quite hot here. The officers are a lot more pleasant than at the last camp. Washed shirt and shorts. Hard work.

SAT SEPT 5

On fatigues today, checking equipment of all tents – 100. Pegs, sheets, poles etc. No extra grub attached to it. Worse luck.

SUN SEPT 6

Still on fatigues. Clearing empty tents out.

MON SEPT 7

Knocking pegs in for tents. Had a good wash down.

TUES SEPT 8

Italian guard died today.

WED SEPT 9

Scilly was "off" tonight.

Thurs Sept 10

Organised march 7.30. took us to a vineyard where we were allowed to get a few grapes. Small but sweet. Walked 5 miles.

Frid Sept 11

Another boring day. Cheesed off all day.

Sat Sept 12

Roped in on clerking fatigue. Making mail lists. Two tables, one bench for 10 men.

Post Office Staff PG73

Sun Sept 13

Working 08.00 – 11.30, 13.30 – 16.30. When on fatigues get extra loaf, but we don't.

MON SEPT 14

6½ hours working. S.M. got ½ loaf each for us.

TUES SEPT 15

Clerking all day. Got sweet F.A. (Fanny Adams)

WED SEPT 16

6½ hours clerking. Canteen opened today after pay. 15 Lires. No back pay 42 Lires overdue. We got apples, tomatoes, onions. Good value.

THURS SEPT 17

Clerking. Parcels come in at night. What a grand surprise. One between two. Everybody happy now.

FRI SEPT 18

Clerking. The tea and English fags are very grateful.

SAT SEPT 19

Clerking. The cocoa is damned good. Had tea of carrots, beef and dumplings. Everything's OK now.

SUN SEPT 20

Had good breakfast of bacon, beans from one of parcels. Tomatoes, onions, apple from canteen.

Mon Sept 21

Clerking. Got our first pay. One loaf.

Tues Sept 22

From Iti news it appears we have surrounded Tobruk. Very cold today with a lot of rain. Got paid 9 lires.

Weds Sept 23

New British armoured division 400 kilometres south of Benghasi. Finished the jam in our parcel. Only magarine left now. Run out of paper at the office. Half day off.

Thurs Sept 24

Germans still fighting in Stalingrad. Now been fighting 3 months in the vicinity. Another day off at the office. Fried some onions in olive oil at night.

Fri Sept 25

Paper comes into office and start work again. Got my foot sores dressed.

Sat Sept 26

Rumours of parcels again. Tippled down at night.

Sun Sept 27

Tippled down all day. Bitter cold at the office. Ground in terrible state, get slutch on boots about 2″ thick.

Mon Sept 28

Parcels come in. Great excitement in the camp. New Zealand parcel between 2. Contents – tin honey, jam, green peas, rabbit and bacon, lamb and peas, cheese, malted milk, tea, chocolate, De Reszke fags (25).

Tues Sept 29

Got my foot dressed. Camp visited by two International Red Cross officials. Had the rabbit, bacon and peas for tiffin. The honey goes down well. Felt really full all day. Rained.

Wed Sept 30

Day off at the office as we have finished off the last batch of mail. Nice to lie in for a change.

Thurs Oct 1

Another day off with loaf. Paid 15 lire. Rumour of parcels.

Fri Oct 2

Had foot dressed. Hard day at office. Canteen issue.

Sat Oct 3

Another intensive day at office. Canteen issue. Shooting at Derna and Altamura. Brought up with Red Cross representative. Parcels to be more regular.

Sun Oct 4

Got foot dressed. 6 and ½ hours hard going at the office. We certainly earn our loaf. We write out 200 numbers and rank names and 400 addresses a day.

Mon Oct 5

Canadian parcel each issued. 40 players 10 Craven A. Made trifle. Biscuit soaked in klim, raisins, prunes and grated chocolate. Cream added. Proved a little too rich after the scilly.

Tues Oct 6

Finished off last week's letters at the office. Had bully for tiffin. Very good. Canteen issue.

Wed Oct 7

Mobile picture show came at night. Iti speaking. One of records before film Gigli singing the Gelida Manina. Had to turn up at the office to file our medical forms. Had foot dressed and got discharged.

Thurs Oct 8

Started work on letters again. Had salmon salad for tiffin.

Fri Oct 9

Another day less. Nearly everyone has crabs. One or two bugs knocking about.

SAT OCT 10

Opened marmalade today. Damned good. Russian winter appears to be setting in.

SUN OCT 11

Great surprise. 1 British Red Cross parcel per man. Amongst other things Peter and I get apple pud, fig pud and cocoa, bacon, sausage. Iti fag issue stopped.

MON OCT 12

Finished off the mail at the office. Shortage of water. Scramble for the water at night. Got my hand scalded but managed to brew the cocoa.

TUES OCT 13

Pete and I had apple pud for tiffin. Delicious. The last word.

WEDS OCT 14

Very cold these mornings. Pete and I debug our shirts in afternoon, Pete caught 51, myself 37. Bad business.

THURS OCT 15

Russians preparing counter attack in N. Smolenskaya and south of Stalingrad.

FRI OCT 16

Bit of work at the office. Rumours of no more parcels. This is too much. Got paid 15 Lires. Canteen issue again.

SAT OCT 17

Received my first letter from home since being POW. Great relief.

Photo's Received

Dad's Mother and Father

Dad's Father at St.Luke's Organ

Dad's Mother at home

Dad's Sister, Alice

SUN OCT 18

Parcel griff turned out to be duff. Thousands of mice in this camp, one got trod on during the night.

MON OCT 19

On Dixie duty from cookhouse. Pete and I carrying big dixies from cookhouse to tent where the grub is shared out.

TUES OCT 20

The General has visited camp and has speared some of parcels. 1 per man taboo. Parcels issued 1 between 4 with the tins punctured. Our parcel contained pea gravy in the butter. Bad show chaps. Instead of the usual cheerfulness at parcel issue, everyone was morose to see our tinned goods being slashed about.

WED OCT 21

The rabbit and bacon in our N.Z. parcel had gone bad due to opening. Dead loss. Made up for it by having pudding with syrup. Couldn't sleep at night due to lice. Horrible business.

THURS OCT 22

Canadian parcel issued 1 between 4. All tins punctured but for sardines. Pete and self cut (cards) with Steve and Chris for choice of articles, I've got meat roll, sardines and cheese as opposed to bully and salmon.

FRI OCT 23

Load of letters came in at night. I've got a damned bad cold. The weather's nippy.

SAT OCT 24

Some silly fool threw a stone at Iti guard. A fool like that can land us all in the cart. God knows the treatment here is very reasonable. Russians appear to be counter-attacking

Sun Oct 25

Still got a rotten cold. Miserable day.

Mon Oct 26

Rained all day. Camp a quagmire. Felt miserable all day.

Tues Oct 27

Steve and self moved our beds to office. Bags of room just four of us. Getting terribly cramped for room over in the tent. Slept better at night. Parcels turned up, 1 between 4, 2 days overdue. Pete and I tossed up with Steve and Chris for parcel. We won cheese.

Wed Oct 28

Pissed down all day. Surface like a skating rink. Everybody browned off. No roll call. Very considerate of Iti's.

Thurs Oct 29

Nice day. Finished work at office in morning. News from desert. Our forces are battering at El Alamein positions. Can't weigh positions up.

Fri Oct 30

Big debugging day. Overcoats and blankets through the disinfector at 8 a.m. Bath at 9 and private kit through the boiler. Walking about in the nude and overcoat till after tiffin. Very cold. Good to feel clean now.

SAT OCT 31

Parcel for Pete and I. Big parade in afternoon. Iti's searched our tents for tins and punctured same. We got away scot free. RAF persons were questioned yesterday. Looks as though they may move us. Curse it.

SUN NOV 1

The fag issue recommenced. 8 fags, 2 day's issue. 3 weeks lapse.

MON NOV 2

Parcels turned up again. Steve and Chris's turn. Clocks put back 1 hour. Scilly in the dark at night. Got paid 16 lire.

TUES NOV 3

The chai at nights is damned good but one has inevitably to get up for a piss. Some blokes get up about four times. I'm not too bad.

WED NOV 4

Southall parcel between Pete and I, lucky again no tins punctured. Got cocoa. 50 Players dished up. Pumpkin pie day as well. I'm getting very partial to pumpkin pie. 1 lire per slice.

THURS NOV 5

Received 4 letters – 3 Harold – 1 Harry. Finished off this week's mail at the office. Bit of rain made the ground untenable.

Fri Nov 6

Parcel issue but not for Pete and I. Lot of rain – no roll call. Sampled the old pumpkin pie from canteen. Only this commodity and onions on sale now.

Sat Nov 7

News from desert – Germans and Iti's at last retreat to Fukka after severe attacks – Alex breathes again. Terribly cold at nights now. These blankets (2) are U.S. Thank god for our great coats. Few fleas and bugs to worry us now in addition to lice. What a life.

Sun Nov 8

Parcel (No.16 London) between Pete and I, jam pudding. Few tins punctured.

Mon Nov 9

Issued with Iti clothing for winter. Certainly need it, it's damned cold morning and night. Jodpurs and pullovers. Look like an Iti now.

Tues Nov 10

More Iti clothing. Towel, handkerchief, shirt, body belt. Jolly decent of them to give us these things.

Wed Nov 11

2 minutes silence for Armistice Day.

THURS NOV 12

18 Hitchin parcel. Pete and I. No punctured tins. Fearfully cold at night now. Bind having to get up for piss at approx. 12 p.m. every night.

FRI NOV 13

Anglo-American troops invade French Morocco from Gibraltar. Admiral Dorlea captured at Algiers. Germans and Iti's occupy the remainder of France except Toulon. Griff says that Canadian parcel consignment is in. Good job for the British supply is running low. We'd be in the shit but for parcels now.

SAT NOV 14

Pete not very well. Gave me some of his scilly. Germans now back at Libyan frontier fighting rearguards. Little organised resistance in Algeria. Mussolini says this is Italy's gravest hour.

SUN NOV 15

Damned cold now. Tobruk reported to have fallen. Going into huts postponed. Drains out of order.

MON NOV 16

Got 17 London parcel. Contained all the things we value. Marmalade, Ovaltine, treacle pud, bacon. Unfortunately Harris's meat roll was bad. And how, nearly stunk the tent out.

TUES NOV 17

Ice formed on the tent in the night. Had ½ treacle pud and custard for tiffin. Axis landing in Tunisia to meet our forces in Algeria. Paid 13 lire for 2 hours musical instee.

WED NOV 18

Water off again at night. Only got ½ mug of cocoa.

THURS NOV 19

Axis now west of Derna.

FRI NOV 20

Canadian parcel. Pete and self. Rumour of moving to hut tomorrow so finished off mail in great haste.

SAT NOV 21

Off day. Wrote some more of my book. Think I have got piles. Rectum bleeds after evacuation. Got a lot of sores round ankles again.

SUN NOV 22

Moving to huts tomorrow.

MON NOV 23

Move to huts. Had to cart 2 blankets, clobber, paliasse full (too full) of straw, Red Cross box, mess tin and water bottle about ½ mile. What awkward baggage. Paliasse bundle disintegrating all the way. Nearly broke my back. Never been as exhausted in my life. Talk about pink spots before the eyes. Huts are Ok. Bunks and lights at night, 92 accommodation per hut. Worked at our new Post Office in afternoon.

TUES NOV 24

Mother's birthday.

Settling down into huts nicely, more comfortable for eating, sleeping, and warmer than I expected. Parcel issue put back 2 days due to moving. Lean day. Not my day for loaf at the office. Fighting in desert at El Agheila past Beghasi, Russian attacks in Don basin.

WED NOV 25

Lights are on all night in the huts; rather disturbing for sleep. Roll call took long time today.

THURS NOV 26

Canadian parcel. Very welcome after delay.

FRI NOV 27

Some bad gen from Red Cross. Parcels to be issued 1 between 4, every 4 days due to transport difficulties. Germans march into Toulon. French gentile half fleet. Unrest which was quelled.

SAT NOV 28

Bloke had his shirt, underpants, vest and pullover outside. Absolutely pitted with lice. Must have been a thousand at least. Was that guy lousy?

I'm not too bad now. Only found 5 yesterday. No one can help having some lice but there's no excuse for gross neglect.

SUN NOV 29

Washed my shirt and handkerchief. Hard work in this cold weather in cold water.

MON NOV 30

Weather very cold now. Frost in mornings. Loaves seem to be getting smaller (7oz standard).

TUES DEC 1

Iti fag issue stopped again. Must be due to bombing at Milan. Roll call was one big balls up. About 1 hour in cold mist. The loaves are depreciating. Smaller and not as good. No hot water for chai at night as scilly turned up late due to water being cut off in afternoon. Crab day.

WED DEC 2

50 Players issued. Thank god. Got paid 13 lires. Had some pumpkin pie after a long spell bart (without).

THURS DEC 3

Had inspection for diptherea in morning. We lose approx. 1 bloke a week from sundry ailments.

Frid Dec 4

Cold working at office these mornings especially since we get no eats till 11 a.m. we sometimes manage to get a bread from cookhouse at 10 when the cooks feel like it. The shower of shit. Cooks are most unpopular men in camp. Big fat cooks.

Sat Dec 5

200 blokes come in from Sicily. 4 days train journey. Looked like men from another world. Forlorn, haggard men with hope lost. We must have looked like that when we came from Altamura.

Sun Dec 6

Southall 16 parcel between Pete and I. Has to last us 8 days. All tins punctured. Scoffed the salmon pronto.

Mon Dec 7

CSM Jones made arrangements for our hut to be spread round the camp to fill vacant places in huts and to leave our hut vacant for newcomers. The blokes objected strongly to being separated from their pals and Jones tried to bullshit us about mutiny. Ultimately we won our point but we had to take our bunks to empty hut and sleep on the deck for the night. Water was off in the afternoon and scilly wasn't ready till 7 p.m. Hungry more than somewhat.

Tues Dec 8

About 80 internees from Vichy France came in, few of them RAF. Looked as fit as fiddles. Bags of kit, tinned goods etc. They'll feel the pinch here. What a contrast to the Sicily crowd. Still on the deck in the hut. Fighting 20 miles west of Tunis. Russians break through at 3 points on Don.

WED DEC 9

Visit from Protective Power. We are going to get 3 Xmas parcels, 1 Canadian between 4 at Xmas. Good show. Should have a good appetite for them as the present issue is a bit of a pinch.

THURS DEC 10

At last arrangements have been made for us to move to 25 hut tomorrow. Been cold on the floor. Turin heavily bombed.

FRI DEC 11

In morning moved en masse from hut 53 to 25. Pete and I managed to get bottom bunks again. Good to get off the floor. Iti fag issue recommences. We only get 25 English in 8 days.

SAT DEC 12

Tried pumpkin pie mashed up with olive oil. Made a lovely spread. Issue of olive oil is 1 spoonful every two days. I revel in it. Must be because we are short of fats.

SUN DEC 13

Cheese bust at tiffin. Hard work making parcel last 8 days between 2 especially when all tins are punctured. Not as cold today.

MON DEC 14

18 North Row parcel. Made tiffin out of chocolate and raisins. Very good with bread. Can't use such things as luxury articles now. Lot of absurd rumours floating about. Russians supposed to be at the Polish corridor. Some blokes actually believe such bullshit. Turkey said to have declared war on Germany. I've long since given over paying attention to such rumours. If Turkey have declared war, I regard it as inappropriate with the desert unfinished. A lot of chaps don't use their reason. One bloke came with the news that we had recaptured Singapore. I asked him what bases we could possibly have used for such an operation. He replied Gibraltar. I think ignorance and wishful thinking foster these rumours.

TUES DEC 15

Iti's kept us on parade almost 3 hours whilst they searched our huts for unpunctured tins. Took quite a few but none of ours. Were we browned off? Scilly was late and cold. News that we were going to get Xmas parcel each unpunctured cheered us up at night.

WED DEC 16

Weather milder this last week.

THURS DEC 17

Felt awful all day. Headache and ached in every bone. Went to bed at 6 p.m.

FRI DEC 18

Felt better today. Roll call in huts. Raining slightly. Axis admit to be withdrawing west from El Agheila and Syrtica. Japs withdrawing in New Guinea.

SAT DEC 19

½ tin of bacon for tiffin. Best meal in parcel. Cold in sandwiches. Got a lot of sores on my left leg. Must be going rotten. The morning coffee is so vile that Pete never has any. As much unlike coffee as anything could be. Scilly is getting thin these days.

SUN DEC 20

Rained on and off all day. Ground in terrible state now. Thank goodness we're not in tents.

MON DEC 21

Russians moving forward in Don sector. Allies still advancing in Syrtica. Still raining. Ground a quagmire.

TUES DEC 22

Parcels failed to turn up in the morning. Rumours that we weren't to get any until after Xmas. Were we crestfallen? R.S.M. Cotman (who has taken over from the useless Benjamin) saw into the matter and the parcels came in at night. We got a Scotch parcel with a North Row lid on. Scotch parcels aren't too good comparatively. Papal Leggett (Pope's representative) visited camp and addressed us.

Wed Dec 23

Our Xmas order of pumpkin pie came in at night. Pete and I have kilo each. Sumptuous.

Thurs Dec 24

Had remainder of the pumpkin for tiffin. 50 fags and parcels dished up in afternoon. Pete and I had Xmas parcel and Canadian between us. Didn't touch a thing in the Xmas parcel. Contents of which, 1 lb Xmas pud, 1 lb cake, ½ lb chocolate biscuits, ½ lb sweets (fancy), ¼ lb chocolate, 1 lb beef and tomato pud, 1 lb beef and macaroni, 3 oz slab sugar, ½ oz tea, ½ size Nestles milk, 3 oz tin of cheese, 12 oz marmalade. Went to carol service at night. Very nice. Good choir. Had supper of cheese and Canadian biscuits. Rained all day.

Fri Dec 25

Xmas day.

Made a communal brew of chai in the morning instead of black coffee. Pete and I arose about 10 a.m. and fried 1 lb sausage and onion in the wash house. Scoffed same with bread and finished off with half Xmas pud each. Tea. In afternoon scoffed sweets, chocolate, apple, orange. Had sweet tea of marmalade bread and butter, ¼ of the Xmas cake and ½ the chocolate biscuits. Twinning's coffee made to perfection. For supper had bread, Iti cheese and a bottle of beer. Good scoff day.

Sat Dec 26

Tea in bed again. Scilly at tiffin. After scilly, fried onions with tomato and steak pudding. Excellent. Brewed cocoa in wash house. Allowed fires in wash house yesterday and today. Scilly for tea. Finished Xmas cake, marmalade and bread. Coffee. For supper had 3 Canadian biscuits and cheese and bottle of beer (⅓rd mug). Felt heavy in the head all day. Took the mail into the Iti compound.

Sun Dec 27

Felt pretty crab today. Must have got a chill. Our group has got a communal brew of tea going instead of individual. It's as weak as piss.

Mon Dec 28

Still feeling crab. Patrol activity in Syrtica. Livelier activity in Tunisia, positions severely contested. Advanced a small way into Burma. Russians still attacking.

Tues Dec 29

Still crab. Had to fetch coffee from cook house in morning. Letter cards come in at long last. Week overdue.

Wed Dec 30

Improved a little. Weather frosty now.

Thurs Dec 31

Snowed during night. 6″ of snow greeted us in the morning. Had good tiffin seeing it was last day of year. ½ lb beef steak and macaroni. 2 oz chocolate and ¼ lb biscuits.

BOOKS READ DURING 1942

Book	Author	Rating (out of ten)
Maid In Waiting	Galsworthy	7
Benighted	Priestley	7+
Flowering Wilderness	Galsworthy	7
Ordinary Families	Robertson	7
Tess of the Durbervilles	Hardy	7
Music At Night	A. Huxley	–
Good Companions	Priestley	9
Nanking Road	Vicki Baum	8
Donaldson	Adrian Alington	7
Ariel	Adres Mansois	7
Don Fernando	S Mangham	7
Hilda Lesswarp	A Bennett	7
Ah King	S Mangham	8

1943

JAN 1 FRI

Bitter cold today. Feeling a bit better.

JAN 2 SAT

Inoculated against diphtheria. Fighting south of Syrtica. Russians attacking on all fronts. Patrol activity Burma-India frontier.

JAN 3 SUN

Paid 6 Lires. Issue of 25 Players to last for 8 days.

JAN 4 MON

Mountains covered in snow presented a rather fine sight on arising. Finished letter cards off today.

JAN 5 TUES

Day off from the office. Had a shower in the afternoon. Fried a few onions, steak and tomato pud on a little olive oil fire I made out of two tins. Small tin containing olive oil and a piece of cloth inside a larger tin with air holes cut in. Very successful.

JAN 6 WED

Soffula's birthday. Letter cards issued. Camp slutchy state due to snow. News – bad weather in Syrtica makes action impossible. Germans reinforce positions in Tunisia. French opposition to Germans in south Tunisia. Anglo-Aussie making new attack on Samatanda in north Guinea. Russians attacking all along front from Caucasus in Arctic (without success).

JAN 7 THURS

Usual daily monotony. Rumours that WO's and Sgts are to go to Austria. Something big in the wind?

JAN 8 FRI

Parcel issue. Got Southall 17. Not much use for 8 days. Got some mail. Weather still bitter cold. Bought carrots from canteen.

JAN 9 SAT

Browned off to hell today. Bitter cold, slutch, lice and monotony get one down at times. Rumours of some big news in next day or two. Griff says there is big conference in Portugal. Roosevelt speech. Will double outpost this year. Confident of 2nd front this year.

JAN 10 SUN

Just another day. Went for walk round compound at night as ground was frozen hard.

JAN 11 MON

Hut gets full of smoke at night with blokes making brews. Some of the fire contraptions are marvels of invention.

JAN 12 TUES

Bread ration 250 loaves short. Waited till it was made up by today's rations which come in at 4 p.m. Didn't get our loaf and cheese till after scilly. 24 hours without grub. Made a brew of cocoa in afternoon in the hut using the Red Cross box for fuel. Crab day.

JAN 13 WED

Another heavy fall of snow. Bread turned up at proper time. Thank goodness. Got issued with battle dress blouse. Bit warmer than tropical tunic. In morning took outgoing mail to Iti office with Iti interpreter and brought back the incoming mail. None for me.

JAN 14 THURS

Clothing issue of socks, woollen drawers and vest. Daren't wear the latter two articles on account of the lice. Deadly situation.

JAN 15 FRI

Visit by Papal Nuncio. Gift of two accordions to each compound. Brought Pope's blessing to R.C's and best wishes for New Year to the remainder. Colonel cancelled all outstanding gaol sentences.

JAN 16 SAT

Parcel issue – Canadian. Said to be the last in the magasin. Rumours of bulk issue and parcels rife in camp all day.

JAN 17 SUN

Dreaming like blazes these days. Generally about grub and feeds. Wake up about 5 times every night.

JAN 18 MON

According to Iti's press, our big offensive has begun in the desert. From Tunisia, Syrtica and Tripolitania. 2nd inoculation for diphtheria.

JAN 19 TUES

Arm very sore and stiff, felt crab generally. Absolutely out of smokes. Poor show. Russians capture Valichi Luchi fort. Big attacks in Caucasus. Fighting in Tripolitania. Another two blokes died at Modena Hospital this week. Average of 1 a week keeps up.

JAN 20 WED

Iti came into our hut to paint our rubbish box, did a deal with me,
1 loaf for 2 bars of English soap. Iti's very keen on this soap for their
senoritas. We have lots of it now. Only thing we aren't short of. Bulk
issue from Red Cross comes in. Short rations because one truckload
has gone astray. 1 tin milk 3oz 1 week's ration – between 2 – small tin
cheese, 7oz herrings, ¼lb chocolate, 10oz jam, ½lb marge. Between
3 – 10oz meat roll, 1lb beef steak pud, 8oz salmon. Between 15, ½lb
bacon, 10 dried peaches, sugar and tea. Another smokeless day.

JAN 21 THURS

Finished off the letters this afternoon. Russians have surrounded
Stalingrad. Heavy air raid on Berlin; retaliation raid on London.
Other fronts – no change. 31 fags issued. Said to be last in stock.

JAN 22 FRI

Iti fag issue recommences. 6 a day to make up for lost ground. Just
about saved our bacon.

JAN 23 SAT

Allies advancing on Tripoli. Germans retreating inside Stalingrad. Made
myself a small trifle from 2 small apples, grated, plus breadcrumbs with
coating of klim mixed thick. Browned off to the back teeth at night.
Arm still very sore from inoculation. 75 blokes leaving for another camp
on 25th. Hope neither Pete or I are amongst them. Things aren't too
good here but don't want to take a chance of striking worse. Laissey-
faire that's us.

JAN 24 SUN

List of names issued. Not amongst them. Breathe freely again. Sorting mail with Steve in afternoon. Tripoli falls. Radio news. Good show.

JAN 25 MON

Chock out of parcel grub now and the magasin empty. Grim times till some more parcels come in.

JAN 26 TUES

Lot of Altimura mail in but none for me. Fell on my sore arm on entering the shit-house. Gave me a shaking. Crab end to crab day. Russians capture Voronesk.

JAN 27 WED

Browned off to hell. Arm still bad. Russians advancing towards Rostov. No sign of parcels yet. Got the bones from the meat. First time in this camp. Grisly do. Not much food wasted in POW camp.

JAN 28 THURS

Got first letters addressed to this camp. Pleasant surprise. Looked at my arm at night – very swollen. Will have to go sick if it doesn't improve.

JAN 29 FRI

Had to knock off work in afternoon as I felt crab. Will go sick tomorrow.

Jan 30 Sat

Attended sick parade at 8 a.m. The MO cut my arm. Said he was going to cut deep and he did. Nearly filled a basin full of puss. Looked like mushroom soup and tomato sauce. Gouged the hole after. Grisly, painful business. Hot formentations and squeezing in afternoon. Got the bones again today. Got a good lot of meat from mine.

Jan 31 Sun

Got my arm squeezed again in the morning. Still getting weak chai from communal brew but no milk or sugar. Rumours of parcels now flying round. End of a long crab month.

Mon Feb 1

News from Red Cross that parcels have been dispatched to camp. Good enough.

Tues Feb 2

Got arm squeezed at infirmary. Remnants of bulk issue given out. $\frac{1}{3}$rd bar chocolate, $\frac{2}{5}$ths tin of jam, $\frac{1}{4}$tr tin butter, $\frac{1}{3}$rd meat roll, $\frac{1}{3}$rd pilchards, 2 biscuits. Better than nothing. Canteen issue at night, carrots and an apple.

Wed Feb 3

Rumoured that 4 truckloads of parcels have arrived at station. German 6th army under Marshal Paulus in south Stalingrad overwhelmed by the ponderous forces of the enemy. Started work at office again as I don't feel too bad now.

Thurs Feb 4

Stalingrad falls. Parcels come up from station. Should be issued tomorrow.

Fri Feb 5

English parcels issued 1 between 4. Unfortunately it isn't Pete and I's turn so we'll just have to wait 4 days. Nice sunny day again. Good weather for Feb. Ground still bad. Got arm dressed again – still mattering freely.

Sat Feb 6

Finished this week's letters at the office. Couple of days off now.

Sun Feb 7

Good weather spell broke up. Rained at night. Letter cards came in. Started work again.

Mon Feb 8

Arm dressed in morning. Still discharging. Camp like a swamp. Carried coffee from cookhouse. Mud over boot tops.

Tues Feb 9

At last a parcel for Pete and I. North row 15. First since 16th Jan. Had salmon for tiffin. On carrying grub from cookhouse.

WED FEB 10

Definite news that parcel issue is going back to 1 between 4 every 2 days. Just the job. Been on the half ration since Dec 1 and felt the pinch. Felt it more when they stopped altogether. Camp in terrible state. Can't go to shithouse without getting mucked up to the nines. Russians still advancing on Kharkov, Rostov and Kirsk. Landing at Novorossiysk. British 8th Army reach Tunisian border from the east. 1st Army and Yanks marking time in Tunisia in west.

THURS FEB 11

Parcels between 4. Not our turn. Got my arm dressed.

FRI FEB 12

100 blokes leaving camp. Not us again. Parcel issue for tomorrow cancelled. 1 between 2 on Mondays and Fridays in future. Good enough.

SAT FEB 13

100 blokes left. Old Wingfield one of them.

MON FEB 14

Arm terribly painful today. Discharged all down my arm making a mess of my shirt. Germans evacuate Crasnodadt – must be evacuating Caucasus. Churchill made speech saying all would be done to make direct contact with enemy as soon as possible.

TUES FEB 15

Got arm attended to at infirmary. Had hot formentations. Arm very painful. Bulk issue in lieu of parcels. Big snag – no milk, tea or chocolate. Plenty of sugar. 2 tins M&V between 2. Tin bully, tin sausage between 3. Tin jam ⅓rd, honey ¼^{tr}, butter ¼^{tr}, prunes, 21 cream crackers, 14 oz cheese between 2, unfortunately mostly mouldy.

TUES FEB 16

Infirmary again. As soon as I took bandage off, arm discharged like a tap all over the floor. Had hot forments. Had to go again for them in afternoon. Good weather spell broke, rained heavily at night. Camp like a shit heap again.

WED FEB 17

Got up at 8 a.m. to go to infirmary. Gale blowing and hail and snow. Ground 8″ deep in parts. Only about 10 blokes went sick instead of the usual 60 or so. Arm a bit easier. On carrying tea and scilly from cookhouse. What a job, wading through the sea of mud with heavy dixy. Right over boot tops – got feet wet through. Rostov evacuated by Germans.

THURS FEB 18

Brilliant sunshine today. Weather changeable more than somewhat. Working in hut since my arm worsened. Pete's birthday. Kharkov evacuated by Germans.

FRI FEB 19

Parcels issued 1 between 2. We get Perth 16. Had big scoff after scilly to celebrate Pete's birthday as we couldn't yesterday. Loaf, bacon, jam and bread, small marmalade pud. Biscuits and chocolate and stinking strong brew of chai. Iti war minister now forbids papers entering POW camp. Have to rely on griff now. Hungary and Romania no longer Axis sympathies, Germans take Bona in Tunisia but 8th Army still advancing from east. Band and concert visited our hut livened things up somewhat. Went to infirmary in morning. Arm cut had closed, had to have it burnt open with caustic pencil. Sting a bit.

SAT FEB 20

Made a brew of Bournvita on olive oil fire. Very good. Navy bloke gave an excellent lecture all night on his experiences.

SUN FEB 21

Finished this week's set of mail off. Made klim tin full of cocoa in afternoon. Macaroni stew tastes ghastly these days. Macaroni and swede. Latest griff, Germans evacuated Warsaw. Russians take Odessa. English troops in Finland. Lot of balls. Expected griff to get rampant when newspapers were stopped.

MON FEB 22

Got arm dressed. Should have been parcels today. First load came in then be danged if they didn't take them out again. Went for shower in afternoon but they weren't working. Swept under bed and unearthed terrible amount of rubbish. Started washing shirt and be damned if the water didn't go off.

TUES FEB 23

Parcels came in. Yesterday's carry on was misunderstanding. We get
a Bermondsey 15. Swopped 1lb tin M&V for apple pud one each
now. Swopped tin of creamed rice for tin bacon. Good show. Finished
washing shirt, towel, socks, handkerchief. Sorted mail at night.
Interesting lecture from New Zealander who escaped from Greece to
Turkey – Middle East, only to get captured at El Alamein.

WED FEB 24

Beautiful day again. Our hut gets the books again today. 1 between 4.
Hope I get chance to read one this time. Had apple pudding each for
tiffin. First rate.

THURS FEB 25

Another fine day. Lecture from a jockey at night.

FRI FEB 26

Got arm dressed. Lot better now. Parcel issue. We got Bermondsey 15.
Went for shower in afternoon – very hot. Colder today.

SAT FEB 27

Swopped 1lb tin of stewed beef and rice for apple pud. One each again
now. Made brew of chai on olive oil stove.

SUN FEB 28

Finished off the mail in afternoon. Brew of chai in afternoon and brew of coffee at night. The olive oil issue is certainly useful. We get a spoon a man every two days except for when bacon fat comes in for the scilly.

MON MAR 1

Parcel issue. We get London 16. Weather glorious. Pitty we've nowhere to go. English fag issue suspended till Friday.

TUES MAR 2

These Iti pants sure get lousy – have to debug them every day or else they'd get out of hand. Had brew of coffee at night whilst I've still got a Player to smoke with it. Russians still attacking heavily. Axis gain some positions in Tunisia.

WED MAR 3

Another beautiful day. Horrible to be behind barbed wire on such a day. Started work on mail again.

THURS MAR 4

Colder today. Swopped a Galantine for a tin of Twinning's coffee. Galantines aren't much bottle, 90% bread crumbs. Bacon for tiffin.

FRI MAR 5

Got arm dressed. Parcel issue. We get London 16. Swapped 2 Cornish pies for 2 apple puds, salmon paste for cheese, jelly jam for marmalade, tomatoes for cheese, tomatoes and cheese for dates. Busy on the stock exchange. Walked round camp at night.

SAT MAR 6

Had apple pud for tiffin. Germans attack in south Russia. Russia still attacking north west of Kursk and north west of Orel. RAF bomb Hamburg and Nuremberg. Jerry bombs London. 1st army attack in Tunisia.

SUN MAR 7

Bitter cold and gale blowing. On carrying chai from cookhouse. Things seemed pretty dead all day. Made brew of coffee at night.

MON MAR 8

Parcel issue. Lea Green 15. Got a sultana pud otherwise like Bermondsey. Started making cakes on parcel days. Grated apple and biscuits, bread mixed with syrup, marge and Nestles. Put apples at bottom of tin and heated by means of margarine wick. Swapped 1 lb beef casseroles for apple pud, meat Galantine for dates, ½lb mixed veg for 2oz of chai. Saving up for my birthday. Rumour says we have taken Crete.

TUES MAR 9

Day off. Had dates and chocolate for tiffin. Brew of chai at night. Bulk came into magasin. Hope they don't dish it up on Friday as we have been mossing bacon and puddings for my birthday, but not containing these items.

WED MAR 10

Some rat pinched 7 of our mail sheets meaning that 100 letters won't be able to be entered. Red Cross parcels getting low in magasin. May have to go back to old issue (1 in 16 days) temporarily. Brew of chai at night – very good.

THURS MAR 11

Bulk issue tomorrow. No milk, tea or chocolate. Have to make it last a week. Good job we've got something in hand for my birthday. Got my first parcel at 16.30. 200 Players. My scilly went cold but I didn't give a damn. Certainly a great surprise. First fag parcel in our section. Gave Pete 50, Steve, Chris, Harold and Jim 5 each and several sundries.

FRI MAR 12

Bulk issue. Between 2 – tin jam, 2 tins M&V, 1 tin bully, 14oz cheese. Between 4 – Tin steak and onions, tin butter. Between 5 tin honey, 12 biscuits, 1½ lb sugar. To last a week. No tea or milk.

SAT MAR 13

Bernard got clothing parcel. Gave me 2 squares of chocolate out of which I made a chocolate ring for my birthday cake. News – In south Russia German counter attack gaining ground. Fighting in sheets at Kharkov. Germans evacuate Viayma. Anglo-American armoured thrusts in Tunisia – held. Recently heavy RAF raids on Hamburg, Berlin, Munich and Stuttgart.

SUN MAR 14

Birthday. Work at post office in morning. Tiffin 1 loaf, ½ tin bacon, 1 apple pud with ½ tin hot creamed rice. P.O. in afternoon. Full pressure work to get mail out. Managed to finish. Dinner scilly – bread and jam, tea. Supper – ½ sultana pud with home brewed coffee on olive oil fire. Late supper – home-made date cake (10 ozs) with another brew of coffee. We had previously saved milk for these brews. Slept well at night, dreamt vividly of Spitfire (Sophulla).

MON MAR 15

Lovely day. Day off. Nowt to do. Rather cheesed off. Lecture at night on civvy prison life. Bit better than this. Had shower in afternoon.

TUES MAR 16

Another boring day. Wrote some more of my book. Sergeants meeting griff. Parcels OK again. Issue as usual on Friday. Thank goodness. Battledress for those with Iti bags on Thursday. Get rid of these lousy bags at last. Walk round at night. Germans retake Kharkov. Bad sign.

WED MAR 17

Tomorrow's clothing issue to be curtailed due to blokes blocking the latrine drains by putting old (or louse ridden) shirts and vests down the shit house. Watched some games of hand ball on the parade ground in afternoon. Five minutes of that game would knock me out. Night time very dreary these days.

THURS MAR 18

Watched hand ball match in evening. Parcel eve tonight. Good show.

FRI MAR 19

Parcels again. We get Paddington 14. Swopped 1lb M&V for apple pud and Galantine for tin of cocoa. Made chocolate cake from bread crumbs, grated biscuit, cocoa, sugar and marge. Had to work at office today as they now dish parcels out in the empty hut caused by recent drafts. Had chocolate and biscuits with brew of coffee at night.

SAT MAR 20

Big parade in morning for checking the roll, lasted from 8 a.m. – 11.30 a.m. Pretty cold on the parade ground. Gave me a big appetite for the pilchards.

SUN MAR 21

In evening watched a game of handball between the cooks and PT class, followed by an amazing display by Sgt Gray and a team showing how the game should not be played. Cpl. Butcher presented the teams with bottle of vino each.

MON MAR 22

Northampton 16 parcel. Had our usual chocolate and biscuits with tea in the morning. (Home brewed chai not communal).

TUES MAR 23

Finished off the mail at the office. Had a brew of coffee in afternoon and brew of cocoa at night. Doing ourselves well these days. 7,000 odd parcels came into camp. Just what the doctor ordered.

WED MAR 24

Day off. On carrying grub. Nice day.

THURS MAR 25

Steve and I on sorting the letter cards. Bulk issue tomorrow so will be working in huts.

FRI MAR 26

Weather colder. No sun. Issue of bulk. Causes bags of excitement and passes the day on. Had brew of tea at night with biscuits and chocolate spread.

War news.

Allies have started their ponderous attacks in Tunisia. Russians attacking in upper Donety and Lake Ladoga.

SAT MAR 27

Nasty day. Drizzle making the ground treacherous. Fell on my back going to the office. Made a fig pudding from my dried figs (soaked), bread, sugar, butter and honey. Filled apple pud tin. Brew of cocoa at night – a snorter.

SUN MAR 28

Rained making camp a shitheap. Had hiccoughs intermittently all day. Spoon of honey the perfect cure but expensive.

MON MAR 29

Parcel issue. We get Northampton 16. Nasty day – pissed down. Had chocolate, biscuits and brew of chai at night – had a brew of cocoa late on.

TUES MAR 30

Weather cleared up a bit in the evening. Naval personnel warned to prepare for a move. RAF next? Hope not. Had two brews again at night – coffee and cocoa. Finished mail off in the morning. Lot of personal parcels being dished out now. Most Atimura ones have chocolate missing – the shower.

WED MAR 31

We have had sugar issued dry from the cookhouse for last three weeks. They vote now for it to go back in the coffee despite the fact that if the issued sugar was used to sweeten the coffee solely it made it sweeter than we had been getting it. Can't understand it. Nice day – dried the ground a bit. Day off from the office so wrote more of my book. Made a new fire stove at night with cheese tin and pudding tin. Brew of strong chai late at night. Ate the fig pudding I made from bulk issue. Best yet.

THURS APL 1

New rule that all have to be out of bed at 8.30. Doesn't affect me as I always have to get up for the office at 8.30 but most chaps stop in bed till grub is called up at 10.30. Went to the camp concert which has just got going at night. Very good. Very amusing with a few classical turns. Jolly sang Prologue Papliacci and Leggett sang Handel's Largo. Both sang duet "Where You Walk" Handel. Beautiful. Had late brew of cocoa.

FRI APL 2

Parcel issue. To our section there were 4 Canadians, 1 Xmas parcel and 5 English. I cut low and missed the Canadian 21. Got the New Mills 16. I made several quick fire swops. Yorkshire pud last parcel for 1lb damson jam, Yorkshire pud this parcel for ½ tin milk and 2oz sugar, 1lb beef steak stew for 1 tin bacon, tin tomatoes for 1 tin cheese, 6½ biscuits for ½ fig pudding. I made two small chocolate cakes in evening and steamed them using marge for fuel and bit of my belt for wick. Brew of coffee with the fig pud at night. Olive oil has stopped, only temporarily I hope.

SAT APL 3

Pete gets his first parcel (100 Churchman) 30 pour moi. Good show. Walk around and brew of cocoa at night. Sentry shot at 2 blokes escaping under wire separating two compounds last night.

SUN APL 4

Quiet day. Listened to Leggett and Jolly at night outside concert.

MON APL 5

Parcel issue. Pete cut a deuce so we had to have what was left.
Bermondsey 12. Good enough. Had a shower in the evening. Pete
got personal parcel (clothing and chocolate). 500 Gold Flake and
¼ Gold Block. Gave me 150 Gold Flake and chocolate. Had walk
round at night then scoffed ¼lb chocolate each and ¼lb biscuits with
coffee. Only just made it.

TUES APL 6

Had the apple pud and creamed rice for tiffin. Our hut got beaten at
handball in evening. Had good walk round compound with Pete and
Lucas who has volunteered for working party as he is cheesed off to
hell. Brew of cocoa at night.

WED APL 7

Dad's birthday.

Finished off mail in the morning. Went on the walk in the afternoon.
My first since October. Good to get out of the pen. Didn't go very far
but had a good long rest lying in the sun on the grass. Pete got two
more parcels today, 500 Gold Flake and 120 Players No.3. Brew of
cocoa at night. We have to brew upon marge now the olive oil issue has
stopped. Penalty for fires, by the way, is 20 days fatigues and 14 days
without parcel. Bit rough.

THURS APL 8

Meant to go on the walk in afternoon but it was cancelled. Must have
been a bit too cold for Iti's. Went to the play "Monkey's Paw" at night.
Jolly good effort.

FRI APL 9

Parcels. Got Paddington 14. Swopped jam pudding for tin of milk and tomatoes for cheese. Only 16 fags issued instead of 50. Parcel supply must be low in magasin. Made a small chocolate cake and steamed it. Had chocolate and biscuits with brew of chai at night.

SAT APL 10

Nothing much doing. News; Big new attack in Tunisia. Jerry driven from mountains. Renewed Russian attack in Donetsk.

SUN APL 11

Opening of football at night. Pitch too small. Civvies seem to take interest in our activities, passing to and fro all evening on their bikes. The soldiers tried to stop them. Girls are certainly well dressed and good looking.

MON APL 12

Parcel issue. Invalid parcels to make up the issue. Our section got 4 out of 10. Pete cut a deuce again and we got invalid parcel. Bags of milk food but no meat scoffs. Had bottle of beer in afternoon. Made Horlicks at night. Got bollocking for untidy bed space – bullshit.

TUES APL 13

Quiet day again. Made a drink of Benger's food in evening and at night had Allenbury's diet flavoured with Canadian coffee. Cleaned our bed spaces out at about 11 p.m.

WED APL 14

Watched football in evening and had Horlicks at night. Finished off the mail.

THURS APL 15

Played practise game of football in morning ½ hour. Didn't play badly but was plain tuckered out at the end. Got our creamola pudding baked at the cookhouse in afternoon. Not a great success. Watched football in evening.

FRI APL 16

Parcel issue. Leicester 16. Had chocolate, biscuits and brew of Allenbury's flavoured with coffee.

SAT APL 17

Quiet day. No sports at night. Absolutely browned off to the back teeth. Got fag parcel. 200 Players.

SUN APL 18

Sports night. The football game was interrupted by roll call which took place on the parade ground. Spoilt the evening. A bloke in the other compound had escaped 4 days ago and has been recaptured without the Iti's having missed him.

MON APL 19

Roll call on parade ground and search of huts lasting from 09.00 – 13.10 hours. Was I browned off. Had headache all day through being in the sun all morning. Parcels issued 18.00 hours. Got Leicester 16. Swopped Yorkshire pud for apple pud, tomatoes for cheese, meat roll for dates, 1lb M&V for bacon.

TUES APL 20

Orders were given out yesterday that we were not allowed to keep any Red Cross boxes. Lord knows where we're supposed to keep our kit, tins, etc. We kept box each to see what happened. Another roll call and search in morning lasting 09.30 – 12.10. No action taken about the boxes. Iti's withdraw our sports gear for censorship at Rome. Things are getting to be a bind.

WED APL 21

Roll call on parade ground. Took ½ hour. Over a thousand letters in today but none for me, 6 weeks since I had any. Pete played rugby at night.

THURS APL 22

Received my personal parcel. Good show. 2lb chocolate. Had a shave with my new razor and had a shower.

FRIDAY APL 23

Good Friday. Parcels issued. We got Perth 16. Swopped oats for apple pud and 1lb M&V for bacon. Steve and myself on sorting mail at night. Pete got 2 parcels, 1,000 Gold Flake and ½lb tobacco.

SATURDAY APL 24

Parcel for me at night. ½lb of Players Medium from Dad. Roll call on the parade ground now.

War News

Still hard fighting in Tunisia. Local activity in Russia. Jap successes on Indo-Burmese frontier. Beginning to lose hopes of being home this year. This camp is now as good as one can expect. Parcels regular. Personal parcels coming through. Weather good. Sports and classes organised. Nothing new to look forward to. Sometimes I nearly go crazy with boredom. Being cooped up in a pen gets on your nerves somewhat.

SUNDAY APL 15

McHaynes orchestra played at night, 3 violins, piano, sax, trumpet, clarinet. Leggett sang "Comfort Ye" Jolly sang "Arm Ye Brave". Enjoyed it. Tantalising to watch girls pass by on their bikes.

MONDAY APL 26

Parcels issued. Got London Y16 with meat roll in lieu of tomatoes. Swopped meat roll and 1lb M&V for 2 tins bacon. Got 4oz chocolate for 40 fags. Had chocolate and biscuits at night. Watched rugby and football at night.

TUES APL 27

Went to the play "The Squeaker" at night. These blokes certainly do well especially the female parts.

WED APL 28

Watched football games at night. Our hut got knocked out of the cup by the cooks (Scilly Bashers). Got my first letter since Mar 9.

THURS APL 29

Had shower and clean change. Rained today consequently there was nowt doing at night. Had a brew to atone for it.

FRI APL 30

Issue of Canadian parcels – first since Jan 16. Welcome change the old klim, butter etc. Had to hand in our Iti aluminium dixies in lieu of which we got a stone basin (flower bowl) a saucer of the same material (red composite) and a tumbler, the latter being superfluous and useless. Bad swap, I'd got attached to the old dixie. Our grub issue has had to be altered. We all queue up independently instead of lining up the dixies for the chief 'lobber outerer' to lob two men's rations in each. Watched football in afternoon as Maurice was playing. His hut 45 won 3-2. Good game.

SAT MAY 1

For the morning chai (office) in place of 4 dixies we used 8 klim tins on a tray. Another difficulty overcome. Semi-finals of the cup at night. 23 (the fit men who really came from France) beat 45 4-0. Good game but 23 had all the luck. Pete got called away early on to collect a parcel. The cooks (the fat men) made a draw with 43 after two lots of extra time. Didn't have a brew at night because we have nearly run out of marge and using butter (for fuel) would be sacrilege.

SUN MAY 2

Rained all day. Ground a mud heap. No football possible. Exceedingly dull day. Brewed cocoa using sardine oil for fuel and Iti shirt for wick.

MON MAY 3

Parcel issue – Canadian. Raining all day again. Boredom sets in again. Brewed coffee with the aid of sardine oil.

TUES MAY 4

Raining all day. Went to bed.

WED MAY 5

Finished off this week's letters at the office. Weather slightly improved. No brew at night. Deadly. Interesting lecture on China.

THURS MAY 6

Day off. Intermittent heavy showers. Washed shirt, 2 pairs of socks and handkerchief. Had a shower in afternoon. Brewed coffee at night on ¾^{trs} spoon of butter. Got to have a brew these dismal nights.

FRI MAY 7

Issue of Canadian parcels. Still showery. Started work on mail again.

SAT MAY 8

Weather better today. Ground dried up a bit. Strong rumours that Tunisia has fallen again (for the fourth time).

MON MAY 9

Diary not legible.

MON MAY 10

Beautiful day. Semi-final of the hut competition re-played at night.
Another draw 0-0 after extra time. Poor game. Watched the girls
passing on their bikes after the match. They are, needless to say, a nice
item. Parcel issue, New Zealand and English. We picked a New Zealand
for a change.

TUES MAY 11

Match re-played at night between cooks and hut 43 (draw 1-1 after
2 lots of extra time. Listened to a bloke talking .... at night.

WED MAY 12

.... parcels come into compound .... Got them out first, enough
on the ...... system. Watched football again at night.

THURS MAY 13

Got a fag parcel in the morning. Had a shower in the afternoon.
The big replay at night. Hut 43 won 1-0 in a very exciting game.

FRI MAY 14

Parcel issue. Swopped ....
Went to concert at night. Not bad but tiring standing.

SAT MAY 15

Got a letter at last. Pete played rugby at night.

SUN MAY 16

Gym display on parade ground in afternoon with Scotch .... at night. Restrained but wise.

MON MAY 17

Parcel issue. Leicester 16. Cup final at night. Lot of tomfoolery before the game. Paddy got debarred. 23 beat 43 3-1. Concert party from next compound came over. Couldn't get a ticket. 3 of the blokes have let their hair grow and were made up as women. The small dark one .....
..... and manly looking but ... . but a good looker. ....

Funny to see the lads gathering round to get a glimpse of her hind.

TUES MAY 18

Had a bit of rugby practise at night. Tuckered out. Boxing in the next camp and seems to be a knock out in the fight. Too vigorous for Pete and I.

WED MAY 19

Finished mail off at the office. Played rugby at night, pace too vigorous. Had a cold shower after game.

THURS MAY 20

Had practise game of football in afternoon. Played rugby at night for hut versus experienced men. We lost 9-6 in an enjoyable game. Feel mighty stiff today, had hot shower in afternoon and cold shower after game at night.

FRI MAY 21

Issue of bulk ....

SAT MAY 22

Played in rugby practise at night.

SUN MAY 23

Big match at night of football, England beat Scotland 3-2. Had a rugby practise at night.

MON MAY 24

Parcel issue at night London 16. Played rugby for our 2nd team vs Sporting Lokov(?) "B" in the knock out.

TUES MAY 25

Big play at night. Trailing 3-0 at half time but they equalised whilst our back was off. We lost in the extra time. Bad luck. Felt bruised all over at the finish.

Weds May 26

Nothing much doing today. .... first team won 24-0 at rugby again.

Thurs May 27

Our first team beat the .... compound team 3-0 in a sterile game.

Fri May 28

Bulk issue. Went to the play at night. Portrayal from a novel. Very good. .... excellent. The ...... take their parts well.

Sat May 29

Our rugger team beat 44 & 45 by one clear try. I had a kick about after the game. Finished the mail so had the day off. Had a shower and washed vest, shorts, underpants and socks.

Sun May 30

Rugger final at night. 23 hut beat our team 3 points to nil. England & Scotland football. England won 1-0 in a poor game.

Mon May 31

Watched some putrid games of football. Started the mail in the morning.

Tues June 1

Listened to the Padie's lecture at night. Revealed some unpleasant incidents concerning Iti's at different camps.

WED JUNE 2

Had rugby practise at night. But was interrupted by thunderstorm and bad light. My feet are in bad condition.

THURS JUNE 3

Usual day ie. office by day. Watching football at night.

FRI JUNE 4

Parcel issue. Finished the mail in afternoon.

SATURDAY JUNE 5

Day off. Had shower in the morning and did washing (vest and socks) in afternoon. Watched our 1st team beat sgts 3 tries to nil at rugby. I was reserve.

SUNDAY JUNE 6

Day off. Did more washing – underpants, towel and handkerchief. Basketball, rugby and football matches at night between WO's and Sgts. vs the Rest. The Rest won basketball 19-4, lost rugby 9-15 and won football 4-1.

MON JUNE 8

Started work at the post office again. Parcels issued. We got Northampton 16. Yorkshire pud and fig pud, good parcel. Made couple of pancakes at night with Yorkshire pudding mixture. Shower at night.

TUES JUNE 8

Went to concert at night. Bit of a wash out. Getting a bit short of ideas.

WED JUNE 9

Had a practise game of football in afternoon. I scored from a penalty. Too hot to be enjoyable. Very sultry and wearying. Made an excellent pancake at night.

THURS JUNE 10

Had hair cut and shower in afternoon. Watched football at night.

FRI JUNE 11

Violent electric storm hit last night ....
....
Managed to get hold of a good book..
....

SAT JUNE 12

Managed to get our rugby practise at night. I played left .... first half. .... Enjoyed it. Had to hand in our RAF greatcoats for .... RAF bloke too much like ......

SUN JUNE 13

Nominal roll call in the huts in the afternoon. Took
....

MON JUNE 14

Nominal roll call on the parade ground in the morning 8 a.m. – 12 a.m. Very hot, gave me a headache for rest of the day.

TUES JUNE 15

Roll call at night took hell of a time. Watched football rest of the night then went to ....

....

WED JUNE 16

Nothing much to report. Watched football at night.

THURS JUNE 17

.... raining today but the pitch was OK for football at night. Had a kick about with the rugger blokes after football.

FRI JUNE 18

Two rugby leagues have been formed. Our hut's A&B teams are in first division and C team in the 2nd. I play for B team. Our first league game at night against our A team. Fought them to a draw 12-12. I scored 1 try.

SAT JUNE 19

Finished mail so day off. Play football for hut team at right half, won 5-0. Certainly like playing in afternoon games.

SUN JUNE 20

Game of wounding rugby at night. Wonder someone didn't get hurt on that hard ground.

MON JUNE 21

Parcel issue. Washed underpants, 2 pairs of socks and handkerchief. Did a bit of sewing at night, rugger shirt. Vest dyed green with red band round waist.

TUES JUNE 22

Started mail again. Steve and I on sorting. Very hot during day and sultry at night.

WED JUNE 23

Work at office by day, watched sport at night. Had a bit of rugger practise late on.

THURS JUNE 24

Anniversary of capture. Nothing happened worthy of note.

FRI JUNE 25

Played rugby at night for B team against Staff which is one of the strongest teams. Forced them to a draw 3-3 chiefly by close marking of the opposing centres.

SAT JUNE 26

Our A and C rugger teams brought off a double victory at night.
23 hut (cup winners) beat 45 (3-0) at football. 45 are present league
leaders. Had roll call in morning whilst our huts were searched. Took
2 hours. Nothing missing.

SUN JUNE 27

Usual Sunday. Special matches at night including all in rugger game
between RAF and Army. Army won 9-3.

MON JUNE 28

Bulk issue. Bit of a nuisance.

TUES JUNE 29

New draft arrived from Brindisi. Played for our B team against
23 A (the knock out winners). Lost 12-3. Enjoyed the game. Good for
defensive play, we only got the ball from the scrum once.

WED JUNE 30

Two blokes in next hut tried to escape early morning, but were both
shot (leg and arm respectively) in between the two wires. No sport at
night due to rain last night.

THURS JULY 1

After many moves the post office is once more established in the camp
office hut. Played for B team against 26 hut. Won 6-0

Fri July 2

Bulk issue again. Only got 1 lb tin M&V to last 3 days.

Sat July 3

Gave my scilly away. Can't face the stuff sometimes this weather. Lost my appetite and found a rabbit's. Reckon my stomach has contracted due to last winter's restricted diet.

Sun July 4

23 hut played rest of compound at football. Drew 2-2.

Mon July 5

Parcel issue. English. Had a crazy session at night with Brewster. I think a few of us are going a bit light.

Tues July 6

Played for B team against 41 hut at 7.30 a.m. Won 9-3 I scored 1 try. Smoked my last English fag at dinner time. Got a fag parcel at tea time. Good egg. Our A team were defeated 9-3 by 23'A'. Finished off the mail at office.

Wed July 7

Played 44 hut at rugger at 9.30.a.m. Won 6-3 after being behind at half time. A team played 51 hut "all in" at night and won 18-3.

THURS JULY 8

Played for Post Office darts team against 45 hut. Won 2 legs to 1. I got the winning double. Very strong wind at night spoiled the football inter unit knock out. RAF beat Lamerons (marine corp?) 2-1 scoring two excellent goals in last 5 minutes.

FRI JULY 9

Played for B team at rugger vs 43 hut won 6-3. Pulled leg muscles got sore foot.

SAT JULY 10

Rugger again vs 26 A team. Was unlucky to lose 9-6. Feeling the strain of these games a little.

SUN JULY 11

C rugger team short of men through sickness and injury so I had to play for them at 08.00 hours. Won 9-0. Sicily invaded by Americans and British. Big scale fighting on Russian front. American initiative in Far East. Beginning of the end?

MON JULY 12

Parcel issue – English.

TUES JULY 13

Finished off the mail in the afternoon. Watched football and rugby at night.

WED JULY 14

Felt down in the mouth all day. Had a shower in the afternoon. Had a horrible dream at night. Dad dead. Terrible thing to dream about.

THURS JULY 15

Played rugger for B team at night. Played "all in" against my better judgment, as our side had no experience of tackling. Lost 21-3

FRIDAY JULY 16

Bulk issue. Not so good.

SATURDAY JULY 17

Secret meeting of RAF discussing policy in event of collapse of Iti's. Rather previous I think. Talked a lot of balls about separating into air crews.

SUNDAY JULY 18

Made a temporary kit bag out of Iti shirt, for in event of a move I would not be able to carry all my kit in bits and pieces.

MON JULY 19

Parcel issue, English. Fried a real egg tonight. 1st for 18 months. Got it from McCorry who purchased it from an Iti when he was in dock.

TUES JULY 20

Played rugger for B team against Sergeant's A team. Big side. Made draw 3-3. Big sports day for 25 hut. 1st football team won 1-0 2nd team drew 3-3. A rugby team won 15-0, B rugby team drew 3-3. Good show. Got some tomatoes from canteen. First of the year. Very welcome this weather, when scilly is practically uneatable.

WED JULY 21

Nothing much doing. 300 men (technical) sent out of camp to working camp. Rumoured in Germany. Sorry to see young Jack Bailey go.

THURS JULY 22

Very sudden thunderstorm at night.

FRI JULY 23

Issue of Canadian parcels. Our rugger match with 36 hut cancelled due to that hut being divided amongst rest of camp.

SAT JULY 24

The post office work ceases to function as the Iti's cannot afford paper for the addressed to be written on. Be at a loose end now. Our extra rations continue until stopped.

SUN JULY 25

Steve and myself sort mail in bundles of 500 in alphabetical order and that's this week's mail finished with. News of heavy Russian attacks. Our capture of Catania. Some POW's killed in a raid on southern Italy. Our C team win the 2nd league. A team 2nd in the 1st league. B team 5th in 1st league. B team would have been 3rd with a better try average.

MON JULY 26

Issue of English parcels. Didn't come in the evening. Had hot shower in afternoon. News comes in that Mussolini has been deposed by Royalist government under Marshal Bagdolio. Wonder what the position will be now.

TUES JULY 27

Rained a bit in evening but had a bit of a kick about with football at night. Very interesting speech by Bagdolio denouncing the Fascist rule of the last 20 years, emanating in a bloody war. Sounds promising for us. The old turncoat.

WED JULY 28

Did a pile of washing in the afternoon. Helped to make up a rugger side for another hut at night. Played hooker. Got the ball out quite a bit. Rather fun. News: Mussolini arrested for murder of a Fascist in 1924. Italy, Romania and Hungary talking peace terms with Great Britain in Portugal. Germans said to be leaving Italy. Hope the latter is true. Give us a chance of Iti's pack in. Lot of blokes expecting their freedom within a few weeks. I still reserve my opinion.

THURS JULY 29

Played rugger practise at 06.00 hours. Scored a solo try. Had a cold shower at 07.30.

FRI JULY 30

Issue of bulk. Very poor. Russians capture Orrel.

SAT JULY 31

Young McCorry challenges me to 100 yds race backing himself with 50 fags. Sinndge beat him with 5-10 yards. Sinndge didn't take the lads fags. Did bit of work at the office today.

SUN AUG 1

Sports finals held at night. Pitch bad for running.

MON AUG 2

Our 1st rugger team drew with the champions 23 hut. 3-3 in a great struggle. English parcels issued.

TUES AUG 3

All RAF had to parade for the Colonel at 8.30. Much speculation as to the meaning of the parade. Some say that he was looking for an Iti. He seemed to inspect our faces closely.

WED AUG 4

Played rugger for B team against 51 & 52 combined. Our 1st match of the new league. Won 3 tries to 1. I scored one try. A good un. News says that Italians have refused peace terms which were pretty stiff.

THURS AUG 5

Watched rugby at night.

FRI AUG 6

Our first rugby team beat Sergeants 6 points to nil.

SAT AUG 7

Got a boil on my cheek. "Ding Dong". Bill squeezed it for me. Left a nasty hole. Rather browned off these days.

SUN AUG 8

The usual exhibition games at night. England beat Scotland 2-0.

MON AUG 9

Canadian parcels issued.

TUES AUG 10

Got up at 6 a.m. and did some sprinting round the compound. Carried coffee from cookhouse. Swept up the hut. Had a cold shower. At night went to the play "Middle Watch". Very good. Some of the female parts were excellent.

WEDNESDAY AUG 11

Had two roll calls in the evening. Lights went out at night presumably for air raid.

THURSDAY AUG 12

Played rugby in morning for 2nd team against Sergeants, a very big crowd. Made a draw 3-3. Rough hard game.

FRI AUG 13

Canadian parcels issued. Affair in Sicily dragging. Have got a very bad cold. Didn't eat much today.

SAT AUG 14

Steve and myself sorted the mail. Appetite very small these days. Generally give my scilly away.

SUN AUG 15

Light orchestra gave open air concert. Quite good. Noticed partial eclipse of the moon.

MON AUG 16

Canadian parcels. Went to the variety at night. Stood up at the back. Not a bad show.

TUES AUG 17

Did a lot of washing in afternoon. Very hot night couldn't sleep.

WED AUG 18

Roll call and search 08.00 – 10.00. Very hot today. New order – anyone outside hut after 23.00 hours is liable to be fired at by sentry. A shot was fired last night over the heads of a group of blokes.

THURS AUG 19

Played rugby at 12.30 for 2nd team against 50 hut. It was hot as hell. After being one down I managed to score with a pretty long run. Managed to win 2-1 at the finish. I was on my knees at the end.

FRI AUG 20

Went on the walk at 08.00 hours in the morning. Good to get outside. Canadian parcels issued. Occupation of Sicily definitely announced. Good show.

SAT AUG 21

Went on the walk again. Saw some smashing dames.

SUN AUG 22

Made my debut for 1st rugby team against 43 hut at 07.00 hours. Won 3-1. I played full back – didn't do badly. Good rugby match at night between 23 champions and 36. Listened to light orchestra for a while at night.

MON AUG 23

Canadian parcels issued. Only two more full issues left in the magasin. Fags are getting short again now.

THURS AUG 24

Did some washing in the afternoon. Felt pretty cheesed off all day.

WED AUG 25

Same as most days. Fleas have started troubling us now we have got rid of the lice. News seems to be pretty good. Russians attacking strongly. We seem to be ready for something big and the yanks are giving the Japs the works.

THURS AUG 26

Just another day.

FRID AUG 27

Canadian parcels. Went on the walk. A bit of mail awaited my return. Went to a recital by the choir at night. Some very good solos. Leggitt sang "Your Tiny Hand is Frozen" Puccini. Roberts played 2nd movement Beety's Sonata Pathetique. Very good.

SAT AUG 28

Heavy downpours of rain in afternoon. Cool all day. Wore my battle dress blouse first time for many months.

SUN AUG 29

Inter compound football matches at night. Home team lost 2-1. Away team (6-a-side) lost 9-3. Our rugger 1st team lost 12-3 to 36. Rough game. I played for 2nd team in morning against 50 hut. Won 7 tries to nil, I scored 2 tries. Got a few bruises.

Mon Aug 30

Canadian parcels issued. Got 40 fags for tin bully. Had a game of deck tennis. Pete and myself were defeated 3 games to nil.

Tues Aug 31

Usual day. Had a bit of passing practise with rugger ball at night. Taganrog evacuated by Germans.

Sept 1 Wed

Played rugby for 2nd team against staff 2nd team. Won 2-1. I made a good try for McCorry after the style of practise the night previous.

Sept 2nd Thurs.

Brewster unfit so had to play centre in the 1st team against staff 1st team. Got beaten 3-1 in good game. Their forwards were too heavy for ours. I knocked my shoulder up and bruised my knee badly, the latter in scoring a good try. Got weighed – 63 kilos almost back to normal.

Sept 3rd Fri

Sports. Should have run in 60 yards relay but was unfit due to yesterday's game. Our hut got knocked out of the event. Sports are a pleasant change from football and rugby. News that British troops have landed in Southern Italy. Slogan – It won't be long now.

Sept 4 Sat

Rained heavily all day. Good job we have now got some pebble paths round the huts. Miserable day.

SEPT 5 SUN

Drying up a bit today. 39 league champions beat 23 4-0 at football.
Good show.

SEPT 6 MON

Did a lot of washing in afternoon. My knee is still very bad or I would
have been running the individual 60 yards and 440 yards at night.
We got our last issue of parcels today 1 between 3. Don't expect we'll
get any more now due to the invasion. Things are going to be mighty
grim shortly. Fortunately we are in a pretty good position for brews.
Letters have been received from the supposed working party that left on
July 21. They are now in Germany. Bad sign.

SEPT 7 TUESDAY

Sports again today. News pretty good. British advancing in southern
Italy. Russians attacking heavily. Yanks and Aussies land in New Guinea.

SEPT 8 WEDNESDAY

Sports finals. Very interesting, 36 hut won. Sensational news at night.
Armistice between Italians and British. Everybody highly elated. Not
sure myself whether it is not too early for rejoicing. Blokes singing all
night. Later news flash that British 7ᵗʰ Army has landed at Genoa. Glad
to know some of our chaps are North of us. Rumours of marauding
German columns. Colonel supposed to have said he is prepared to arm
us against their interference.

GERMANS
TAKE OVER

SEPT 9 THURSDAY

Woke up at 7 a.m. to find the camp surrounded by Germans. What a nasty awakening. During the course of the day they relieved the Iti's of their arms and took over the camp. The Iti's were put in No.3 sector. It was afterwards stated that an Alpine division had been sent against the Germans last night and got cut up. A patrol received the same treatment and in the morning the Germans were dug in round the camp.

There was no confirmation of our troops landing at Genoa but Americans have landed at Naples. They'd better get here quick now. The next few days will be anxious. Can't see the Iti rations continuing and we are almost out of parcel stuff. The lads were rather glum today after last night's brief hilarity. Will the German's stay be brief or is it possible they will get reinforcements through the Brenner?

SEPT 10 FRIDAY

Another anxious day. Civvies outside seem cheerful. One of them threw half a loaf over with a message in it, "To our English friends – the Brenner Pass is closed by British and Italian troops. The whole of Southern Italy is in British hands, the Germans are retreating north and many POW camps have been relieved. At the most you will be freed in 2 or 3 days".

English MO got some wireless news from Carpi hospital. Italian Navy given over to us. Italian air force flown to North Africa. British invaded western France.

The suspense is rather wearying. No rations came in today. We got ⅙th invalid food parcel. Gift from the Gods. I had 3 biscuits ½ tin salmon and bit of bread I had saved all day.

There is to be a roll call tomorrow. Lot of blokes are getting rather gloomy as to the prospects of freedom.

SEPT 11 SATURDAY

Lot of blokes escaped during the early morning, someone having cut a fairly big hole through the barbed wire. Blokes were in a queue to get out until a machine gun burst put an end to proceedings. Roll call went off all night and 17 blokes were missing although there were quite a few hiding in the camp for fear Jerry might move us off.

Had our last good meal from the parcel at night M&V with fried onions. Fortunately jerry took the Iti contractor to get the bread. Iti civvies have volunteered to send vegetables in.

Blokes spend most of the time sitting by the wire shouting lewd remarks to the Iti girls who seem to like it. A lot of women beckon for us to get out of camp. Bet they are taking care of some of our chaps. Things cheered up when the bread came in.

SEPT 12 SUNDAY

Had an issue of parcels, 1 between 6, these having come from officers camp. Germans had the rifles at the alert all day. Had thin vegetable broth for dinner. Meat roll and bread at night. We can brew up with immunity now. Two Italian girls contrived to get some news to us. One distracted the guard and the other came to the wire and gave the news. The British landed at Trieste this morning. We have not landed at Genoa but are advancing rapidly from the South. Can't come too quick for us. A lot more wire cutting and escapes during the night. Several long bursts of machine gun fire were heard later on. Hope none of our chaps were hit though rumour already says that 2 blokes have been killed whilst escaping.

SEPT 13 MONDAY

No confirmation of the Trieste landing. Still fighting round Naples. Things don't look too rosy. Went to the play "Rookery Nook" at night. Not bad. More machine gun bursts at night.

SEPT 14 TUESDAY

Things took a very ominous turn today. 600 chaps in set 4 were marched to the station at 13.00 hrs. We were told to prepare ourselves to move. Looks as though we'll finish the war in Germany after all this suspense. Too bad.

SEPT 15 WEDNESDAY

Another day of anxiety and little grub. Just about finished our parcel grub. Scilly ½ loaf is the days ration. Civvies haven't been as cheerful lately. A girl gives us the griff each day. We have bypassed Rome where there is a big battle. We did attempt a landing at Trieste which was driven off. A lot of shooting goes on these nights.

SEPT 16 THURSDAY

Another ghastly day. Scilly like dishwater. Made some porridge – the last of our parcel stuff. Civvies throwing bread over this afternoon, I got a piece – very welcome. Chap got shot last night going for piss in his pyjamas. Think some of the Jerries were drunk with vino.

The news states that we have landed reinforcements at Naples and are fighting South of the city. Americans are North of Barri. Yugoslavia supposed to be clear of German troops.

SEPT 17 FRIDAY

These are ghastly days. Not enough grub and nothing to hope for
except a trip to Germany although some blokes are getting hopeful
again. Gerald McCorry escaped in the rubbish bin but got caught.
A crowd of blokes watched the cart go past on the road giving Jerry the
tip that someone was hiding therein. When the rubbish was tipped the
other chap gave himself up and Gerald got away. Good luck to him.
No improvement in the news except from Russia.

SEPT 18 SAT

Issue of Canadian parcels. Not quite enough for 1 between 2. Most
of camp got 1 between 2 but we were unlucky in the cut and got
1 between 3. What a relief to get a bit of grub. Kelly (the parcel man)
nearly made a balls of things by trying to escape when he went out for
the parcels.

The Jerries were very talkative round the wire tonight. One was
promising to throw over a bottle of vino at 12 o'clock. A good laugh
was had at the expense of the Italians. Mussolini has now set up a new
Fascist party. Talk about the Vicar of Bray.

SEPT 19 SUNDAY

As usual on Sunday our Carpi friends came to see us. When the crowd
on the road got too great Jerry dispersed them with machine gun fire.
A bit too free with the use of his guns. As last night Coulson, with a
crowd of blokes round him, talked to the German guards for an hour
or so. Whilst guards were thus preoccupied a chap cut the wire 20 yards
away and went through the wire. 4 blokes followed him but the 5th was
seen by the guard and then the bullets began to fly. He was however
captured without injury.

SEPT 20 MONDAY

Curfew is now imposed at 8 p.m.. these days are pretty deadly. Washed my shorts in afternoon. The camp is going to rack and ruin, bloke having taken wash house and shit house doors and window frames for brewing up. No news today as Carpi wireless set has been discovered by Jerry.

SEPT 21 TUESDAY

Steve Caddy got out in a wagon load of straw that was going to a farm. Good luck to him. Civvies helped him. Griff says that we have landed at Fiume and are advancing in the South. Bit of air activity today – unusual.

SEPT 22 WED

At last comes what I've been waiting for. Suddenly at 8 a.m. comes the announcement that we have to be ready to move in ¼ hour. Eventually we marched to the station at 12 a.m. The kit bag weighed more than somewhat before we finished the 3 mile walk. The accommodation was 40 per cattle truck as usual. I think we passé through the Brenner at night. What a bloody night, couldn't stir.

SEPT 23 THURS

Travelling all day. Got 2 mugs of barley and wheat at different stations. Another uncomfortable night.

SEPT 24 FRI

Guts bad this morning. Had to have a shit or bust. Held on as long as I could but as jerry doesn't open the doors much I had to do it in a Red Cross box. What a stink. Threw it out when the door was opened in the afternoon. Jerry hasn't shown much consideration for the calls of nature. We had to piss in tins and  pour it through the grating. Arrived at our destination at about 6 p.m. Marched us into a compound (saw some Serb civvies taken for a run). There were some huts but not sufficient for us all. We (Pete and myself) had to sleep outside. Very damp and cold. Continuous queue for the one shithouse throughout the night. I had to wait for an hour.

ARRIVAL AT
STALAG LUFT IVB –
MUHLBERG, GERMANY

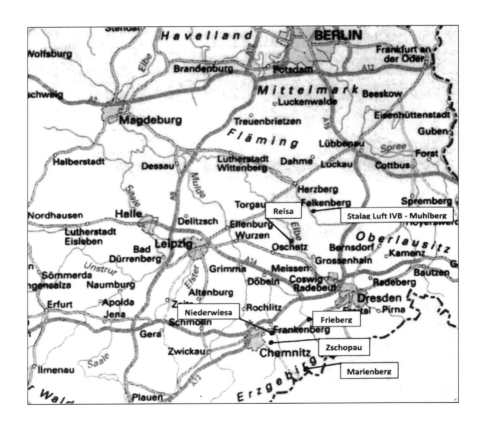

SEPT 25 SAT

Had a scilly at 11 a.m. consisting mainly of swede. At 5 p.m. we got
$\frac{1}{5}$th big loaf and bit of margarine. Had to have our hair sheared off.
Looks like Sing Sing now. First time I've had mine off. Was just ready
to go to sleep outside when it began to rain. There were as many chaps
outside as in the huts for which there was a dash by the unfortunates
in the rain. There was much commotion and dissension and an
uncomfortable night was spent by all. Must have been about 300 in
the huts. Lot of different nationalities here – Russians, Italians, Dutch,
French and Serbian bandits.

SEPT 26 SUN

Meals – good amount of potatoes boiled in their skins with spot of gravy, ¼ᵗʳ loaf with margarine and small piece of polony. Bitterly cold today. Crushed to death in the hut at night. What an existence.

SEPT 27 MON

Should have moved out this morning for fumigation and baths but this was cancelled due to the great numbers of Iti's passing through the camp. Funny to see all these Iti's prisoners. Our former Iti officers are here. All the various nationalities seem confident about an early finish of the war. Romania is said to have asked for peace.

German children, about 10 – 12 years old, passed the camp in uniforms with packs and rifles. They yelled 'swinehund' at us – the young rips. We are told we are moving to another compound tomorrow. Let's hope it's better than this. Another horrible uncomfortable night.

SEPT 28 TUES

Reveille at 5.30, marched off at 6 o'clock it still being dark. Went to a new compound in which there are 10 huts in lieu of 6. 200 men per hut. Managed to sort ourselves out. Very tight fit but better than previously. Was very hungry today and was glad when spuds came up. Got spoon of jam in lieu of margarine. Had a better night.

SEPT 29 WED

Orders of the day. Reveille 05.30. Roll call 06.00 (it is dark until 06.30). Inspection, beds in line etc 09.00. Roll call 19.30. Fancy bull shit in a place like this. 1 wash tap in the compound. No room to stir in the hut and we've got to have our kit tidy. Another 15 blokes came in the hut before nightfall, so that whereas we were crowded before we are now crowded more than somewhat. These are horrible days.

We get loaves, 1 between 4 and 1 between 5 alternately. The weather is cold and the appetite keen. Spuds and gravy today. Filling pro tem.

SEPT 30 THURS

We arise before 6 o'clock and don't get any grub till 15.00 hrs. It was good when it came, being peas on thick gravy. 800 more blokes came in today and bivowacks had to be erected for them. What a life!

OCT 1 FRI

Orders prohibit fires but blokes have been brewing up in our hut ever since arrival. Jerry paid a surprise visit this morning and found the brews in full swing (I had just got the fire prepared for ours). We were, consequently, turfed out of the hut, bag and baggage for the day. After a day in the open, it was fine fortunately, Jerry let us back in the hut after the roll call at night. Will now have to be satisfied with the German brew of cinnamon tea which tastes of FA.

OCT 2 SAT

Another uneventful day. A news bulletin came round. Russians attacking on all fronts. Smolensk and Kiev in Russian hands. Heavy attacks to cross the central Dneiper. Germans retreating to plan in Southern Italy. Naples still in German hands. Getting bitten to death by fleas. Orders that we are going through the disinfestor starting at 12 midnight. Later cancelled but at 3 in the morning blokes were aroused from their slumbers to be disinfected.

OCT 3 SUN

No more blokes went out to the disinfestor this morning. Another crab day. Bread has been 1 between 5 since Friday. 1 wash tap for over 2,000 men. Job to get a wash.

OCT 4 MON

Got grain scilly and ⅕th loaf and bit of marge. Just about equivalent to Iti rations today. Felt hungry. Griff says that we have invaded France and the Russians are on Polish soil. Hope it is correct.

OCT 5 TUES

Got bread 1 between 4. New shape of loaf. Spuds for scilly. Better than yesterday. No confirmation of invasion, afraid it must be duff. It is said that German newspapers have been stopped. If so, it sounds to me as though it must be political differences rather than war news is the cause of the repression. (Lice have started again).

OCT 6 WED

Got turned out of the hut early with our kit preparatory to going through the disinfestor. Late afternoon we were marched to the aforesaid. The fumigator was a gas affair and all our kit was put through without damage. We had a good shower, after which we were painted with some disinfectant under the arms and balls. We were then marched to another room where we were vaccinated and inoculated in the left breast. We then went into a big drying room to dry off whilst our clothes were still in the fumigator. We eventually collected our kit which was searched (mine wasn't looked at). We finished up in a big compound. The huts contain bunks of 3 stories and 2 men have to sleep in one bunk. The bunks are small in comparison to the other bunks and are barely adequate for one man. Blokes were also sleeping on the floor. Must be about 400 in the hut. We are locked in at night 7 o'clock. Days rations – a poor scilly, ½th loaf with bit of carroway seed cheese and marge.

OCT 7 THURS

Got registered today. What a palaver. Like a labour exchange. 8 forms were filled in for each man. Finger prints and photographs taken. Got the worst scilly ever today. Seemed to have bird seed in it – very watery. Bread 1 between 4. Oval loaves. Must be months old (had March on the box so it's said). Tastes like solid sawdust. Marge and bit of meat paste (tasteless). Bunk collapsed and Brewater has to sleep on floor and I sleep with Pete who was fortunate to get a bunk to himself. Tiring day.

OCT 8 FRI

Bitterly cold today. Made a brew in the hut in the afternoon – jolly good. Rations better today. Spuds and stewed cabbage, ⅕th loaf (better bread) with jam and marge.

OCT 9 SAT

Grub was a bit late today. Spuds and stewed cabbage, ¼ loaf and marge. Good. Vaccination appears to be taking swelling and pains round the shoulder.

OCT 10 SUNDAY

Was rolling a fag from a bit of shithouse paper when the Jerry guard came up and slipped me a packet of cigarette papers. Good show. Rations ⅕th loaf, spuds and scilly. It appears there are 3,000 parcels in camp and they are to be dished out to the semi-permanent members of the camp, as the transit blokes are liable to move off any day and get parcels at a permanent camp. We (the RAF) are included as we have to stay behind here. Are the privates kicking up a row about it? NCO's and RAF unpopular again. Nice day but cold. Only got bit of tobacco now and have been relying on home rolled ones for several days now.

OCT 11 MONDAY

Got a Canadian parcel between two. Moved over into RAF compound this being the fourth we have now occupied. We are again cramped for space and are on the floor (brick floor). The lighting is better and the blokes stop up fairly late. There is no water in the wash house during the day as the cookhouse tap is off. Mostly air crew in here. A cosmopolitan crowd, Indian, Australian, Canadian (French), English, USA, New Zealand. Some line shooters amongst them. They haven't been captured long. Grand to get a bit of parcel stuff again.

OCT 12 TUES

All our army friends left today for different camps. News – Germans have evacuated the Cuban bridge head. Good show. Crimea must be in danger. Brilliant weather but cold. Water came on at 8 p.m. so had a good wash. Water position is damned awkward.

OCT 13 WED

Issued with the Iti dixies. Pete got his pinched within an hour of getting it. Got another Iti blanket (3 now). Had the shits today. Had to get up in the middle of the night. All RAF under rank of corporal had to parade at 2 a.m. It turned out to be for digging fatigue so I dodged off the end of the column.

OCT 14 THURS

Was on digging fatigue this morning 8 to 11. Didn't overwork myself 50 men are required for the work every morning and afternoon and there are only 70 of us under rank of corporal out of 700, the sergeants have volunteered to take their turn with the spade. Good show. Esprit de corps at last. Jerry is complaining that he can't get on with RAF. We don't cooperate as the army do. Someone pinched the valve off his bike. He came in the hut in a hell of a temper and slung someone's bed on the floor. Washed socks late night when water came on.

OCT 15 FRI

Another wasted day.

OCT 16 SAT

Moved early this morning into the next hut. 5th hut since arrival. Got a bunk. Not enough lats but have to make them do. Some chaps arrived who have not yet been captured a fortnight. What a sell for them. Better off than we were when originally captured.

Back left to right: Dave, Jimmie, Bernard Scholfield
Front left to right: Peter Squires and Dad

Oct 17 Sunday

Big parade at 9 a.m. when a big knob announced rules of camp. No fires, no interference with German women etc. Heard it all before. Got a hot plate on the stove. Bit of competition to get on it. Got letter cards.

Oct 18 Monday

Issue of parcels one between two. We got English parcel, there were some Canadian. This camp is very oppressive. Bare and stark. Felt depressed today, get fits of depression occasionally. Washed a shirt and underpants. Was the water cold.

Oct 19 Tues

War news. Overwhelming British and American forces attacking north of Naples. Russians still attacking west of Smolensk and central Dneiper. Warmed up steak pudding and potatoes on hot plate. Hope some more parcels come in before next week.

Oct 20 Wed

Good weather just lately. Bread 1 between 7 today. Oblong loaves. Better bread but not as much as the oval sawdust loaves. Heavy air raid nearby (Liepzig?) strict blackout observed.

Oct 21 Thurs

Washed two vests and had a shave. Weather quite warm. Good library here. Got one book between three. The blokes recently captured are lucky to get books so early. We had to wait for nine months and then we had to give tin of biscuits and tin of jam for two books. Was on hut fatigue making coal bricks. There is a slack heap in the camp and with the aid of water we make coal balls for the stove.

OCT 22 FRI

Another nice day – wasted. Got bird seed scilly today. Get soup twice a week in lieu of spuds. Poor do, thin and tasteless.

OCT 23 SAT

Made porridge in morning. No news of any more parcels coming in. Out of fags and bacca today.

OCT 24 SUN

Band came into hut at night and gave us a bit of music and some jokes. Bloke next to us (recently captured) doesn't smoke much and he gave Pete and myself 5 fags each. Bolt from the blue. Had our last tin from the parcel today – egg flakes.

OCT 25 MON

A very thin day. Bird seed scilly and bread, 1 between 5. Announcement at night that 8000 Canadian parcels have come in and that they will be issued 1 a man tomorrow. Bucked us up somewhat.

OCT 26 TUES

Parcel a man issued, Canadian. We marched to the magasin and collected our brew. We live again. ....
Had some good brewings today. Good to have some smokes again. Wrote 3 postcards.

OCT 27 WED

Lot of rumours flying about today. Russians in Romania and Poland.
Continental invasion. Government of Germany taken over by army as
opposed to party. Rumours like these leave me cold now but a lot of
new blokes believe them. They'll learn in time. Lot of bartering going
on with Italian prisoners. Bit one sided for a lot of our blokes were
taking the Iti stuff and clearing off without giving anything in exchange.
Makes me sick. The Iti's are a lot worse off than we are now for they
get no parcels. Some of these blokes are worse than the Iti's were.

OCT 28 THURS

Grub wasn't up till 2.30 pm. Good job we had parcels to keep us going.
....

OCT 29 FRI

Got some toothpowder issued. Oblong loaves today between 5. Better
bread. Had some toasted with sardines. Lovely. Do a lot of toast since
we acquired the hotplate. Greatly improves the sawdust bread.

OCT 30 SAT

Bitter cold wind in the morning. Oat and barley scilly for dinner.
Fried meat roll for tea. Strong rumour RAF are moving on Tuesday.
Wait and see.

OCT 31 SUN

Cold again today. Made bully spud hash for tea. Bread has been the
better type lately. Gerry food issue not bad, better than .... meat
issue.

NOV 1 MON

Issue of Canadian parcels 1 between 2 late afternoon. Collected coal dust for coal bricks.

NOV 2 TUES

Went for shower in afternoon. Wonderful showers, pity we don't get them more often. 2nd since arrival.

NOV 3 WED

Went for X-ray in the afternoon. Couple of frauliens there, not bad ones either. What the reason is for X-raying us is, I don't know. Most of these new chaps here keep their underclothing in filthy condition. Before they know where they are they'll be lousy. In last two days 3000 Xmas parcels, 3000 invalid and 3000 milk parcels have arrived. Not an issuable parcel in the lot. What a to do. Be lucky if we get 1 between 2 on Monday.

NOV 4 THURS

Bitter cold today. All washing outside frozen stiff.

NOV 5 FRI

Had big wash in morning. Shirt, heavy vest, underpants and socks. Hard work. Cold spell continues.

NOV 6 SATURDAY

Was on fatigue of wood collecting for the camp. This lasted from 8 a.m. – 12 a.m. and consisted of 15 men dragging a cart 3 miles to the place where the wood was stacked and then drawing the loaded cart back to camp. There were 10 carts all told. What a trek. Fatigued me more than somewhat. Smoked my last fag at night.

NOV 7 SUN

More news that a lot of parcels are on their way. Out of everything bar milk and sugar.

NOV 8 MONDAY

A lot of classes commenced today. I have put my name down for French, English and music theory. Went to the latter class in the afternoon. Promises to be interesting. Blokes are to be admired for getting classes going under very adverse conditions. The lecture room is empty but full of empty bunks which have been moved to form separate enclosures. News that 4000 parcels are at the station. Was issued today with 50 fags borrowed from Xmas parcels. Craven A – poor fag compared to Players, Capstan.

War news

From German communiqués it is apparent that the Germans are cut off in Crimea, though the inevitable successful defensive actions are being fought. In Italy we are making heavy attacks but Germans still hold Rome.

NOV 9 TUESDAY

8 more truckloads of parcels arrive at the station. A lot brought into camp. Issue of 1 per man at night, Canadian. Just the job. Got tea for a change. Can't beat it. Jerry cheese issue today, stunk the place out. Uneatable.

Nov 10 Wed

Went to English class in afternoon. Very interesting lecture, the stages of the Russian front since 1941 at night. There are rumours that the British navy have entered the Black Sea. This would coincide nicely with the Germans trapped position in the Crimea. It is known that Eden has had troops in Turkey.

Nov 11 Thurs

2 minutes silence observed. Went to French elementary class in morning and music class in afternoon. Had salmon and potatoes boiled in klim. Tin of sardines each on toast. Made ...... cake from 3 biscuits, prunes, jam and butter. Big eats. Full .... somewhat at night. 8,000 more parcels come in today.

Nov 12 Fri

20 French fags (Elegante) issued today sent from officers camp. .... Moved all the lads round in the afternoon to get more space and light. Before we were very cramped for space in between the beds and it was also very dark.

Nov 13 Sat

English class in afternoon. 21,000 English and .... Australian parcels come in. .... instead of Monday as the parcels are getting ......

NOV 14 SUN

Been raining last few days and roll calls have been in the hut.
Anti-parochial weather. Mention of bitter encircling movements west
of Kiev on the news bulletins.

NOV 15 MON.

Went to French class in morning. Left the elementary class for a revision
class. Enjoyable. Music classes have unfortunately been cancelled due to
lack of chalk and blackboards.

NOV 16 TUESDAY

More parcels come in today. There is now over 60,000 in stock.
Finished Cronin's "Keys of the Kingdom". Very good. Changed it at
the library for Walpoles "Jeremy".

NOV 17 WEDNESDAY

Went to English class in afternoon. Very dry. Freezes every night now.

NOV 18 THURSDAY

Went to meeting of French classes. Lecture at night on Beveridge's
Plan. Seems a good scheine. Very interesting. Light went out about
8.30 p.m. and in the dark the thief or thieves, who have been at work
some time now, pinched someone's parcel. The lousy bastards. There
has been a lot of pilfering of Red Cross food stuff lately.

Nov 19 Friday

Went to concert in the other half of the hut at night. The comedian sent me in stitches. Had a wonderful shower in afternoon. Pity we don't get them more often. Repaired my bed. Put extra wooden side pieces in as my lats are too short.

Nov 20 Saturday

Went to French class in afternoon. Barley scilly again today. Third time this week. Dead loss. News mentions German counter attacks on Russian front. Hope they aren't serious.

Nov 21 Sunday

News that classes are being discontinued until the Red Cross supplies arrive. Very disappointing. Went to another hut to see the concert we saw on Friday. Everybody has got the song "I Like Coffee I Like Tea" on the brain.

Nov 22 Monday

Our hut leader, a New Zealander, escaped three days ago. Today the Jerries got wise to it resulting in a long roll call. Parcels were therefore up late in the afternoon. Lights went out at 7.30 p.m. due to air raid. This is becoming too regular.

Nov 23 Tuesday

Roll calls in future at 6.30 a.m. and 8.00 p.m. Escape measure. Lights went out at 7 p.m. and night roll call was dispensed with. Saw a horrible sight today. A Russian was taking Red cross tins from the rubbish dump and running his finger round the insides of them. Reminds me of Altimura days when blokes used to search for ears of corn in the paliasse straw.

NOV 24 WED

Mothers birthday.
One of those depressing days when one feels that the war may go on for years. Progress in Italy is really disappointing. Saw a map and it appears that we aren't a great distance north of Naples.

NOV 25 THURS

Got issued with pair of socks, laces and braces. Red Cross. Had a strip down wash in the wash troughs. Cold but worth it. Lights went out at 8.30 p.m.

NOV 26 FRI

Nothing much doing. News; heavy raids on Berlin. Bitter fighting on eastern front. German counter attack continues west of Kiev. In Italy, Germans retreat in west but repulse Americans in east.

NOV 27 SAT

Due to lack of storing accommodation we got Canadian parcels issued today. Amusing lecture at night. "..........."

NOV 28 SUNDAY

Typical bleak November day. Good griff announced at night. On eastern front Germans in full retreat on 120 kilometre front. Berlin raided 6 times in 9 days. Germans retreat in Italy where British are prepared for another big push. Yugoslavs still causing trouble. Yanks capture more islands in far east. Chittagong in Burma captured.

NOV 29 MONDAY

Went to play at the French theatre in afternoon. "Blythe Spirit" Noel Coward. Very good. The deportment and dress of the women was perfect.

NOV 30 TUESDAY

At night there was a variety show (radio) in the other half of the hut. Done behind a screen. Very good. Very rainy weather just now.

DEC 1 WED

Had haircut at French barbers. Cost me 2 English fags.

DEC 2 THURS

Lot of army left today taking with them the musical instruments. Going to bugger up the concerts. Lights went out at 7.30 p.m.

DEC 3 FRI

Watched football match in afternoon. Our compound won 8-0, chap called Jeffrie is really first rate. On fatigue late afternoon carrying Canadian parcels from one compound to ours. Just about creased me. At roll call at night one bloke was fast asleep when Blondie came in to count. When the chap got up to join the ranks, Blondie greeted him with a humorous "Good morning".

DEC 4 SATURDAY

Terrific frost in the morning.

DEC 5 SUNDAY

New commandant called a big parade at 9 a.m. at which all the old bullshit was read out. Tone however was conciliatory. Big football match, British vs Continentals. British won 7-2. Jeffries scored hat trick. Our lads played very clever football. Bitter cold today.

DEC 6 MONDAY

Canadian issue. Pete and I got tobacco in lieu of 50 cigs. We swopped both chocolate bars for 25 cigs each. Finished up with 50 fags each and 1oz of Players Medium.

DEC 7 TUESDAY

Was on coal brick making fatigue. Very cold to the hands. Our hut was defeated at football 4-3. Should have been 2-1 for us, 4 goals were offside.

DEC 8 WED

Very frosty. Pool in the French compound is completely frozen over. Blokes skating on it. Lecture at night on chain stores.

DEC 9 THURSDAY

Snowing today. Helped in the transfer of Red X parcels from our compound to a hut by the gate. 2 boxes of fags were pinched 4,000 in all. Pilfering from the Red X supplies is getting too common.

Dec 10 Fri

Jerry guard lost his temper in the morning and knocked one of our blokes about. Turned out he had lost his wife and family in Leipzig. Got a shower in afternoon and some of the chaps were inoculated.

Dec 11 Sat

Had a game of football in afternoon. Ground covered with compressed snow like a skating rink. We lost 5-2. I scored a good goal. Much fun was had by all due to sliding about uncontrollably.

Dec 12 Sun

Had another game of football in afternoon. Lost 5-3. I played outside right as yesterday. Ground was more slippy than yesterday. Bags of fun. Later in afternoon I watched a French team beat an army side 4-0. French forwards all keep forward and look very dangerous on attack. Well worth their win.

Dec 13 Mon

Issue of Canadian parcels.

Dec 14 Tues

On shit house cleaning fatigue. Lecture at night on Spanish Civil War.

Dec 15 Wed

Played a 2 hour football game in the morning. Played left half. Draw 8-8

DEC 16 THURS

Lecture at night on 'Tripoli to Italy' lights went out at 7.30 p.m. but came on again at 9 p.m.

DEC 17 FRI

Quiet day on the POW front.

DEC 18 SAT

Played football in the morning at inside right. Lost 4-1. Pulled a thigh muscle. Marched to Muhlberg to carry Red X parcels to the magasin down there. 6 miles there and back. Road was like glass and we slipped and staggered the whole way. Terrible strain. Guards were in a nasty humour and used their bayonets and daggers threateningly. Was dark and very cold coming back and I was at the finish plain tuckered out. A change to see a bit of civvy life. The kiddies are quite attractive and gave us coy smiles. A lot of very young boys were in uniform. Saw a propaganda poster showing Union Jack, Stars and Stripes and Hammer and Sickle with a Jew in the background.

DEC 19 SUNDAY

Usual bullshit parade at 9 a.m. The commandant gave us the message that at Xmas time it was usually Peace in IVB and we would have freedom of the camp Xmas week. In afternoon football match between Army & RAF vs French etc. Good game until Yugoslav International goalkeeper objected to a goal after which he refused to attempt to stop any shot. Spoilt the game. British side won 7-1. Very bad display of sportsmanship. Curtain show at night. "Hay Fever". Very good.

Dec 20 Monday

Issue of Canadian and English parcels. Another trip to Muhlberg in afternoon. Fortunately it has thawed since last trip and the walking wasn't as bad. Made 3 trips to magasin with 2 parcels a time. Tiring walk. The children seem to like us. Was tuckered out on the return journey.

Dec 21 Tuesday

Issue of Xmas parcels. Not the excitement it was last year.

Dec 22 Wed

Serbian rebels brought in ages 9 to 80. In separate compound. English alone allowed to give them extra food. German commander kicks up a fuss about various electrical gadgets chaps have made. Tells us that when we go to Muhlberg we must not sing whistle or smoke (or walk too fast for the guards who are either C3 or wounded). Lights out at 11 p.m.

Dec 23 Thurs

Made a cake in afternoon. Heard hundreds of kites go over late at night. Heavy Berlin raid.

Dec 24 Fri

Christmas Eve. A bit dead. Gave a Russian two slices of bread and jam and a cigarette. Mug of beer at night. Weak tack. Went to carol service in afternoon. Stayed up til midnight.

Dec 25 Sat

After much fuss and palaver about the concession he was going to grant
for Xmas, Jerry had roll calls at 7.30 a.m. and 8 p.m. Saw Scotland beat
England 4-3 in morning. Ground slippy and wet, spoiled the game.
Had 1 lb tin beef steak and macaroni and half Xmas pud for dinner. Felt
full after it. Nothing interesting at night. Lot of blokes tried to scoff
too much and Russians gained by what they couldn't eat. Xmas cake
competition in morning. Some clever designs. Two Serbian children
came round and saw the cakes. These kids are very pleasant looking and
can't be any more than 9 or 10. Damned shame.

Dec 26 Sun

Football match in morning. Dutch beat Ireland & Wales 3-2 after
leading 3-0 Exciting game. Ireland & Wales should have won with their
chances. Dutch were chuffed with their win and celebrated after the
match and a friendly spirit prevailed. I gave half my Xmas chocolate and
a fag to a Russian. Had big meal again at dinnertime. 1lb tin (rissoles,
rice and peas) with fried spuds ½ Xmas pud. Went to variety show at
night. Show not so hot but the hut was very crowded like sardines.
Couldn't get to my hip pocket for my fags.

Dec 27 Mon

Roll call at 6.30 again. Issue of Canadian parcels and 50 fags. Ground
swampy. Had strip down wash in the sink with cold water at night.

Dec 28 Tues

One of those miserable oppressive days.

DEC 29 WED

Saw rugby practise in afternoon. News that Scharnhorst has been sunk. About time. Pretty deadly day.

DEC 30 THURS

Watched South Africans rugby practise. Not bad. Blustery and cold today.

DEC 31 FRI

Shower at 7.30 a.m. 3 weeks since we had one last. Cleaned under my bunk. Collected cookhouse hot water and washed shirt, vest, underpants, socks and towel. Bit of entertainment at night. Best turn was by some South Africans who came in with spears and shields and represented Zulu warriors, their bodies blackened for the occasion. They sang Zulu war songs etc. Saw New Year in with a cup of chai.

1944

JAN 1 SAT

Terrific blizzard outside most of the day. Changed to rain at night. Bread 1 between 9 today due to damage to bakery. Water and electricity went off in afternoon but came on later. Lights on till 1 a.m. but I went to bed at 9 p.m. Poor start to the New Year.

JAN 2 SUN

Shitty weather. Miserable blank days just lately.

JAN 3 MON

Issue of parcels. We chose 2 English. Swopped 2 bars of chocolate for 40 fags, tin of oats for 30 fags, jam for 30. Drew tobacco in lieu of 50 fags. 2 curtain plays at night. Adaptations. Very poor.

JAN 4 TUES

On fatigue of shifting Red X parcels from one magasin to another. 300 yards distant. Made six journeys, 3 parcels a time. Very tiring work. Lecture at night on "Life as a Guardsman" What a load of bullshit.

JAN 5 WED

Frosty today. Received my first letter – Harold.

JAN 6 THURS

Ground hard with frost again. Lecture on Zulus at night.

JAN 7 FRI

Was going to play in rugby practise but rain cancelled the game.

War news

Russians are 40 kilometres and 25 kilometres inside the Polish borders at certain points. Also they are 40 kilometres off Besarabian border. Bulgaria seem to be after a separate peace. Only communications Germans have from Crimea is by sea to Odessa. Heavy raids on Toulon, Bordeaux. Civilians of occupied countries warned to keep to their shelters when invasion starts.

JAN 8 SAT

Frosty morning. Had a good walk round.

JAN 9 SUN

Raining most of the day. Ground swampy. War news still good. 150,000 Germans captured in Kiev salient.

JAN 10 MON

Jerry stops parcel issue due to blokes not marching in orderly fashion to the magasin. Got a good bit of food in reserve. Got my 2nd letter from mother.

JAN 11 TUES

Got our 50 fags issued. Good job too. Walked round French and transit compounds 10 times today. Good exercise.

JAN 12 WED

Took all our clothes and blankets to the fumigator. Had a shower after which we had to dry off in the nude in the drying room until our clothes were ready. Took more than an hour. The fumes from the clothes got on my chest and every fag I had for the rest of the day tasted chlorinated.

News

Russians at one point 60 kilometres inside Polish border. Germans are having to withdraw 60 divisions from Dneiper bend. Heavy daylight raid over France and West Germany. Parcels issued – English. Gave meat roll to Russians.

Jan 13 Thurs

Heavy fall of snow.

Jan 14 Fri

Air raid at night. 3 bombs (light) dropped quite close.

Jan 15 Sat

Classes starting again shortly. Have put down for maths, bookkeeping and French. Concert at night in the other half of the hut. Just a succession of filth. Terrible.

Jan 16 Sun

Game of rugby in afternoon. Played right centre. Very hard game. We lost 4 tries to nil. Not bad considering all the experienced men were on the other side.

JAN 17 MON

Played football in hut practise match. Winning 1-0 till punctured ball stopped play. I played centre forward. Was stiffer than I've ever been before due to yesterday's rugby. Rumours of us moving to Memel.

JAN 18 TUES

Got 50 fags yesterday but no parcels. Saw a 1st rate rugby match between British 15 vs South African 15. Britain won 24 points to nil. British backs were excellent.

JAN 19 WED

Gave tin of salmon to Russians. Parcels issued. We got one English and one Canadian.

JAN 20 THURS

Very bright day today. Rugby match between our hut and the Anzacs. Poor game. Draw 6 points each. Raid at night. Lights went out.

JAN 21 FRI

Fine again today. Went to bookkeeping class. Another raid at night.

JAN 22 SAT

Saw football match between Army and RAF in afternoon. RAF won 2-1 a high wind spoiling the game. The Iti's (our former captors) now clean our shithouses out in place of the Russians. Sergeant Walker who escaped from DG 73 gave a lecture at night. He got to the German front line before he was captured. The Iti's were very helpful to him, accommodating and feeding him.

JAN 23 SUNDAY

Bullshit parade at 9 a.m. Jerry kept us waiting for almost an hour consequently the blokes were restive when he arrived. He refused to take our parade due to the chaps pissing about. A parade was called later on and he kept us waiting for ¾ hour at which time all the chaps went back to their huts before he arrived. As punishment we were locked in the compound all day but someone pinched the lock off the gate and put it down the shithouse. Jerry threatens to keep us in our compound all week pending return of the lock.

Very miserable day. English and American troops make landings South of Rome. Russians striking from Leningrad capture Novgorod.

JAN 24 MONDAY

Issue of 50 fags. Good walk round in afternoon.

JAN 25 TUES

Another weary day. Deep depression over IV B.

JAN 26 WED

Parcel issue. News at night that we are moving to a Luft camp tomorrow morning. Rumoured that we won't move but will just be searched.

JAN 27 THURS

Up at 6.30 a.m. and outside with kit packed at 7.30. Put everything in my kit bag. Very heavy and bulky weight. Nearly creased me carrying it to the gate. We were searched systematically. I was lucky in the kit search and the personal search but some chaps had to strip and had their kit turned inside out. Knives and notebooks were taken but I got through with my three diaries. Back in the hut which had been cleared out at 2 p.m. 6 ½ hours in the cold and showers of rain. Air raid at night. Went to bed early in the dark. What a bloody awful day.

JAN 28 FRI

Book keeping class in morning. Maths class in afternoon. Went to the concert at night. Bit disappointing. Hut has been converted into theatre. Not bad place.

JAN 29 SAT

French class in morning. Poor teacher.

JAN 30 SUN

Windy and rainy. Air raid at night.

JAN 31 MON

Good football match between RAF and the Army (recently returned from Zeitung). Draw 1-1. Jeffries was outstanding. Went to show in the other hut at night. Piss poor. No talent whatsoever.

FEB 1 TUES

Played in rugby practise at 9.30 a.m. Rather a scrappy game. Played right centre but the stand-off was so poor that the ball rarely reached the backs. Got some good tackles in. Shower at 11 a.m. just the job.

FEB 2 WED

Played in another rugby practise at 9.30. Much better game than yesterday. Played stand off and saw a lot more of the ball. Bruised my knee but enjoyed the game. Our blokes had been pinching coal systematically from Jerry, having made a skeleton key to fit the lock of the coal shed. Tonight Jerry caught them and one chap got shot in the knee trying to escape arrest and two of our chaps were put in jail. On roll call at night the Jerry made quite a joke of it and said we should bribe them before pinching.

FEB 3 THURS

Nasty day. Scratch side beat Anzacs 2 tries to nil. Pete was playing.

FEB 4 FRI

Book keeping class in morning. Maths in afternoon. Meaningless parade in afternoon in which Jerry took a shufti at each individual. Was on fire watching from 12 to 1 at night. Very cold.

ALL STUDIES COMPLETED DURING CAPTIVITY (WHETHER AT THE SAME OR DIFFERENT CAMPS) SHOULD BE ENTERED ON ONE CERTIFICATE USING THE BACK IF NECESSARY.

PRISONERS OF WAR CERTIFICATE

NAME OF CAMP .... Certificate No. **8005**

THIS IS TO CERTIFY THAT ....

P.O.W. No. .... REGIMENTAL No. .... RANK ....

HOME ADDRESS ....

has regularly attended the undermentioned lectures and classes while a prisoner of war in the above camp.

Subject/s of Lectures, Classes or Physical Work (to be noted separately)	Total hours worked	During the period From	To	Lecturer's Signature with Rank or Qualifications
	30			
	10			
	11			
	11			
	89			
	19			
	15			

OR, being class:—
PRIVATE STUDY, BOOKS READ.

Pre-war ....

In Camp ....

Give particulars of any University or other public examination passed

If no public examination passed in camp, indicate here the degree of proficiency attained in the subjects of the course

Signed .... Camp Leader

Signed .... Officer or O.R. i/c Education

THIS CERTIFICATE IS NOT A GUARANTEE OF EMPLOYMENT.

It is a record of educational studies pursued by the holder whilst a Prisoner of War. As such it may be helpful to the Ministry of Labour and National Service in suggesting the most suitable type of employment for the holder. It may also be a useful guide to a prospective employer in assessing the qualifications of the holder for the particular appointment he wishes to fill.

This Certificate should be retained by the holder for production at the appropriate Office of the Ministry of Labour and National Service or to a prospective employer after the holder has been demobilised.

It must not be used in any way whatever whilst the holder is still a member of H.M. Forces.

FEB 5 SAT

Went to the show at the Empire in the afternoon. "Boy Meets Girl"
Very good.

FEB 6 SUNDAY

Saw Anzacs make a draw with British side 3 points each. Now got goal
posts on rugger pitch. The show "Swing Time" came into the hut at
night. Mostly composed of Dutch players. First rate. First time I've
enjoyed an accordion. Bill Rae returned from Zeitung gave a turn.

FEB 7 MON

Played right centre for 1st rugby team against 48a. I scored a try under
the posts from a pass by Pete. It was converted. We won 16-6. 4 tries
2 goals to 2 tries. Good game. Enjoyed playing with good backs, 3 of
whom were from old 25 hut, Brewster, Pete and myself.

FEB 8 TUES

Saw 2nd rugby team defeated 16-0. Fatigue in afternoon. Spreading sand
on the pathway.

FEB 9 WED

Book keeping class in morning. Weather cold.

FEB 10 THURS

Snowing. Miserable day. French class in morning.

FEB 11 FRI

Frozen hard and snow.

FEB 12 SAT

Frozen hard. Had a walk round. Dutch band at night. Jolly good. Violinist top class.

FEB 13 SUN

Blokes in the hut gave a show at night. Not bad at all.

FEB 14 MON

Book keeping and Maths classes. Ground unfit for sports.

FEB 15 TUES

Rugger game cancelled due to frost.

FEB 16 WED

On fatigue at 8 a.m. Collecting sand for the roads. Very cold at nights. Meningitis and diphtheria in camp.

FEB 17 THURS

French tutor failed to attend the French class. Had a run about with rugby ball.

Feb 18 Fri

Pete's birthday. Took rugby ball out again. Ground hard and covered in snow.

Feb 19 Sat

Show at night "Piccadilly Madness" with Bill Rae. Bloke did rumba dressed as a woman. So realistic as to excite one. Some of these chaps are terribly convincing as women.

Feb 20 Sun

Took rugby ball out and tried some drop kicking. Sunshine all day but ground still frozen and covered with snow.

Feb 21 Mon

Got some classical records in at night. Eine Kliene Nachtmusik, Chopin studies, Apres Midi d'un Faun, Pagliacci overture. Very enjoyable. Brought back memories.

Feb 22 Tues

Gave tin of bully and packet of prunes to Russian collection. Usually give salmon but got New Zealand parcel which contained two tins of corned meats.

Feb 23 Wed

Had shower in afternoon. Swing records in at night. Lousy.

FEB 24 THURS

On coal carrying fatigue in morning.

FEB 25 FRI

Still freezing at night. Otherwise weather good.

FEB 26 SAT

Show in the other hut "Knee deep". Very good.

FEB 27 SUN

Ground thawed a lot today. Be fit for rugby shortly.

FEB 28 MON

Got English parcel and bulk issue.

FEB 29 TUES

Typhus in the camp. Precautions by M.O. – barracks to be evacuated 8.45 – 9.45. All sports and plays cancelled for 12 days to prevent crowds. We had to go out without our morning brew. Had a severe headache all day.

MAR 1 WED

Roll call now outside at 6.30 a.m. Still go back to bed till 9 a.m. No point in making day longer than needful.

MAR 2 THURS

Classes stopped to avoid crowding. Typhus. 185 to 200 blokes in a barrack and they gather about 8 to 10 blokes in a classroom.

MAR 3 FRI

Very slutchy outside and my boots let water. Had a strip down wash under the cold sprays. Pretty cold too. Finland considering peace terms.

MAR 4 SAT

Nothing of interest.

MAR 5 SUN

Beautiful day. Ground thawing.

MAR 6 MON

Canadian parcels. Did a lot of washing.

MAR 7 TUES

On fire watch 04.00 – 06.30 hrs. Kept the fire going all night and made two brews. Had strip down wash late afternoon.

MAR 8 WED

New order. No one to be out after 8 p.m. At 10 p.m. a bloke got shot at. He was coming to our hut for some water from the next hut.

MAR 9 – 13

Life pretty dead due to quarantine restrictions. Weather terrible.
Snow and rain.

MAR 14 TUES

Birthday. Received 2 letters from home. Boots let water so unable to
walk out in the mud.

MAR 16 – 23

Still quarantine restrictions. No sport, classes, concerts etc. Snow almost
every day. Chap committed suicide hanging himself in the wash house.
Lot of huts in separate quarantine due to scarlet fever and diphtheria.
1st day of spring – blizzards all day. Playing a lot of chess and draughts.
Had my boots repaired by a Russian for a tin of bully. Good job.

MAR 24 FRI

4 huts out of 8 in our compound are in quarantine. Diphtheria and
scarlet fever. That is in addition to the general restrictions for typhus.
We carry their grub and do their fatigues.

MAR 25 SAT

On fatigue shifting rubbish from incinerator. Russians in Bessarabia.

MAR 26 SUN

Weather improved. Still cold.

MAR 27 MON

English parcels issued. Stock low. 40 fags.

MAR 28 TUES

Coal carrying. Just about creased me.

MAR 29 WED

Coal carrying again. On my knees.

MAR 30 THURS

Sun shining most of the day.

MAR 31 FRI

Blizzards all day. Had shower.

APR 1 SAT

Volunteered for tin fatigue. 6 of us had to load a truck with tins and push it to a dump a mile outside the camp. Snow storm all the way there. Covered from head to foot. Sun shone all the way back.

APR 2 SUN

Beautiful day.

APR 3 MON

Ban on sport etc. lifted. Issue 1 Xmas parcel and 1 English. Grand day.

APR 4 TUES

Played rugby for 1st team against Whitehead's team. Lost 6 points to nil. 2nd team beaten in afternoon 26-0 by 48 hut.

APR 5 WED

Went to "Outward Bound" at theatre. Very good acting.

APR 6 THURS

Watched rugby and football matches.

APR 7 GOOD FRIDAY

Roll call at 7.30. on fire watching 10.30 – 1.30 at night.

APR 8 SAT

Watched RAF beat Army at football 4-3. Good game.

APR 9 SUN

Army beat RAF at rugby 3 points to nil. Scrappy game.

APR 10 MON

Roll call 7.30. Amateurs drew with pro's at football 2-2. Excellent game.

APR 11 TUES

Went to Bookeeping and French classes.

APR 12 WED

Had a bit of practise with rugger ball. Thigh easing up a bit. Very warm. Went to Arts and Crafts exhibition. Blokes have made clocks which keep good time. Also a small loom which weaves. Odessa falls.

APR 13 THURS

Played rugby for "Saints" against 49A one of the best teams in camp. Defeated 6-0. Good defensive game.

APR 14 FRI

Commenced doing PT and running in the morning.

APR 15 SAT

Wore shorts for first time. Weather good.

APR 16 SUN

Saw Springboks defeat Anzacs 21-0. The former have a splendid side.

APR 17 MON

Training in morning. Our 2nd rugby team Exciles were defeated 28-0 in afternoon.

APR 18 TUES

Played rugby for Saints against Casuals. Losing 3-0 half time. Never got the ball from scrums. Equalised and then got knocked out and was off field for 5 minutes. Turton (hooker) got injured. Partridge (scrum half) got knocked out and went to hospital. Consequently we lost 14-3. I went to hospital for treatment after game. Terrible headache at night. Missed the music concert.

APR 19 WED

Headache all day. Went to bed soon.

APR 20 THURS

Felt bit better today. Soccer team won 2-0.

APR 21 FRI

Resumed training again.

APR 22 SAT

Scotland beat England at football 3-2. Scorers Jeffreys, Morgan o.g., Hanlon, Steen. Gusty wind spoiled the game.

APR 23 SUN

Wales vs England at rugby. Draw 3-3. Windy.

APR 24 MON

English parcels issued.

APR 25 TUESDAY

Rained heavily early morning. Showers during the day. Pretty miserable.

APR 26 WED

Did lot of washing in afternoon.

APR 27 THURS

Training with rugger ball.

APR 28 FRI

Played rugger against the crack camp team. Lost 12-0. 2 tries and 2 penalties. Hard defensive game throughout.

APR 29 SAT

Our 2nd rugger team lost 3-0. Bad luck.

APR 30 SUN

Recently aircraft have been using this camp as a target for dive bombing or straffing, flying dangerously low over the huts. Today the expected happened. Junkers 88 caught his wing in telegraph wire, ploughed through the barbed wire, killed one chap, Canadian, knocked half his head away, injured another, managed to recover and flew away. Bad business. Went to Chamber Music concert given by Dutch string quartet. Excellent.

MAY 1 MON

Roll call at 7.30 a.m.

MAY 2 TUES

Blondie kept us out on roll call from 6.30 to 9.30 for being late. Drew his revolver in a temper and brought two guards to watch us. When the guards went the lads gave them 3 cheers and someone brought Blondie a chair in mock politeness. Parcels issued today. Coal issue has been cut down so we had to hand all brew materials to cookhouse. Hut fires are lit once a day for cooking.

MAY 3 WED

Amateurs beat pros at football 3-1 in a high wind.

MAY 4 THURS

Played rugger for Saints, got beat 8-0. Very windy. Carpenter played stand off and wouldn't let the ball out. Should have won.

MAY 5 FRI

Exciles gained their first point drawing 3-3.

MAY 6 SAT

Sports. Not nearly as interesting as at 73 (Italy).

MAY 7 SUN

England beat Anzacs at rugby 9-0. Gale spoilt the game.

MAY 8 MON

Played in a practise game of rugby against 36B. Won 12-0. 4 tries. Very cold but enjoyable game. Pulled off some good tackles but handled badly due to cold.

MAY 9 TUES – MAY 14 SUN

Brilliant and warm weather. Nothing out of the ordinary happened during the week. Rugby practise every morning. On Sunday Springboks defeated England 17-3. Wonderful team.

MAY 15 MON – MAY 21 SUN

Very warm weather most of the week. Were defeated by Heathens 6-3. Springboks defeated Wales at rugby 17-3 their backs giving another marvellous display. Identification parade during week. Lot of army blokes found out who were taking place of RAF blokes who have gone out on commandos with a view to escape.

MAY 22 MON – JUNE 5

Springboks defeated the rest of the camp 9-0 on 31st May. Played for Saints against Wanderers and spoiled their 100% record making a draw 3-3.

JUNE 5 SPECIAL.

Today the invasion of France took place. Landings at Le Havre and Cherbourg. Everybody a lot more optimistic. Been waiting 18 months for this. Rome captured.

JUNE 7 WED

Went to show at Empire. "Let's Raise a Laugh" Pretty poor in spite of stage contraptions.

JUNE 8 THURS

The big match, Saints vs Exciles. Saints won easily 11-3. Dance at night 3 blokes got made up as girls.

JUNE 19 MON

Played rugby for Saints. Draw 0-0.

JUNE 27 TUES

Cherbourg captured by Americans.

JUNE 28 WED – JULY 12 WED

Army chap shot dead from point blank range whilst pinching strawberries inside the camp. Death roll now four. Two shot, one suicide, airplane accident.

JULY 11

Carantan and Caen captured. Russians capture Minsk. Nearing Ancona and Reghorn in Italy.

Went to see "The Man Who Came to Dinner". Best show up to date. Play and acting superb. Heard Gus Valten's Dutch orchestra. Very good. Heard violin and piano recital by Dirk Hol and Dave King.

JULY 12 AND 13

Took exams for French, English, Book keeping and Maths.

Germans discovered tunnel which had been dug from recreation hut to outside the wire. 200 blokes were believed ready to go shortly. Gerry is now pumping shit into the hole. Make rather a stink in the reccy hut.

JULY 13 THURS – JULY 21 FRI

On Thursday played in rugby practise game. Alan Bolt's orchestra gave a concert. Violins weak. Wind instruments, flute, clarinet, saxophones, trumpets, trombones were good. Played Beethoven's Egmont.

JULY 21

Played rugby at wing ¾ for Saints vs Offspring. Lost 3-0.

British capture Leghorn and Ancona. Break through east and west of Caen. Russians near east Prussia, Brest, Llitovok and Lemburg.

JULY 21 -31

Played three games of rugby. 2 at wing ¾ and one at centre. Saw variety show "Flash". Not very good. The bugs and fleas are getting deadly now. I get bitten every night.

July 31 we evacuated the hut 07.00 – 20.00 hours for fumigation. The gas was so strong that I couldn't stay in the hut and I slept in 45A.

AUG 1 – AUG 11 FRIDAY

In France Yanks branch out from Cherbourg peninsula and cut off Brest peninsula capturing Lorient. Now striking towards Paris capturing

Le Mans and Laval. Russians near Warsaw. Turkey has broken off
diplomatic relations with Germany. Fighting in Florence in Italy.
Attempt on Hitler's life. Many generals executed.

Played 2 games rugby and one of football. Weather hot.

AUG 12 – AUG 31 THURSDAY

Invaded the south of France and captured Toulon and Marseilles.
Reached the Swiss border to the north and Italian border in the east.
French patriots capture Lyons and numerous places in the interior
and places on Spanish border. From the north the army driving south
reach Bordeaux and the armies driving north capture Paris and cross
the Seine in several places. 5 armies now driving on towards Belgium,
Luxembourg and Germany. Romania capitulated and Russians make
big advances in that sector. Bulgaria too making peace overtures,
Russians refuse us bases in Russia to help Poles fighting in Warsaw.
Some dissension on policy in Poland. Not much advance in Italy. Big
search this week after which we (the RAF) get locked in our compound.
Classes stop and sport also ie. for the RAF.

SEPT 1 – 18

Bulgaria capitulate and declare war on Germany. Tito's forces meet with
the Russians. Finland capitulate. German troops leaving the country.

Metz, Nantes captured, Meuse crossed. Most of Belgium captured
and Holland invaded. Aachen captured. Seigfried line penetrated and
according to Germans the allies are at Koblenz on the Rhine.

Played rugby against Nomads for Saints and Against Barbarians for
Exciles. 2 of the best teams in the camp. The Rest beat South Africa at
cricket by 140 runs.

SEPT 19

News that we are going to a working camp on Saturday. School has been taken down for accommodation purposes.

SEPT 21 THURS

Played my last game of rugby for Exciles at stand-off. Lost 3-0.
1 penalty goal.

SEPT 22 FRI

Got debugged in morning. Went into straffi compound in afternoon and got searched. Our hut brought us our brews to the compound. Miserable day, raining, got all our kit wet.

SEPT 23 SAT

Up at 4.30 a.m. and walked to the station. 40 of us in a cattle truck. Left at 9 a.m. Door kept open with 3 Jerry guards who were quite good humoured. They got quite a lot of food and cigs from civilians. Later we were locked in and slept the night on the truck. Great discomfort was suffered by all.

SEPT 24 SUN

Arrived at destination at 9 a.m. very short march to the billet. Took us 24 hours to travel about 80 kilometres. There are 76 of us and we are billeted in a chapel. Seems to be very clean and the beds are a big improvement being 2 tier bunks instead of 3. The Koblenz news appears to be duff.

SEPT 25 MON

No sign of any parcels here and it also looks as though our rations aren't organised. All we got today was cabbage soup, bread and marge and coffee. Start work tomorrow.

SEPT 26 TUES

Up at 4.30 a.m. Party of 26 of us marched 3 kilometres to railway line. Worked 2 hours with forks and picks cleaning stones from between sleepers, then the rains came. Good job too for the work was awkward and tiring. Sheltered in a shed for 6 ½ hours whilst it rained then did another 2 hour's work and walked back to the billet tired, wet and hungry to receive some watery millet scilly. These rations are deadly to work on, all we had with us on the job was bread and marge. The whole business is a wash out. Heard that we had captured Cologne.

SEPT 27 WED

Fine day. Worked all day picking and shovelling, levelling the railway lane. Damned hard day left at 5.40 and returned at 5.30. Can hardly write tonight. Getting blisters. Heard we captured Amsterdam.

SEPT 28 THURS

Worked all day harder than yesterday. Guard took Pete and my names, he caught us having a short rest after a hard spell of work. I'm just about browned off with railway sleepers, stones and levelling lines. Eat, work and sleep and not much eat. No time for anything at night.

SEPT 29 FRI

As a result of having our names taken, Pete and myself have been put on the Neiderweisa party. Not a very good change. Work consists of laying a new line. Taking all the old sleepers out, putting new sleepers in screwing in the bolts, knocking the stones under the sleepers and levelling the line. Did 4 hours solid pick work in afternoon.

SEPT 30 SAT

Travel by train. Expected the half day today and only took breakfast which we had at 8.30. At 10 o'clock we were told we had to work till 5 p.m. or come on Sunday. I was for leaving the work at 1.30 as originally arranged since we had no food and then we could have refused to work on Sunday. Some of the blokes fell soft and we had to work till 5. Bashing pebbles under the sleepers continuously for all the day. Complete dead loss. No news of any Red Cross parcels.

OCT 1 SUNDAY

Day off. What a relief. Did some washing, reading and bookkeeping.

OCT 2 MON

Working with the pick continuously all day. Are my hands sore?

OCT 3 TUES

Pick work all day. 9 solid hours picking stones under sleepers. My God what monotony. My back is just about breaking and my hands are blistered and aching.

OCT 4

After another hard days pick work we went to a nearby lager and collected three parcels each for our commando. We rushed back to the station in a lather of sweat and just caught our train. After the march up to the billet I was just about buggered. Issued with a parcel a man for a fortnight.

OCT 5 THURS

Picking all morning and in the afternoon filling in the gaps between the sleepers with stones. Just about cheesed. Had to collect the remainder of our month's issue of parcels. Tuckered out again. What a life. Gen about Cologne appears to be duff.

OCT 6 FRI

Filling the line in with stones all day. Cheesed off to hell. Last the day better now we've got a bit of parcel stuff. It was pretty deadly working on scilly, bread and marge. Looked at myself in the mirror tonight and I'm just a mass of ribs. Don't remember looking so skinny since Altimura.

OCT 7 SAT

Again we work Saturday afternoon. I was loading old sleepers onto a truck all day. I lifted over 300 sleepers during the day. Four of us swung the sleepers on the truck. Heavy and dirty work.

Air raid during the day. Oderon party had to go and repair line at Frieburg. They have to go out again tomorrow.

OCT 8 SUNDAY

Day off. Got up about 8 a.m. Did a lot of washing. Sunday dinner is quite a good effort. Boiled spuds, a rissole and brown gravy. A change from the weekday scilly. Went a walk in the afternoon there being about 25 of us. Pretty dull.

OCT 9 MONDAY

Bath day. Another day off work. Unbelievable. Went for baths in the morning. 11 baths in separate rooms, hot water. Best bath for 4 years.

OCT 10 TUESDAY

Back to the grind. Pick work and shovelling stones in morning. In afternoon marched 3 kilometres up the track and cleared stones from between sleepers. Not much time for anything in the evening. Eat scilly, drink of coffee or brew, put grub up for following day, make bed, have wash and shave and then time for bed. Leave billet at 5.45 a.m. return 6.15 p.m.

OCT 11 WEDNESDAY

Working up the line again. Nice walk in morning but bloody tiring coming back at night. Working with garble (fork) in morning and with schlagel screwing up bolts in new sleepers in afternoon. Finished the day with ½ hour with jinnbo (a long log for bashing the line straight). Very tiring. Hands very sore and stiff.

OCT 12 THURS

Taking old sleepers out and putting in new ones. Lot of unscrewing of bolts, digging out stones and picking etc. Away from billet 12½ hours no time for anything on return. Fingers very painful.

OCT 13 FRI

Another day at the old grind.

OCT 14 SAT

Our half day goes for a shit again. Could have finished the stretch of line earlier but the gaffer hung on until we missed the early train. The lousy bastard. Apparently our last day at Niederweisa for we are moving to Chemnitz on Monday to a new job, said to be a bensine factory.

OCT 15 SUN

Day of rest. Good dinner again.

OCT 16 MON

Packed up the kit and marched to the station at 12.30 a.m. Travelled by cattle truck to Chemnitz. Kit conveyed to barrack by lorry and we marched. Quite a surprise. New hut with good lavatories, wash basins, tables and stove for cooking. Big snag the bedroom. Double decker beds. No room to turn between beds. 2 thin blankets, no mattress, very close at night as there is no ventilation.

OCT 17 TUES

Did a bit of coal carrying in the lumber yard. Start work tomorrow I am on air raid shelter party. Pete is on different party, the Feldwebel having picked parties alphabetically. Only get 320 grams bread here as against 400 at Gorblesdorg. Scilly was poor. Heard that Hungary has surrendered. Aachen fallen at last.

OCT 18 WED

Reveille 5.15. Leave at 6.15. Started work 6.45. Static water place, digging clay all day, 20 minutes break for breakfast and 30 minutes for dinner. Gaffer was pleased with our work which isn't as arduous as the railway. Rations 320 grams bread and scilly. Not so good. People seem quite well disposed to us. Good sign.

OCT 19 THURS

Same as yesterday. Still digging terraces out of clay. Boring work. We get back not long turned 5 p.m.

OCT 20 FRIDAY

Same work. Not hard but tedious. Fingers getting very stiff. A cut in the bread ration 290 in lieu of 320. Big drop from 400. Felt weak with hunger after work. First time I've felt like that in Germany. Air raid in afternoon; went down shelters. Some nurses in the shelter sang songs – very nice singers. Heard that women 18-24 are being armed in big cities. Is this for protection against foreign workers when the end comes or is it a last defence resort? I favour the first.

Oct 21

Knocked off work 12 noon. Just the job. Had a sleep in afternoon.

Oct 22 Sun

Got our first letter cards since leaving IVB. Spuds issued in their jackets. Had fried kam and spuds for tea.

Oct 23 Mon

These rations are ridiculous for working 5.30. One slice bread. Work 6.30 – 8.30 two thin sandwiches. Work 9-12 two thin sandwiches. Work 1-4.30. Scilly at 5.30, 1 biscuit 7 p.m. No wonder I felt weak at the end of day. Feldwebel is trying to get us increased bread ration. He seems to be a genuinely good bloke with a sense of humour.

Oct 24 Tues

Another routine day. Not many are expecting war to be over for Xmas now. Seemed a cert a couple of months back. German civvies and guard are getting quite well disposed towards us and more than a few hope for the war to end quickly. If I read the signs correctly, they can see the end of the war coming quickly and want to be on good terms with us when that contingency arises.

Oct 25 & 26 Wed & Thurs

Same old routine. Every few days bread is $\frac{1}{6}$th in which case the working day ration is 3 sandwiches. Some of the lads lifted some spuds which are helping out nicely.

OCT 27 FRI

Out of smokes. Got a cigarette given and started smoking it on an empty stomach. Made me dizzy and had to nip it.

OCT 28 SAT

Intermittent rain in morning and we refused to work in the rainy periods as we only have one set of battle dress. The guard tried in vain to deter us but the gaffer didn't seem to mind when he returned. When we got back to the billet parcels had arrived and were issued 1 between 2 untouched, the Feldwebel refraining from puncturing tins against orders. We smoke again. Sold our chocolate for 25 fags. Received 9 letters. Some canteen goods arrived, matches, fag papers etc. also 2 bottles of beer each. Quite a good day.

OCT 29 SUN

A quiet day, washed socks, handkerchief. German officer visited us, quite humorous. Said our shithouses were "luxurious".

OCT 30 MONDAY

Rained solidly from 9.30 onwards, no work during that period. Was enjoying myself digging out a step lined with tree stumps which I chopped out with a pick. Extra bread ration comes through. Now get 355 grams. Improvement.

OCT 31 TUES

Ground too muddy to dig. Worked down at factory removing new doors on a truck. Bitter cold today. 65 personal parcels come in for the 75 of us. Wasn't one for Pete, Dave, Jim, or myself. Rank bad luck will be out of English fags, but are hoping for Serbian tobacco issue and French cigs. Norway invaded by Russians. ⅔^{rds} of Greece in our hands. Heavy attacks in Holland and East Prussia.

NOV 1 WED

Another 27 personal parcels came in today and still no luck. 2 chaps who we didn't know previously gave Pete and myself 40 fags. I got a few odd ones from other chaps.

NOV 2 THURS

Bitter cold today. Rained on the way home. Feldwebel took our photographs.

NOV 3 FRI

Air raid warning at 12.15

NOV 4 SAT

Half day off. Long game of chess with Pete. Managed to win after being on defensive all game.

NOV 5 SUN

Feldwebel gave us a bollocking for bothering him with minor complaints. I was in sympathy with him for he has done a lot for us, but all the time he was talking, our dinner was burning on the stove. At night Feldwebel showed us some lantern slides with his cine-camera. Don't seem to be able to settle down to anything these weekends. Too many odd jobs to do. Washing socks, darning, sewing buttons, writing letters, cooking, hair cut etc. Last five days have been very cold.

Nov 6 Mon

Off to work again. Intermittent rain gave us a few breaks.

Nov 7 Tues

Another day cut short by rain. Very cold wind.

Nov 8 Wed

Feldwebel brought us our photos. Not bad. Talking of Xmas he said our people should move on, they were all waiting for it.

Nov 9 Thursday

Worked in the factory stacking wooden partitions in the rain. Due to being wet we had the afternoon off in the barrack.

Nov 10 Friday

Went to work on our water hole near the school today. Did a total of about 3 hours work due to the weather. Snowed heavily in the afternoon and we returned to the barrack about 2 p.m. Had a kip to avoid the numerous odd jobs which crop up.

Nov 11 Saturday

School today. Snowed heavily and we returned 10.30 a.m. bulk issue very poor. 1 Tin M&V, 1 tin sausage, 1½ tin of jam, egg powder, ⅔rds packet of prunes, sugar tin, 1⅓rd bar chocolate, 2 packets biscuits (1 tin milk, 1¼tr lbs butter for fortnight) all between 2 for 1 week. Beat Pete at chess in evening after a hard defensive game.

IMPRESSIONS OF THE WEEK

Weather terribly cold but not much work done. Over 100 personal parcels arrived here up to date and not one for Pete, Dave, Jim or myself. Jerries seem as anxious for war to end as we do. The bitter fighting in Holland is my chief hope though some favour Joe's push in Hungary and Czechoslovakia.

NOV 12 SUNDAY

Played Lexicon in afternoon, washed socks, darned socks, cleaned boots and had a shower at night.

NOV 13 MONDAY

Worked at the billet today. Sawed wood in morning and peeled spuds at coal house in afternoon for 3½ hours. The latter was a bind.

NOV 14 TUESDAY

Fine today and worked all day at school. Pete has now got on my Commando.

NOV 15 WED

Work at school. Some personal parcels in at night. Jimmy got one and gave Pete and myself 30 each. Got 8 letters. Most blokes have had personal parcels.

NOV 16 THURS

I'm getting a bit cheesed off with shovelling clay for 9 hours a day.

NOV 17 FRIDAY

Last full day of work. Time didn't pass too badly. Made a trip to the barrack with a truck in morning, broke the monotony.

NOV 18 SATURDAY

Rained in the morning. Good old "David". Returned to barrack at 10.30. Got a job of coal carrying in afternoon. Damned annoying. Beat Pete at chess in evening. Kept him on defensive. Bulk issue was ½ lb cheese, 1 tin M&V, ⅓rd lb bully, ⅓rd packet of soap powder, packet of tea and tin of milk powder from emergency parcel, 8½ biscuits. Poor for a week.

SUMMARY OF WEEK

Bitter cold weather for work. Had snow. Disappointing no personal parcel. Most of chaps looking to next spring for end. Rumours of a new big push in Holland, also attacks east of Metz. Jerries have got a wireless in their room and put the speaker in our room occasionally but there doesn't seem much hope of any news from it. Spud issue cut from 600 grams to 500 grams a day. Not that we ever saw 600 grams as they are a swindling lot at the cookhouse. Lucky if we got 500 grams all week. Very poor scillies. The bread doesn't go very far and the food situation would be grim but for a box of spuds Jimmie gave us.

NOV 19 SUNDAY

Football practise in morning, would have played but my left foot is going flat (like the right one was at Compton). Read music book in afternoon and played Lexicon at night.

Nov 20 Monday

At school site. Felt very lethargic all day. Rained at 4 p.m. and we
knocked off temporarily to the grave displeasure of the boss. At night
received 19 letters from Italy and 1 for this year.

Nov 21 Tuesday

Showers all day. No work in morning. Marched to another site and
removed some drainage pipes. Rained, stopped work and we returned
to billet a 3 p.m. to find that Red Cross Commission had arrived
together with Chemnitz Kommando leaders. We were therefore
marched to factory, the guard taking us to boiler room where we rested
until our return at 4.15 p.m. More parcels have arrived at 4F. We are
advised to "stay put" in case of armistice.

Nov 22 Wednesday

Work at school all day. Returned to find that all four of us had got fag
parcels. Pete got four.

Nov 23 Thursday

Rained in morning and we stayed in the hut. In afternoon ground unfit
for work on the hole and we cleared the site up somewhat.

Nov 24 Friday

Mother's birthday. Worked all day despite ground conditions. Job
practically finished. Took railway to bits and stacked the lines etc. in
the yard. Received my July 11 personal parcel at night. Just the job.
Certainly needed the chocolate, been feeling the shortage of rations this
week (decidedly weak). Shoes, underclothes just what I needed.

NOV 25 SATURDAY

Job at school finished, spent morning clearing up and preparing everything for removal. Canadian parcel between two.

WEEKLY SUMMARY

Bumper week for post. Italian mail interesting. Fag and clothing parcels just the job. News says Metz, Belfort and Strasbourg captured and new push in Italy. Hope it is reliable. Still a chance if they keep pushing.

NOV 26 SUNDAY

Washed socks and handkerchief. Scrounged 4 post cards and wrote 5. Don't seem to be able to find time to settle down to much at weekend.

NOV 27 MONDAY

Frosty this morning but quite pleasant working. Got paliasses and a long lecture from Feldwebel at night.

NOV 28 TUESDAY

Still working at the school cleaning up the debris. Severe frost felt the cold more than yesterday.

NOV 29 WEDNESDAY

Most of us sent down to factory until new water hole site is found. Bind of a job – 20 minutes for breakfast and 30 minutes for dinner. Timed by a hooter. The work isn't very hard (apart from loading bags of cement) but the atmosphere is deadly. Too many bosses round the place. Received 1lb Capstan at night.

NOV 30 THURSDAY

Work at the factory. Loading and pushing small wagons about all day. Air raid lasting from 1 p.m. – 2.15 p.m. gave us a good break.

DEC 1 FRIDAY

Another day with the small wagons. Some of the wood has been soaked in some horrible mixture which has made rather a mess of my clothes.

DEC 2 SATURDAY

Four volunteers wanted to stay in and clean up etc. I volunteered like a flash for I am cheesed off with the factory. Swept out bedrooms, brought laundry and went a long trip up hill and down dale to bring the beer (15 crates on a small wagon). There were six of us and at that it was hard work up hill. Had a shower at 12 a.m. The factory party went to the forest and didn't arrive back till 2 p.m. Good luck to me.

WEEKLY SUMMARY

News (supposedly authentic) says that the Americans have crossed the Rhine at Strasbourg and two other places and are fanning out from a 25 kilometre front. Cologne virtually surrounded. This news gives new hope if true but time is getting a bit short for the end of the year.

SUNDAY DEC 3

The usual darning, washing of socks etc. Read "The Growth of Music". Had many brews, 2 bottles of beer and 2 of lemonade, consequently pissed more than somewhat.

MONDAY DEC 4

New digging site not ready. Pete and I were amongst the forest party and did a spot of lumberjacking, sawing logs and heaving them into piles with crow bars. High gale and blizzard stopped work for a period. Had to clock in and out of factory.

TUESDAY DEC 5

Went to school, collected spades, marched to another finished site and loaded tractor with wagons, lines etc. Marched to factory after breakfast in air raid shelter and there loaded lorry with timber etc. Went to new site and unloaded. Travelled to school, loaded more stuff, wheelbarrows, lines etc. and travelled back to new site. At 4 p.m. travelled to a building and loaded blocks of stone, after which had to march ¾^{trs} hour back. Bitter cold day. What a relief to get back.

WED DEC 6

New site, near slaughter house on outskirts of town. 50 minutes march. Spent most of day moving stone slabs by means of our small trolleys. Slabs weighed about 7 cwt. Heavy work, enjoyed riding down the hill on the trolley. No parcels in at night. Had a shower. Long walk tiring.

THURS DEC 7

Another day on moving the stone slabs. Heavy work. Wagon came off the rail 3 times when I was riding on same, twisted my knee slightly in one accident. The walk there and back is a terrible bind. 3 miles. Feeling a bit better these days due to getting extra bread by various means.

FRIDAY DEC 8

Shifted the rest of the stone slabs and laid part of the railway line. Heavy work. Just about played out at night.

SAT DEC 9

Laid the rest of the lines in the morning. Just about ready for the week end, my right foot is giving me hell due to the long walk and being on my feet all day.

WEEKLY SUMMARY

Crossing of Rhine confirmed from some sources and denied in others. A real mix up don't know what to believe. Felt exceedingly exhausted and cheesed off this weekend. One of those moods when one could imagine the war lasting for years. Gaffer been a bastard all week. Work been very heavy and weather bitter cold.

SUNDAY DEC 10

Called out with 9 other chaps to unload a wagon of sand at factory. 9 a.m. – 11.30 a.m. What a bind. Sunday dinner was an improvement. Beetroot, boiled potatoes (peeled for a change), gravy and a small piece of pork (very tasty). Played Chinese Chequers at night. I won.

Monday Dec 11

Day passed quite quickly. I am on the railway gang and distributor of earth from the wagons. Air raid at midday. Also was one last night.

Dec 12 Tues

Air raid at night, 2 during the day. The walk is taking hell out of my feet. Had shower at night.

Dec 13 Wed

Misty cold day, miserable for working.

Dec 14 Thurs

The afternoons get colder and colder. Looked like snow but didn't get any.

Dec 15 Fri

The gaffer, after being affable all day, made us work 20 minutes later at night.

Dec 16 Saturday

Bright sunshine. Knocked off 11.15 and arrived barrack at 12 a.m. just after air raid siren sounded.

WEEKLY SUMMARY

Been air raids almost every day of the week. My feet are crippling me due to the walk (left heel and right sole). Developed a bad cold at weekend. Been a miserable week. Seems to be a stalemate in the war. I no longer believe we are across the Rhine. I'm in one of those moods when I think the war could last to next July. May not be far wrong at that. Got a gramophone this week, old records best of which Solveig's Song (Grieg). Was being played too fast till I adjusted it.

DEC 17 SUNDAY

Visit from padre. Nice service with a sensible sermon. My cold is worse.

DEC 18 MONDAY

Frosty, clear, sunny day. Rather enjoyed working. Day passed quickly. (1 air raid warning).

DEC 19 TUESDAY

Went to factory, loaded wagon with firewood, then went to school site and loaded railway lines. It was 10.30 before we had breakfast. I helped transfer wood from roadway to hut by wheelbarrow and then stacked it in the hut. Easy day after bad start. (1 air raid warning).

DEC 20 WED

Still frosty, ground hard to pick. Pete got 500 fag parcel on return. Just the job for Xmas.

DEC 21 THURS

Frosty in morning turning to cold mist in afternoon. Cruel working.
My cold much worse at night. Long lecture by Feldwebel.

DEC 22 FRI

So cold today that the gaffer gave us 5 minutes "powser" (rest in the
hut to warm our hands) after filling each wagon. We filled more than
usual. Bitter cold in late afternoon. Heard that we were the last RAF
Kommando to leave IVB and that they have 4 month's supply of parcels
there. We have 1 month's. Just our bloody luck.

DEC 23 SATURDAY

Bitter cold again. Gaffer gave us 5 minute breaks as yesterday and we
knocked off early. When we got back to barrack we were issued with
1 invalid parcel a man and the usual ½ Canadian. Splendid Xmas issue.
The invalid parcels were a reserve but were getting damp in store.
Contain Horlicks, Ovaltine, Cocoa, Tea, Yeastex, Bovril, lemon curd,
Bemax, soup powder, oats, cheese, egg flakes, milk, sugar, greengages
(tinned), 2oz chocolate.

WEEKLY SUMMARY

Biggest sensation of the week was the German offensive which has
made good progress into Belgium and Ardennes. What a blow. Very
unsettling news. The invalid parcels are just the job for Xmas. No mail
for a month. Coldest weather yet this week. The lake we pass has been
frozen all week.

Dec 24 Sunday Xmas Eve

Jimmie brought us coffee in bed. Breakfast at 8 a.m. Macaroni scilly for dinner time. Egg flakes on toast for tea. Had many brews and biscuits with marmalade and lemon curd. Feltwebel's wife came in at night. Lights were put out and she stood before table lit with candles and wished us a Merry Xmas and Happy New Year, hoping we would be home for the latter. Later in the evening she sang for us. She seemed to be a very nice woman, smart but quietly dressed.

Dec 25 Monday. Christmas Day

The decorations were magnificent and a credit to the decorators. Paper chains from coloured paper and salmon tin labels gave colour to the barrack and the decorated Xmas tree and small fir trees on each table (all of which were lined up end to end) added artistry to the general appearance. White paper centres were on the tables. The day was one succession of meals, but we didn't overeat although we were satisfied. The sweets were not as good as their appearance implied. The trifle looked good on top, the surface covering a biscuit duff. The pastry (tarts and pasties) was made of meal and proved to be dead weight and the consistency of putty. This caused great merriment on our table. New illness rife – Pastry on the Chest.

Radio show – mouth organ band, piano and a short play, was given at night. Quite good. Feldwebel's wife came in to dinner and cut the cake (I suggested getting the two handed saw for the cake was very sad and plain). She shook hands with most of us before leaving, I managed to get a handful. The Feldwebel gave me a cigar. Spent most of day in bedroom reading as we had to keep out of the way of the cooks. Enjoyed the day better than two previous Xmases. Afterthought – we have been saving up for this for the last month, giving in ½ tin bully, ½ tin salmon, ½ packet cheese, 4 biscuits, prunes and raisins. Cigarette collection over 1,000. The latter enabled us to obtain flour etc.

DEC 26 BOXING DAY TUESDAY.

Didn't get up till 10.30 a.m. First lie in since coming to Germany. Very quiet restful day. Some of us played Chinese Chequers.

DEC 27 WEDNESDAY

Back to the grind. Boss had poor Xmas. No coal etc. Turned out to be a fine day; sunshine; the usual daily air raid warning. Temperature at nights is -15°C and the ground is frozen hard making pick work difficult.

DEC 28 THURS

Colder today. Work difficult, like chipping at granite. I've got indigestion terrible – "pastry on the chest". Everything I eat passes a hard knot half way to my stomach. Snow in afternoon.

DEC 29 FRIDAY

Improvement in stomach condition. Weather bitter cold. Roads difficult due to yesterday's snow.

DEC 30 SATURDAY

Bitter cold in morning 15° below. Sun came out later. Hands frozen stiff. Lights out at 12 p.m. Digestion still troubling me.

WEEKLY SUMMARY

Xmas grub was disappointing considering what we gave in, the flay pastry ruining my digestion for a week. The German offensive in the west appears to be slowing up, there being talks of 6,000 bomber attack on the attacking troops. They are, however, in Luxembourg and South East Belgium. The Germans are supposed to have surrounded an American army, and are themselves threatened by armies on either flank. Confusion is manifest. Cruel working in the bitter cold.

DEC 31 SUNDAY

Lots of singing. New Years Eve and plenty of brews. 2 bottles of beer. Guards seemed to have a pretty good time too. Rather amusing. Nobody dare say much about getting home next year. No confidence due to previous disappointments.

1945

JAN 1 MONDAY

Had to get up at 11 a.m. and fetch the grub from cookhouse 20 minutes walk away. Heavy fall of snow made progress with the cart difficult. Stitched collar on to shirt and mended my gloves. No laundry, so had to wash shirt, vest, pants and socks.

JAN 2 TUESDAY

Snow deep. Trudging through the snow fatiguing more than somewhat. The railway is on a slope over 100 yards and we get a smashing ride after filling each truck. Shot off the rails at the bend going full speed. Chick Young took a swallow dive into snow and finished up on my back. No one hurt. These rides are better than the Big Dipper. Very cold.

JAN 3 WED

Another hard bitter day. Wrote letter in French to M.O. for Tomlin our Con. Man. Got month's supply of parcels.

JAN 4 THURS

Not quite as cold today. Usual air raid warning went. Saw inside the slaughter house. Many newly killed carcasses spread-eagled on the floor; these were being hacked about whilst those awaiting their doom watched on. A grisly business.

JAN 5 FRI

Not quite as cold today thank goodness. Blasting operations took place to remove the frozen crust of earth. Very ineffectual despite the technical efforts of 10 smartly uniformed officers and men of the German demolition service.

JAN 6 SAT

Taking the last truck of the day down, Jock Hey lost grip of the breaking pole; I was riding on the back and attempted to avert disaster by treading on the brake (this worked on previous occasion), this failed and Pete and I jumped clear as the wagon jumped over the block at the end of the line and landed down the clay slope. We managed to get it back by means of rope tug of war fashion. Jock got hell from Sommer.

WEEKLY SUMMARY

Very little news this week. I think the German offensive halted or slowed down, it also appears we are trying some encircling moves. I'm resigned to another 6 months at least.

JAN 7 SUNDAY

Got name taken for staying in bed. Very cold at night, 2 blankets. No coal now, having to economise on fires.

JAN 8 MONDAY

Was fire maker in the billet. Up at 4.30 a.m. No coal, all wood damp. Spent all day chopping and drying wood and keeping the fires going. Quite a rush job as there is no laundry I rushed through some washing. Day passed quickly.

JAN 9 TUESDAY

Out on the job again. Bitter cold in morning turning warmer in afternoon.

JAN 10 WED

Bags of snow greeted us in the morning. Took us over an hour to walk to work. Had to clear the snow from the site before we could start work. Am now wearing my balaclava. Weather bitter.

JAN 11 THURS

Snowed during day making work unpleasant. Couple of breaks during heavier downfalls. Miserable day. Scilly is terrible these days. Getting about 50 grams of spuds, the ration should be 600 grams. Disgraceful dishing that stuff up after a day out in the cold on 5 sandwiches.

JAN 12 FRI

More snow last night. Warmer during day, thawed a bit. The walk back at night just about finishes me off. Watery scilly again.

JAN 13 SAT

Road treacherous. Cold wind. No beer again. Did my weekend wash at 10 p.m. Laundry caput – no coal.

WEEKLY SUMMARY

A bitter cheesing week. I am wearing underpants, vest, shirt, 2 pullovers, scarf, tunic and balaclava. Very cold in bed with 2 threadbare blankets. Got another blanket issued Saturday. News vague and unreliable. Monty supposed to be counter attacking capturing $\frac{2}{3}$rds of ground taken. Russians commenced long awaited offensive in east Prussia, Warsaw and Cracow sectors. Agreement arrived at in Greece. No air raids this week probably due to weather.

JAN 14 SUNDAY

Clothing check in the morning, lasted 9 -12. Rather a bind. Not much real enjoyment at weekends, merely the relief of being in from work.

JAN 15 MONDAY

Was at sick bay 8-11.40. waiting for dental treatment. Got a temporary stopping in my tooth. Go again Thursday. Ate all the day's sandwiches (5) at dinnertime. Wasn't too full, when I'd finished swept bedroom, repaired pullover and went for grub in afternoon. Received 200 fags and 4 letters.

JAN 16 TUES

Back to the old site. Ground mist all morning – very cold. Sun came out later. Overhead warning of an hour coincided with our dinner hour. Dead loss.

JAN 17 WED

Six of us had to load wagon with wood at the factory and push it to work. Heavy work. Breakfast time when we got there. Bitter cold wind blowing all day. Every day is a positive ordeal these days.

JAN 18 THURS

Went dental sick and got my tooth drilled. Another temporary stopping put in. Not painful. Digging air raid shelter in afternoon.

JAN 19 FRI

Bitter cold wind blowing all day. Slight blizzards. Got a very bad finger due to accident with heavy hammer.

JAN 20 SAT

Snowing all the way to work, stopped as soon as we got there. Sun came out later in morning. Air raid (overhead).

WEEKLY SUMMARY

This week an ordeal due to weather. Good job I had two days at the dentist. War news improves again. Russians are making big advances in Poland. Cracow and Warsaw evacuated by Germans. Russians reaching borders of Upper Silesia. Heavy battles on western front north east of Strasbourg and Ardennes. We are on the attack in Italy. Lot of blokes optimistic again and some Jerries are saying 1 or 2 months. It will need some astounding good news to build any hopes up again.

JAN 21 SUN

Had to hand a blanket in, leaving us with two. Nicht grub. Made a biscuit duff in afternoon. Not bad.

JAN 22 MON

Arrived at work usual time. Sommer not there and he hadn't left the key for us. Walter, the postern, took us to No.2 site where we had breakfast, after which we went back to barrack. No work. Just the job. A film show in the evening. "Native Soil" German speaking, English subtitles. Not very good but a change.

JAN 23 TUES

Another blanket taken from us in the morning. Now only one blanket. Deadly position this time of year. We are allowed to keep our trousers out of the store at night. Not quite as cold at work.

JAN 24 WED

Tomlin came back from Hartmannsdorf with the grim news that there are no parcels there for us. We have only ½ issue for the week left. God knows how we are going to work on Jerry rations. The railway position in Germany is critical so we don't hold out much hope.

JAN 25 THURS

Snow in morning and we packed in work for the day thereby incurring Herr Sommer's grave displeasure. We can't afford to get our clothes wet as we need tunic, pants and greatcoat for the bed. In future, however, we have to apply to postern before packing in. We were threatened with loss of bread for our action.

JAN 26 FRI

Bit warmer today. Snowed in afternoon and when it came on heavily we stopped work through the legitimate channels for 1 hour. Yesterday Pete got personal parcel. 4 kilometres for ½ lb choc.

JAN 27 SAT

Took us over an hour to get to work. Cold morning. Trouble with turntable due to snow. Washed towel, shirt, vest, underpants and handkerchief in afternoon, also had a shower. Had our last parcel issue till? Bought bully and sardines for 40 fags. Our stock stands at 430 and 1½ lbs tobacco.

WEEKLY SUMMARY

Work didn't go too bad this week. Horrible news about Red X parcels. God knows when we will get more, the railways are supposed to be in terrible state. The guard keeps our bedroom fire going at night, so up till now one blanket position is not too bad. Position on west front obscure. Don't know who is attacking or where. Russians fighting round Breslau, Posen and are near to Danzig. They have advanced 250 kilometres in fortnight and are that distance from Berlin and here. The blokes expect the end in month or so, but I expect a halt in the near future. Confirmed pessimist.

SUNDAY JAN 28

On fatigues at 8.30 taking bins back to cookhouse (20 mins walk). Darned my gloves and made a biscuit, prune, raisin duff.

MONDAY JAN 29

Commenced snowing on arrival at work. Bitter wind blowing, my hands and feet ached with the cold. Slight blizzard stirred up, causing stoppage of work after ¼ hour. Returned to lager in heavy snow at 10.30 a.m. it having been decided that snow had set in for the day, which it had. Did ¼ hour wood sawing in afternoon. Quite a good start to the week.

TUESDAY JAN 30

As soon as we arrived at work it started snowing heavily. Never left the hut to work. Walter, the postern, telephoned and we returned to the barrack at 9 a.m. Did ¼ hour sawing again. Had 2 games of chess with Pete in afternoon. Won 1 each.

WED JAN 31

Inspector decided conditions not fit for work so we returned to barrack at 10.30. Repaired my shirt and had shower and change of clothes.

THURS FEB 1

Reported dental sick but Dentist didn't turn up. Went to company cookhouse with Walter the postern. Made two trips to our cookhouse in afternoon, once with tins and then for grub. Thawed a lot today and rained.

FRI FEB 2

A full day of arbeit. The site is now a mass of slush. What a change from the frozen hardness. Very cheesing throwing wet clay about. Parts of the lake have thawed relieving the ducks who have been sitting on ice for 2 months.

SAT FEB 3

Not very cold again today. Half day. $\frac{1}{8}$th of parcel a man and 1 cigarette being the last of our issue.

WEEKLY SUMMARY

Food position bad. Pete and I have 200 fags and 1lb tobacco. Russians still advancing and rumour states them at 40 kilometres from Berlin. Although this is hardly credible the advance is terrific and some people expect the end within a few weeks. Apparently a big attack is expected on Western Front but I don't think we are able to make much impression on the strong defences this weather.

SUN FEB 4

Did my weekly wash. Over Feldwebel called us outside on parade and bollocked us for not getting up at 7 a.m.

MON FEB 5

Went dental sick, got the same tooth drilled and another temporary filling put in. Went very near the nerve. Chopped wood and collected some coal in a cart.

TUES FEB 6

Went to work. Very muddy. Overhead warning went at 10.45. We rejoiced for it meant stopping work for a while. To our immense surprise bombs started dropping at 11 a.m. and then afterwards we were in for it. We went into the slit trench and sat tight. As each flight dropped their load it sounded like numerous express trains rushing through a tunnel. They seemed to be coming straight for us every time. One lot dropped about 100 yards away and debris came within a few yards of us. The raid stopped at 11.45, quite a harrowing experience. Rained after which we returned to lager. Electricity and water off. The damage got gradually worse as we approached the barrack and I was thankful to see it still there, there being a score of hits within 100-200 yards of it. Lot of factories and flats were hit. Must have been 200 aircraft (afterwards heard 500). Went to bed 7.30 p.m. slept like a log.

WED FEB 7

After dinner went to fill in a bomb crater on the railway track. Four hits right on the line, nearby factory being brought to the ground. Worked till dark. Came back through a wood which was pitted with bomb craters. Must have been a terrific amount of bombs dropped. The area round the camp is in a bad state, many detours having to be made.

THURS FEB 8

Arose 5.30 left at 6.30 and started work on the craters at 7.15. Heavy rain gave us a long freistich. Eat out in open but sheltered in a railway truck. Sunshine in afternoon. Knocked off work to our surprise at 4.15. Not bad working, lorries bring the debris and we deposit it in the hole. Got a clothing parcel on my return. From Italy, all the chocolate except ½ lb stolen. Curse it, could have done with the chocolate these hard times. Only got a few raisins left from parcel. Further cut in rations.

FRI FEB 9

Work on the bomb crater again. Overhead warning at 11.15. Everybody dispersed quickly. Pete and I sheltered in bomb crater in a swede field. Raid was quite near and lasted an hour. We collected some of the bombed out swedes to augment our meagre rations. Nearly filled the hole today. Some Polish women came to our site, four of which refused to work having had no grub for 3 days. One of them was quite nice and spoke a bit of English, reminded me of Mary Chadwick. Most of these women are a pretty tough crowd and carry sleepers about and such like.

SAT FEB 10

Worked all day. I worked hard until mittach (afternoon), placing sleepers, shovelling and screwing bolts etc. Scrounged a lot in the afternoon. Heard that we are going to get parcels on Monday. Hope a raid doesn't upset arrangements. Working tomorrow. Worse luck.

WEEKLY SUMMARY

Raid upset us more than somewhat. Widespread damages. We no longer look forward to an overhead warning as a rest from work. Finding work rather wearing without much parcel grub. Strong attacks in west. Fighting between Mass (Maastricht) and Rhine in Holland. Russians 60 kilometres from Berlin and widening their bridgehead over the Oder west of Steinan. The atmosphere of crisis has passed however.

Sun Feb 11

Out to work again, digging out an electric cable in some fields near a factory. Field pitted with bomb craters. Bitter wind blowing. We were supposed to work till 6 p.m. but due to agitating and getting a statement of the work required to be done, we got away at 2.30. The extra time off was very welcome. Water came on this morning and we were very grateful for shower.

Mon Feb 12

Working on the railway again. Pushing a truck about till 9.45 in a cold, misty wind. Absolute murder. Unscrewing bolts in afternoon. Rotten day. The expected parcels did not arrive due to Sarro refusing to loan us the lorry to go to Hartmannsdorf. The lousy bastard.

Tues Feb 13

Parcels were brought by horse and cart. 1 a man for a fortnight. American. 100 fags a man.

Blokes have been getting a day off by rota and today should have been my day off. Saaro found a job for us digging out a gas pipe on

Leipzigstrasse. Gas set on fire from a spark from a pick; warmed the place up a bit. Rotten eating friestich and mittach on the job, very cold.

The overhead warnings at night 9.30 to 11.30 and 1 a.m. to 2.30 a.m. Very harrowing in the small shelter all the time. The first raid sounded terrific being on the outlying districts and hundreds of aircraft passed overhead. Very nerve racking expecting the bombs to come down at any moment. The second raid was worse; we sat tight whilst at least a thousand aircraft passed directly overhead taking over half an hour emitting a heavy drone all the time. Made the blood feel a bit thin.

FEB 14 WED

Working at the same job, got down to water but, uncovered the pipe. Air raid at 11.30 a.m. Outlying districts and parts of the town were bombed. Luckily our site is on the outskirts of the town and we sheltered in a big tower. Didn't hear much noise apart from the aircraft engines. Four chaps in a neighbouring commando were killed by a direct hit on a shelter. Made a collection for their dependants. Gave 30 marks. Total 1,300 marks for 75 men. Hard luck on them. Some of our chaps had the job of digging them out. A D.A. dropped within a few yards of some of our chaps and another went off 50 yards from them. One of the chaps fainted. This air raid business is telling on the nerves of all of us. At night we had two more raids, 8.30 – 10.30 and 12 – 1 a.m. Both were on South Chemnitz. Incendiaries were used; the fire from which created a terrific red glow in the sky. H.E. was then dropped, some felt quite close. Allowed to stay in bed till 6.30 due to loss of sleep.

FEB 15 THURS

Working in water again today. Very unpleasant. Warning from 11.30 to 1. Nothing dropped in Chemnitz. Sheltered in the tower. Two women there, were very pleasant with us. Very grateful as a lot of people have been shouting "Swinehund" at us today. Mostly people who are removing their belongings from the town. Very pathetic can't help feeling sorry for them.

FEB 16 FRI

Got my day off in barrack. Swept bedroom out before breakfast. 8.30 – 12.30 working on air raid shelter. Had an hour sleep in afternoon then went to cookhouse for grub. No warnings either during the day or at night. Rather a relief after six raids in 36 hours.

SAT FEB 17

New job with the waterworks. Digging out a pipe on the roadside near Auto Union works which has recently been target. Get some black looks from some civvies these days. Near us some convicts are digging out an unexploded bomb. 10 days off their sentence for each bomb. 4 miles walk to this job – too far. Issued with 1 American parcel between two. Last of the issue.

SUMMARY OF WEEK

Very nerve racking this week. Not much change in war news, Slight advances by Russians and very heavy attacks in west. Our position here is very strained.

SUN FEB 18

Pete's birthday. Had cereal and prunes for breakfast and beef and beans
with boiled swede at night. Work same as yesterday. Ours was the only
commando that didn't get half a day today or yesterday. Cheesed off to
hell.

MON FEB 19

Got put on No.5 kommando for the day. Clearing away rubble from
some of the Town Council buildings. Not a bad job only ½ hour walk.
Deadly cold today. Alert went today but they left us alone. (warnings at
9 – 9.39 and 3.45 – 4.30. horrible having to get up at that time.)

TUES FEB 20

Working on No.5 again. Have our meals down an air raid shelter. Table,
chairs, lights. 'In the vicinity warning' went in afternoon and we went
to the shelter, civvies came in with us. Warning 9.15 – 9.45 in the
evening but no aircraft came overhead. Most blokes go into our shelter
on the 'vicinity warning' I don't take any chances these days.

WED FEB 21

Rained all morning and we worked in it. Got wet through. Absolutely
miserable. Alert went in afternoon.

THURS FEB 22

Still clearing away rubble. Overhead warning 11.45 – 1 p.m.
Went down shelter and I had a snooze.

FRI FEB 23

Carting buckets of sand to the top of the building all day. 83 steps. Made my leg muscles feel like water. Feeling the lack of food. Two warnings (immediate) lasted from 10.30 – 12.45 with 3 minutes in between. Rest from work. Alert at night 8.30 – 8.45.

SAT FEB 24

Carrying buckets of sand up the 83 steps again. Carried up a bag of cement (1 cwt) Just about killed me. Knocked off work 12.45. Rested in afternoon. Alert 1.15 -1.30.

WEEKLY SUMMARY

Nervous tension, perpetual arbeit, short rations are playing havoc with us. Scillies have been very thin and the bread just about makes 2 decent sandwiches for a whole days work. Felt absolutely devoid of stamina. Big attacks on Western front towards the Rhine in Holland, Duren sector towards Bonn. Russians advancing more slowly. Drive towards Gorlitz is in our direction about 150+ kilometres away. Water has been off for 10 days. Can't do any washing or have a good wash or shower.

SUN FEB 25

Nice morning and the usual alert. Took some cement up the steps and cleared a yard of rubble. Knocked off 12 a.m. Had a good meal at night. Turnips, soup powder, M&V and prunes. Our last till goodness knows when, though it is rumoured that there are parcels at Hartmannsdorf, though these were intended for Silesia, they are awaiting confirmation for issuing from Geneva.

MON FEB 26

Back on No.3 the water pipe job. A circus is quite near and I saw the animals. Not very good specimens. Met Lucas, haven't seen him since IVB over twelve months ago. Quite a chat in the afternoon. Didn't do much work. Rained all way back. Miserable.

TUES FEB 27

At last my day off. Swept bedroom out, chopped and sawed wood all morning. Immediate warning went 12.30 and heavy formations passed over till past 2. All clear 2.30. Ruined our afternoon. Managed a bath and washed some clothes in stream water. Made some prune jam – short of spreads.

WED FEB 28

Went on no.1 kommando at the railway goods yard. 3 miles. Pretty cushy. Blokes clear off into the fields when alarm goes. It went at 3. All clear 3.15 and we went back to barrack. Not bad.

THURS MAR 1

Back on builder's labourer job at No.5 carrying bricks up the 83 stairs all day. Monotonous and exceedingly tiring. Immediate warning 9 p.m. – 9.15.

FRI MARCH 2

On No.5 again. Easy day shovelling rubble. Air raid on Chemnitz 9.45 – 12. We were in a deep shelter and heard nothing. I slept. After "all clear" planes dived low and bombed (one quite near us) during another immediate warning. Caught everyone on the hop. At my old commando No3 Dick Walters was blown into a hole by blast, 2 chaps (not ours) next to him being killed. Dick recovering this evening. Water came on early this morning but was off again on our return. Blast it. I guided a blind man to the shelter this morning. Had a good talk in French to a Frenchman who had recently come from Berlin which is flat. No raid at night – snowing.

SATURDAY MARCH 3

Our usual sojourn of 2 hours in the shelter 10 – 12. Bombs on Chemnitz again. Some dropped about 50 yards from us leaving a big fire. Like being in a submarine with depth charges dropping. Didn't feel as safe in this shelter as hitherto. Knocked off work at 12.30. bombs dropped near No 3 job again. Another 2 immediates, 4 – 4.15 and 8.30 – 9.

WEEKLY SUMMARY

A horrible week with the raids coming again very trying on the nerves. Parcel stuff finished except for margarine and coffee. Going to be grim next week. The Yanks dropped news leaflets and food coupons. According to the leaflet, we are advancing all along the Western Front. Taken Duren, 25 kilometres from Cologne. Most promising advance is between Nass and Rhine in South Holland where we are very near the Rhine at Emmerich. Russian advance appears to have slowed up a lot. It is imperative for the war to be over shortly, I'm just about at the end of my tether, I have no hopes of an early end. Can't do any washing – will be getting lousy shortly.

SUN MAR 4

Expected to be off up till 10 p.m. when we were told we were to be sent out on demolition. At 8 a.m. we went to Feldwebel's house which has been damaged. Clearing the road in blinding snow till 1 p.m. Miserable. Before I could get into barrack, I was sent to cookhouse for grub.

MON MAR 5

My day in the lager. Didn't get a spare five minutes. Sawing wood, carrying water from the stream 3 times, fetching the grub. Boiled some clothes and had a good wash down. Air raid 9.30 – 11.30. Bombs dropped on Chemnitz. Saw a few formations through the clouds. Sirens and electricity put out of action and no drinking water even at the pumps. We got the heaviest raid yet by the RAF, commencing at 8.30 p.m. I was standing in the doorway when the first few aircraft dropped flares which immediately lit the town up like daylight. I rushed to the shelter whilst incendiaries were falling. Then commenced half an hours intensive bombing most of it very near us. Bombs were showered down from all angles. Lot of D,A's, H,E's incendiaries and some cookies. What a din. When it was over the Feldwebel ordered us all out and we marched in the snow to the forest as a precaution against a later raid. Looking back on the town, the place was a mass of flames making an awe inspiring sight. Spent an exceedingly uncomfortable night, returned to billet at 5 a.m. and slept till 10.30. A lot of fires were 100 yards from the barrack and we could consider ourselves very fortunate to get away unscathed.

TUES MAR 6

Didn't get out to work today. Did a bit of snow clearing outside the lager. Feltwebel has lost his flat, and one of postern's his wife and children. Fires still burning. Alarm went at 8.30 and we marched to the forest over 2 miles away. Nothing came over Chemnitz and we returned after the all clear. We have to do night watches for distant sirens as none are working in the town. I was 1.30 – 2.30. Very cold.

WED MAR 7

No outside work again today. Did some wood sawing. Tried to get a bit of sleep. Alarm 11.45 – 12.45. Went up to forest 7.45 – 10.30 as precautionary measure. Immediate alarm 9 – 10. Heavy raid on some nearby towns. Zwickan or Planen. Another alarm 1.30 a.m. – 1.45 a.m. This is worse than a day to day existence, it is alarm to alarm. Very cold in the forest.

THURS MAR 8

Went out 8 a.m. clearing the streets. The damage is terrible. Block of flats blown to smithereens, lot of dead in the cellars along the street. Looks like a dead city. Everyone looks in a daze. Returned to barrack 11.30. As regards grub, we have reached rock bottom and there has been no German magasin issue for 2 days. Stood by from 8 – 10 to go to the forest in case of alarm. Fore alarm went but no "immediate". Had a good sleep.

FRI MAR 9

Went out working from 8 a.m. – 2 p.m. clearing the streets. Desolation everywhere, the town is in ruins. Chemnitz is certainly out of action.

Electricity and water still off. Looking round we can thank God that we came through that raid in safety.

SAT MAR 10

Clearing streets. A very high side of a building collapsed across the road within 20 yards of us. Knocked off 12.30 p.m. got ½ Canadian parcel today. Tomlin getting them from Hartmannsdorf yesterday having to walk there and back with a hand cart. These parcels are not intended for us and were issued against Geneva orders due to our urgent need. We can hold no hopes of any further issue. Went to forest on alarm.

WEEKLY SUMMARY

Definite news states we have reached the Rhine but rumours are rife about fall of Koblenz, Bonn, Koln and Dusseldorf. Feel a bit more hopeful about the end. Can't understand the easy week's work but Chemnitz appears stymied, almost every street we've been on has been burnt to the ground. No lights or water yet or signs of it.

SUNDAY MAR 11

On alarm watch 3–4 a.m. Miserable – raining. Street clearing 8 – 12. Had a cold wash down and change of clothes in afternoon.

MONDAY MAR 12

Off to work 7.30 On the water works job near the circus. Terrible long walk. Back at 5 p.m. barely time to put up tomorrow's sandwiches before dark. Didn't go to forest on alarm for first time since raid. Too tired. Scilly at night was macaroni. Thin as piss. Disgraceful expecting work on these rations.

TUES MAR 13

Same job. Scrounged a bit of animal bread at circus. Dry bread tastes good these days. Scarcely a building in town has escaped damage. Nothing but ruins along our 5 kilometre walk.

WED MAR 14

Birthday.

Managed to get 1 ½ kilos animal bread for 10 fags and bar of soap. Stewed prunes and klim at night and the chocolate which we have saved. One of the guards used his butt on Walsh and Johnson. Usual warning at night, was on alarm watch 1 a.m. – 2.

THURS MAR 15

On way to work saw Polish women doing the same work as we do, digging out the water pipes. Beautiful sunny day. Felt listless and weak. Managed to get some animal meat at circus, cooked it at night. Train depot is a mass of matchwood. Went to forest at night.

FRI MAR 16

(Luftwaffe refused to work with us)
Beautiful day. Civilians and soldiers being stopped and examined by Gestapo. Felt very weak again today. Went to forest on the evening alarm.

SAT MAR 17

Colder today and rained. Warning at 11.15 terminated the day's work. Aircraft passing over all the time during the march back. Passing over for a solid hour, thought we were in for it.

WEEKLY SUMMARY

Only sure news is that we have actually got bridgeheads across the Rhine. Feltwebel has changed from "5 to 12" to "2 mins to 12" Hope he is right. Scillies have been weak and thin all week. Impossible to work on these rations. Lights, water still off.

SUN MAR 18

First Sunday off for 6 weeks. Did washing and had wash down. Some chaps are getting lousy already.

MON MAR 19

Same job. Warning 12.30, 14.45. Thousands of kites passed over. One leaflet supposed to have been seen by Feltwebel's wife saying RAF were going to raid again on 19th, we went to forest for first time since big raid.

TUES MAR 20

3 p.m. seems to be regular finishing time. Got hold of some spuds today, beetroot yesterday – augments rations a bit. Felt off colour today.

WED MAR 21

Worked till 4. Beautiful weather.

THURS MAR 22

Another beautiful day. Absolutely incapable of work. The walk alone puts me on my knees. Talked with some Belgians.

FRI MAR 23

Really hot today. Managed to get some beetroot.

SAT MAR 24

Beautiful weather again. Worked till 3.30.

WEEKLY SUMMARY

Scillies have been terribly thin. We have no parcel food and are in a very weak condition. Don't know how long we can keep this up. Our boys are across the Rhine and attacking, lot of Germans give it 2 weeks to a month. If only they were right. Russians appear to be attacking again.

SUN MAR 25

Day off. Darning, had wash down, carried grub. Beautiful day. Absolutely out of smokes. Terrible position.

MON MAR 26

New site. West Strasse – same job. Only 10 minutes walk, but I was walking all day, with 2 warnings and having to bring a mobile shithouse from No2's old job. Feel very weary and weak. Reports of parachute landings on Western Front. Managed a smoke from tobacco dust in Pete's trouser pocket.

TUES MAR 27

Same job as yesterday. Horribly boring. 20 fags a man from pooled personal parcels that had gone astray. We smoke again, being issued 5 a day. Confirmation of yesterday's news. Yanks 260 kilometres away. Lights came on in the evening, been off 22 days.

WED MAR 28

Working at new water pipe hole on the hill. Spent a lot of time helping women up the hill with their water carts. Tomo went to Hartmannsdorf brought back 40 French fags a man. No hopes of parcels. Americans advanced to Wurzburg south east of Frankfurt.

THURS MAR 29

Same as yesterday. Some kids gave us 10 spuds; gave them 3 marks, marks being no use to us. Rained a bit today.

GOOD FRIDAY MAR 30

Worked till 12 a.m. Peter is ill and off his food. I had a good sleep in afternoon.

SAT MAR 31

Worked till 1 p.m. M.O. visited Pete who is still very bad. He ate
nothing today.

WEEKLY SUMMARY

Our boys seem to be advancing quickly in the west having passed
Frankfurt, spearheads at the approaches of Nuremburg. Place reached
136 miles from here. Heavy attacks from Monty in direction of Munster
and Cassel. Russians advancing in north-west Hungary; captured
Danzig. Am feeling weak and listless (as one does after long illness).
It is to be hoped this state of affairs doesn't last long.

SUNDAY APL 1

Allowed to lie in till 10 a.m. I had to go to Company cookhouse, took
1 ½ hours. Didn't feel too good today. Talked to 2 Frenchmen at
kitchen and they gave the war another month.

MONDAY APL 2

Clocks put forward 1 hour. Very surprised only to work till 1 p.m.
Collected stream water and washed my hair and had a bath. Did stack
of washing yesterday. Feldwebel told us of fall of Cassel, Munster,
Heidelburg; nearest place to here 100 miles. Wave of optimism in
barrack. Can't arouse enthusiasm.

TUES APL 3

Work 7 – 3.30. Very cold and windy. Unpleasant working.

WED APL 4

Same as yesterday. Very cold and windy. Got cold on the stomach. Had temperature at night. Limbs felt like jelly. Tomo went to Hartmannsdorf. No issue of the mis-directed parcels but Xmas parcels came in last night and the factory commando collected ours later in the day and they were issued 1 between 2 at night. What a glorious surprise. Ate ¼ Xmas cake and brew of tea with a Players. Beautiful. Recent conditions gave us maximum appreciation. Pity I didn't feel in good form. News that we have reached Jena, 120 kilometres from here. Munster fell without fight

Ran up high temperature at night.

APL 5 THURS

Went sick this morning. Got a stack of pills and 3 days bed rest. Just what I need. Pete got arbeit. There were 2 immediates last night, 1 this morning and fighters came over straffing this afternoon for half an hour. Good sign but I fear the next few weeks till our blokes come (most people Germans and Kregies think it a matter of days) will be nerve racking. Told today that the Yanks are 70 kilometres east of us and Russians have commenced driving towards Dresden.

APL 6 FRI

Stayed in bed till tea time, apart from the warning 10 – 11 during which thousands of kites passed over. The rest did me good, stomach being a little upset still. Upsetting news that the drive towards here has been driven back.

APL 7

Dad's birthday.

In bed till nearly midday. Did some washing in afternoon, had shave. Good meal at night. Heinz beans on toast, half Xmas pud with custard and slice of bread with honey, mug of tea. Pudding tasted wonderful after the base fare we've had for the last few weeks.

WEEKLY SUMMARY

Great hopes at beginning of week when Yanks were advancing apparently at 20 kilometres a day. Rumoured 70 kilometres away Thursday. According to German news 120 kilometres away at Gotha. Pete is very confident of our release week after next, but a lot of chaps are a bit pessimistic again due to the halt. Monty is doing well in the North. Munster, Cassel, advance on Bremmen and Hannover. Attempt to cut off Germans in north Holland by northern advance from Arnheim. Russians in great drive captured the remainder of (north west) Hungary and are on outskirts of Vienna heading for our drive to Nuremburg. Really a splendid week for news. I felt better for my rest but stomach still painful.

SUNDAY APL 8

Day of rest. Had a good feed from parcel at night. Tin of pork and stuffing with some spuds saved from dinner. Yorkshire pud with the remainder of the honey, brew of tea and cigarette. Later had ¼ Xmas cake each with butter and another brew and cigarette. Nothing left but ½ custard powder, fags finished too. Felt very well satisfied. Had ½ bar of chocolate in bed. Enjoyed this parcel more than any previous parcel. Certainly needed it. News of German counter attack due west of here.

3 immediate warnings today. As last night terrific flashes to north west and ack-ack but no sound of bombs. Surmise paratroops.

MONDAY APL 9

Arbeit at Leipzigstrasse. Very tedious. Cold. According to news gleaned from various sources, Monty is making great strides in north. 8 kilometres from Bremmen and on autobahn to Hamburg. 30 from Brunswick, 10 from Hannover. Yanks advancing on Weimar contrary to Germans who say they have pushed us back 40 kilometres in that sector. Joe is 50 kilometres west of Vienna and we are 50 from Nuremburg and 20 from Stuttgart. Paratroops landings near Leipzig. Very good news if reliable.

TUESDAY APL 10

As yesterday. Cold morning, warm afternoon. Very tedious and tiring. Whipped some turnips off the back of a cart. Deadly without smokes. Warning 10-11.30 at night. Some kites bombed Chemnitz after 11 and caught most of us in bed. Flares and a few bombs.

WED APL 11

Warm and sun shining today. Fighter did some straffing. New order, we work 7-5. Ration of bread cut 310-286, spuds 450-250. Can't stand 10 hours on that grub let alone work. Feel extremely weak.

THURS APL 12

Went dental sick and got my tooth filled. Walk to Revier to company kitchen and our kitchen just about killed me. Griff today; Hannover fallen. Brunswick and Magdeburg reached. ¾trs Bremen captured. Patton commenced new attack driving towards here and Liepzig.

110-120 kilometres from here. 100 kilometres from Berlin. News that there are no parcels for us this week.

FRIDAY APL 13

Arrived at work 7 a.m. When we marched up the road to Friedrick, Volkstorm were making a road block with fallen trees in feverish haste. Civvies were running about all morning buying in large quantities of bread and food. Lot of army transport coming down Liepzigstrasse. Tension in the air. Feldwebel came out at 10.30 and took us all back to lager. Heard that Liepzig had fallen and Yanks 60 kilometres from here. At 12 tommo came back from Hartmannsdorf telling us that he had managed to get issue of parcel a man and was going to collect them this afternoon. Also told us that tanks were expected any hour at Hartmannsdorf. Straffing by fighters most of afternoon, some gunfire. Tommo returned after late start with parcels. Between 4 of us we got 1 Canadian, 1 English and bulk. Chocolate, biscuits with cheese and jam and butter and brew with cigarette. Wonderful to smoke and eat again. Everybody in high spirits. Tommo says our troops are 6 kilometres from Hartmannsdorf, 20 from here. Had a good scoff at night. Artillery fire all night.

SAT APL 14

Parade 6.30. Told we're being evacuated at 10 a.m. to place 25 kilometres south of here. Pete and I got packed and escaped through wire and with some more chaps hid in shelter near empty factory. Panzer alarm went and woman found us. She ran off in panic and brought a civvy. We got out of shelter and came up the line and bumped into postern. Went back to lager and Feldwebel has altered plans of waiting 10 kilometres outside town, which we didn't like and he proposed taking us to his flat and hiding us in his cellar till town taken. Very decent of him. Drew rations having to give the lousy cook

200 fags for same. Needed these as we were out of bread. At 1 p.m.
went to the flat and 65 of us were distributed in 5 small cellars. Bit
cramped. Had good meal, Moton's apple pud, diced bananas and klim,
cheese and biscuits, ½ mug tea. Settling down when Walter, postern,
came back with news that Chemnitz had been declared open city. On
strength of this we returned to lager though I personally was dead set
against this. Posterns rifles unloaded, blokes singing as they straggled
back, but I was unable to feel any elation. Not long after we returned,
gunfire opened up in the forest again. We thought at first it may be
spiking of guns, but soon doubts began to assail us. Overhead warning
went. Hopes of the entry of Yanks tomorrow fell and the ration position
looks like troubling us. The Feldwebel is in a funny position if enquiries
are made. Queerest day of ups and downs I've known. Got wireless
in and heard news. Very good, 7 miles past Chemnitz, by-passed
Leipzig. 100 kilometre from across Elbe, heavy fighting near Bremmen
approaching Hamburg 45 miles. Russians 30 miles west of Vienna
(captured), probing attacks across Oder in direction of Berlin. See what
tomorrow brings.

WEEKLY SUMMARY

Got steadily weaker every day. Wonderful day Friday when I did my last
stroke of arbeit, the end looked actually in sight and Tommo brought
life giving parcels from Hartmannsdorf. Head in a whirl Saturday. Hope
they don't make another effort to evacuate us and that the Yanks enter
the town and relieve us from this intolerable uncertainty.

SUNDAY APL 15

Yesterday's doubts justified, heavy shelling most of day, some small
arms fire heard. Anyhow had quiet day till evening when Feldwebel
announced that he was obliged to carry out his previous orders due to

certain enquiries. He proposed to divert from them by marching 10 kilometres south west instead of south to Marienburg. Jimmy Webb and Dave Brewster attempted to escape at night (they returned only this morning), failed, Jim got away but returned. Later it was announced that we were to go to Marienburg and an hour later, 10 p.m., Tomlin announced that he was being left in sole charge as the Feldwebel and guards were going. This surpasses all the previous sacrifices the Feldwebel has made for us. He has turned out aces high. It is to be hoped the Yanks come shortly as we have only about 3 days supply of food and we will not get any more as we have to lie low to give the appearance the lager is deserted. Jimmie and Scotty pinched 2 hens which we boiled up for six of us, with carrots, spuds (also pinched), pea flour tin of M&V. It was wonderful. Very close shelling as I write 11 p.m. Nervous tension high. To bed.

MONDAY APL 16

After a sleepless night due to continuous shelling, Feldwebel aroused us at 4.30 a.m. Plans seemed to have changed overnight. We were to march off (Feldwebel said west) at 9 a.m. Just before 9 a terrific bombardment of the city commenced and we all rushed for the shelter. Shelling of city main roads continued intermittently throughout the day making the march impossible. Thank God. Spent most of the hottest periods in the shelter. During the day the posterns kept disappearing to return later in civvies. Walter seemed very pleased. In afternoon Feldwebel changed into civvies and Tomlin was left in sole charge. Food situation grim, two thin slices today. Jimmie saved the day by getting some carrots and together with some spuds we swiped yesterday made a good stew. At about 6 p.m. fighters came over and dropped leaflets telling people to put out white flags or else. White flags began to appear and about half an hour later some fool shouted "They're here" but it was a false alarm. A car with a white flag was seen to go out on the road to the east. Most blokes think the city has surrendered. It looks like it as there has been no more shelling and straffing, and it is now 7.30. I still daren't build up too much after Saturday's affair. Bit of a scare when some Jerry kites came over and ack-ack was showered at them. Didn't realise what was happening. Pandemonium for few seconds. Heavy artillery duels across the city all night. Our guns seem to be only 1 or 2 kilometres away. Slept the night from 2 a.m. onwards in the shelter. Went with Webb for some rabbits during heavy shellfire – what a caper. Everybody's nerves in shreds.

Tues Apl 17

The expected Yanks did not arrive with the dawn. Everybody is edgy and in low spirits. Had the rabbit stew with carrots and spuds. Very good. Terrific panic when a Feldwebel came to gate, blokes diving out of the escape hatches and doors at back of barrack. He only told us that he thought town was surrounded. My God I wish they'd come and relieve this tension, it would be terrible to be taken away at this stage. Little gunfire during the day, increased at night. Sounded like tank fire close by at one stage. I slept in a cellar in the yard. Quite comfortable. Lofty guard, Mandel and small Feldwebel came in for the night with uniform on. Don't trust any of them.

Wed Apl 18

At the crack of dawn 3 Feldwebels roused us out of our hiding places with revolver shots. Hopes immediately zero. We were marched out of town straight away and 10 minutes rest every hour. Most of way was very steep and hard going, weather hot, full kit and overcoats on. Arrived at Schapen 18 kilometres away at midday. Rested 2 hours and marched further 15 kilometres landing up eventually at a rest house near Marienburg where we slept the night. Gunfire still sounded near during day. At one of resting points found full milk can and had a butter tin full. Tasted lovely, first for over 3 years. Only grub Peter and I set out with was 6oz bully, 6oz cheese, ½lb marge, little butter, klim, tea. Most of this went on the march. Had a brew which refreshed us at night. No German rations for 4 days now. Looks as though we are in for a very thin time from now on.

THURS APL 19

Marienburg apparently full of Kregies, we stayed the day at the Guest House. Rest welcome. Got our first bread for five days. 400 grams to last 2 days and some tinned meat (I tin between 8). We had great difficulty getting this bread, shortage of food being acute in the district. The weather is beautiful, the countryside is magnificent, rolling wooded slopes and green fields and the accommodation is reasonable, but the general position doesn't bear thinking about. The country back to our lines is terribly difficult, don't think we could make it in our condition without food.

FRI APL 20 MORNING

Still at Guest house. The little girls are very interested in us and they do us many small services, they are very lively and cheer the place up. The woman of the house boils water for us and cooks spuds for those who manage to get them. Peter and I are the 'have nots'. Jerry officer demanded English battledress for suit of civvies; said he would take it forcibly if not given. Wonder what his game is – he can't speak English. In the evening Peter and I walked into village entered a shop, bought coffee and exchanged bar of soap for 5lb spuds. I asked for a little margarine which was given. Very nice woman. Postern caught us coming out and kicked up a row. Ignored him. Feldwebel reprimanded us but we were satisfied with our reconnaissance. 14 more blokes came in including Ted Jesop. Slept well on hard floor.

SAT APL 21

Boiled up some spuds in morning and made a brew of coffee. Rained in afternoon. More rations came up. 600 grams of bread $\frac{1}{10}^{th}$ tin of meat for 33 days. Had scilly made from scrounged spuds, swedes and carrots. We might survive if we muddle through like this. At night went out in rain made a fire and brewed our last brew of tea after which we smoked our last cigarette. Wonder when we will get any more.

SUNDAY APL 22

Roused up at 6.30 and told to be ready to march off at 8. Few blokes pissed off through the shithouse window; seem to think Chemnitz has fallen, though a Jerry soldier came in saying he had travelled from Chemnitz by bike last night and all was quiet. Don't know what to think or do for the best. Snowing and raining today and the terrain is arduous. More blokes went during the day, one lot were reported to Willie the Volkstormer but he didn't seem inclined to make any effort to stop them. The Jerries say the Yanks have returned from Chemnitz but the French, notable 'duff gen wallas', say they are 30 kilometres from Dresden. From German press there is good news of a drive south from Hof which should keep us from going to Munich. Russians and us sandwiching Berlin. Now 5.30 so it doesn't look as though we are moving today. Jock and Ginge returned from their escape, Jock finding the weather too bad. Lights off tonight.

MONDAY APL 23

6 inches of snow on the ground. High altitude. Return of the escapees. Tomo, Vidler and Merrick returned with policeman reaching a point 10 kilometres south west of Chemnitz. Lewis and Fisher came back late afternoon. New M of Con. Since Tomo escaped, viz Eric Hall.

TUES APL 24

30 men wanted for work. Digging slit trenches at the side of the road. Supposed to be for civilians. Did no work today due to heavy fall of snow. Got another 2 days bread issue, 400 grams.

WED APL 25

Work did not materialise thank goodness. Tried to go out on the scrounge but guards on front and back. Very hungry today; scilly contained no veg (few beans and barley). 3 days more bread issued in evening – ate some of it. Similar rations to Benghasi and Altimura. Strong rumours of 4 day conference at Ribbentrop in America.

THURS APL 26

For the fourth night in succession I dream't of cigarette and food. I am not taking too easily to the cigarette famine, especially when guards and blokes who aren't really smokers are still smoking. Beautiful morning, cleared snow away. Heard today that Russians and Americans have met at Torgan, north east of Liepzig. Hope it is time. Tommo gave Pete and I a French fag to join at. First time I really appreciated a French fag. Got ¾trs kilo bread for a shaving stick, ate it all today and still felt hungry. Must get out on the scrounge tomorrow, we can't lie here and starve slowly. Had 2 games of chess with Pete, I won both.

FRI APL 27

Early this morning Pete and I got out with a pack and the soap. Our first attempt was frustrated by the guard and we were called back on the 2nd attempt but we kept on walking. We had a fine walk over the knoll and through the wood and we eventually dropped down into a village after a walk of about 5 kilometres. I asked for spuds for shaving stick at a farm and met with refusal. I then asked a woman who gave us a sandwich of fat each and a bowl of spuds. I talked with a Russian at another farm, he took us to his bed sitting room and his wife brought us a bucket of spuds. A Pole took us to an adjoining room and his wife gave us a big plate of potato scones in batter, with a frying pan of peas, coffee with milk. To crown it all the Pole gave us a roll of bacon to finish off a good meal. Before we went he gave us a hunk of bread each and quite a bit of home grown tobacco. Felt very weak on the way out due to the last 9 days poor rations, felt better on the return journey. Had a lie down on the fringe of the wood, very nice to feel free and listen to the birds with a satisfied stomach. Were away for 5 hours. Shook the cobwebs away a bit. Scilly today was just barley water. Very hungry again at night. A bit of extra food gives you an appetite for more. Lights came on in the evening after being off for 6 days.

SAT APL 28

In a dream I smoked the lettering off a Player's No.3. Raining. Very dismal, boring day. Ate a few of our spuds, bread and barley soup. No strength giving qualities. Feel like a very old woman when I climb the stairs. Good to smoke a few rolls of the old dried grass.

WEEKLY SUMMARY

Growing steadily weaker due to poor and little food. Certainly a cure for the nerves after shelling, bombing and sirens at Chemnitz. Russians are all round Berlin and terrific battle is raging. German press says future of Reich and Europe depend on this struggle. Hope so. After period of despondency following our move blokes are coming round to the view that the war cannot last more than a month, let alone possible release.

SUNDAY APL 29

12 of us went for walk with Feldwebel. Intermittent sunshine, strong cold wind. Walked 7 miles at a brisk pace; bit too far but I felt much better for it. Bean scilly, better than usual.

MONDAY APL 30

Only enough spuds for today so necessity once more sent us out on the scrouge. Dodged the guard easy enough and visited a village the other side of the Annaberg road. It was like flogging a dead horse. Some of our blokes must have been there before. All we had to offer was marks which obviously aren't worth anything to anybody. We must have asked over 30 farm places, most of them gave us about 6 or 7 spuds but we were met with a few refusals. Only one woman accepted our marks and she gave us quite a few spuds. An old woman gave us each a slice of bread and marge. Called at 4 shops. One lady shopkeeper gave us an iced cake (6th size) and it was very good, ate half in the fields and the other half when we got back. A man gave us some salt, 2 Maggi's soups and a few spuds. At a bread shop a woman gave us a kilo of bread for a shaving stick. Most people were quite friendly disposed towards us. Surprised at my cheek begging from door to door, felt a bit degraded but when it is a question of starving it's got to be done. Feel sorry for some of the blokes who can't pluck up the courage to go out, they must feel the pinch. Returned to Guest House 2 p.m. having been away 3½ hours. Well worth the effort. Ate our scilly (barley) the remnants of our previous spud supply, ½ the cake and some bread with a mug of coffee and felt quite satisfied. Swopped a soup and 6 spuds for 4 Players and by jove the first one tasted wonderful, profound satisfaction. It's going to be grand when we get a regular supply again. Chatting with a Frenchman who told me that Berlin was nearly finished and that Himmler had asked for peace with British and Yanks (capitulation) but

we had replied capitulation must be to the 3 powers. Tommo came in
with same griff said to be BBC.

TUESDAY MAY 1

Sunshining but bitter cold wind. Like a nice day in January. Went with
coal party with horse and cart to Marionberg for the Guest House's
coal. Had Maggi's soup and spuds for dinner. The scilly was nothing
more than soup. Annoyed to get honey, marge and cheese powder in
today's rations. Ate a kilo of bread between us but weren't satisfied.
Could eat bread all day. Rumoured that Munich fell after 48 hours
ultimatum. Advance on Innsbruck, fall of Trieste, Verona. Most of
Berlin in Russian hands. In all this time, war should be over in a
fortnight.

WED MAY 2

Supposed to be heard on this morning's radio that Hitler has been
killed in Berlin, Admiral Donity superceding. Snowed all morning.
Read essays, sewed button on tunic. Had cold bath at night. Very cold.
German radio – heavy street fighting Munich; pockets of resistance in
Berlin. Deadly life without smokes. Could end any day.

THURS MAY 3

Only one day's supply of spuds left so had to go out on the scrounge
again. Called at our Polish friends and got a rather stony welcome.
Made us feel like we were – scroungers. Rather a shock after last week's
benevolence. They were cooking, but we got up to go and Anton gave
us quite a few potatoes rather shamefacedly. We found all the shops in
the village closed and returned to Guest House at 12.45. Griff, Berlin
and Munich finished and Hamburg surrendered. Yesterday's paper news
admits heavy fighting in Munich, pockets of resistance Berlin, retreat of

German army in Italy, advance of Yanks to east of Pussan 60 kilometres from Linz (the Russians being the same distance from there over three weeks ago). Advance south 10 kilometres from Innsbruck. Germans have nothing left to fight for.

FRI MAY 4

Nice day, a bit cold. A lot of Yank fighters came over during the morning straffing the roads. Saw some of them quite close, a grand sight. First signs of action round here since we came. In afternoon heard wild rumours that Yanks were 4 kilometres other side of Schopan. Proved incorrect by underofficer coming from Chemnitz. Supposed BBC news says that over a million men capitulated in Austria and Italy. Germans capitulated in Norway and Denmark. Everywhere but this god-foresaken spot about which no one seems to care. Navy capitulated.

SAT MAY 5

Run out of spuds again so had to go out. This next week's rations, 7 days, are poorer than the previous issue for 4 days. Scilly rations negligible. Rained all day and we put off going out till afternoon. Called at all the shops in the first village and got tea, coffee, salt, matches; soup powder unobtainable. One shopkeeper gave us a sandwich each of fat (very nice) and another gave us a few potatoes. This village no good for obtaining spuds so we went over fields in search of another. Passed through one which contained hotels being used as reserve lagerets. Came across another village further down Annaberg road and went to work with the marks. Didn't do badly at all. I had the cheek to ask one farmer for some tobacco and I got a nice supply of home grown. Quite good stuff considering. Relieve smoke situation for few days. All the people we encountered were very pleasant with us, some asked us when we were going back to England. Some asked why we didn't make for Zwickan or Chemnitz. Had a good meal of spuds on our return. Were

wet through and had to dry all our clothes in front of stove. Tommo
came in with griff that war was over at 12. Can't help laughing.

WEEKLY SUMMARY

Everything happened this week except the end of war. Every area of
importance lost by the Germans and we still look no nearer to getting
released. Reckon we'll be in last thousand kreigies to be released.
Dreamt about cigs or grub over 8 times since coming here. Spuds are
increasingly difficult to obtain and the Jerry's rations wouldn't keep
a fly's strength up. Weather been terrible all week. When I had cold
bath, woman of the house (30 odd) came in wash house and caught me
stripped; I didn't care two pins but Willis rushed up and covered me
with towel. The girl (14) opened the door 5 minutes later and retreated
laughing. Must have lost my prudishness for I was very unconcerned.

SUNDAY MAY 6

Rained all day, so had a day in. Ate plenty of spuds as our bread is
finished. News this morning that the Germans in Bavarian sector have
capitulated. When are they going to capitulate in Saxony? Tommo
heard the Czechs appeal for aid over Prague radio asking for our
support or paratroops. Later in afternoon, German broadcasted from
Prague – looks as though they have taken part control of the city again.
Late German radio says that British and Russian paratroops have been
dropped in Zeeland and that British are up in arms against Soviets.
Hope this is propaganda. Wish I knew what was really going on.

MONDAY MAY 7

Went out for more spuds today. Went about 7 kilometres up the
Annaberg road. Found 3 farms nicely off the beaten track and did well

at all of these. Had an interesting chat with a farmer who had deserted from the army a month ago. Had another talk with a young woman who was scared stiff that the Russians would arrive here first. Got 2 eggs for tin of Vaseline. Visited a few more farms and finished up with quite a haul. Weather was beautiful and warm, had a rest in the fields and a smoke. Very nice. On the way back up the road we met the German army in a schnell retreat. Gharries racing back from Reisa. Talked with a Jerry soldier who looked as though he had been on the march for days, he told us the Russians were advancing fast. Was going to try to flog soap at bakery in Hilmersdorf but found our way blocked with tanks. The village was packed with military transport, all S.S. troops. Talked with one of them. Near the lager we saw our cooks disembowelling a horse that had been shot (because of wind). It was cooked in the evening and it tasted like beef and was really tender. Packed my kit in event of moving; think we will, hope it is the right direction. Boiled the eggs and ate most of tomorrow's bread. Cooked some spuds for tomorrow. Tommo announced that we are going to march to Chemnitz tomorrow to meet the Yanks. Some nearby gunfire during night, probably Russians.

LIBERATION

TUESDAY MAY 8

Boiled spuds to take with us and had some cold horse meat for breakfast, saving some for the march. Set off 9 a.m. kit weighing heavy. After walking a kilometre we turned left into fields to cut across Annaberg road. Walked slap into 4 Russians with machine guns. Imagine our surprise. We advanced waving, the posterns were non-plussed but the Russians made up their minds for them relieving them of their rifles and sending them along with us (there were some civvies with us too). The Russians gave us Deutsche fags and after much hand shaking they proceeded down Annaberg road and we continued on our way to Chemnitz. Ruskies looked a pretty tough proposition. Everybody straggled along at sixes and sevens and soon Pete and I were on our own. Still some armed Jerries in the villages but they paid no attention to us. Beautiful country to Zachopan, pine trees with a river winding it's way through the valleys. The villages were a fine sight nestling amongst the hills and woods. Had a good drink of beer at a Guesthouse and ate some spuds and horse flesh at another 2 kilometres from Zachopan. In Zachopan we called at a beer house and I got talking to a Frenchman; he took us to his lager and gave us some scilly, spuds and bread. His friends gave us bread and we recommenced our journey with 1½ kilos bread at 3.30. Road out of village steep and tiring. Very hot now. A boy pulled our kit 2 kilometres on a go-cart, Pete gave him 20 marks, his mother gave us drink of cold coffee, no milk or sugar. Nearly 8 p.m. when we arrived in Chemnitz very footsore and weary. Russian territory apparently but didn't see any.

Yanks are on autobahn. A very nice couple put our kit in their go-cart and helped us to find our destination. After much chasing about they handed us over to an official of sorts who took us up Liepzigstrasse. To our great pleasure and surprise we saw our first Yank vehicle and Jeep; they stopped for us and we happily jumped on and sped away. Got some Yank fags and boy did they taste good. They had a bottle of brandy (most people in Chemnitz were drunk) and a few swigs put us in high spirits. Yank staff car stopped us and officer bollocked our driver for having trespassed into Chemnitz. Good job for us they did or we wouldn't have made it tonight. They took us to a transport place and we finished the bottle of brandy. We got on to a lorry with blokes from our lager, Serbs and Ities. One of the Serbs was gloriously drunk and sang at the top of his voice; I was a bit squiffy myself and really entered into the idea of this sudden freedom after all the suspense of the last few months. At Limbach we stopped for the night at a lager. Finished off Tony's special (3 days ration in one) scilly (the first thick one we had) but the horse fat made it sickly and I was sick and felt better for it. Slept with my clothes on. There were bags of blankets so I needn't have taken the trouble to have brought mine. Heard that we get flown home – too good to be true. Never felt as tired in my life. Feet terrible. Lager dirty and stinks.

WED MAY 9

Another beautiful midsummer day. Just getting dry bread and scilly here. Getting cheesed off waiting for transport so visited American sub HQ and enquired. Told us they had no spare transport but had us in mind. Chatted to passing Yanks all through the day and they kept us going in fags. In the afternoon a lorry turned up, full of Red X parcels, English, and at 6 p.m. we were issued 1 a man with 2 extra between the six of us (these were given to us by one of the Frenchmen on the lorry for 2 bars of chocolate). Also got tin of butter and klim, no cigs but I noticed that all the French were smoking cigarettes whereas they had been rolling them in the morning. Had a very big feed at night, chocolate, 2 oatmeal bars, tin of carrots and an M&V with the scilly, 2 tins of creamed rice with Nestles and bread and jam, mug of tea and cigarette. Had to loosen my pants at the front. Just the job. Feel in a much better frame of mind now. Cleared out a waiting room and slept there at night in preference to the stinking lager. Bags of fresh air and quite warm; didn't sleep too well due to rich food. The French in charge here are a niggardly crowd, playing fast and loose with Red X stuff and dishing us out with poor rations. French liaison officer in charge.

THURS MAY 10

Were invaded early morning by a lot of our fellow countrymen. They commandeered our tables and chairs, drew Red X parcels without it putting them in good humour, demanded some bread from Pete (bread for which we had exchanged our cocoa) one of their men not having a ration due to one of his own blokes double shuffling. They took the place by storm but moved after a short while, thank goodness, leaving a bad smell behind them. During the day French civilians invaded our shack and borrowed all our utensils without asking. Spoke to a very nice Dutchman who recounted some of the Russian atrocities in Dresden. Got talking to a Yank at night and he took us up to his billet to meet a Scotsman. We listened to the wireless, drank champagne and smoked cigarettes and talked. Scottie told us of a convoy that was going 130 miles west tomorrow and advised us to get a lift on it (the last bloke he arranged a lift for was dropped near an airport and flown home the same day). Think we will take the chance as we are cheesed off waiting for official transport.

FRI MAY 11

Got up to the transport yard at 7.45. convoy of Jerry vehicles. I sat in front of staff car with a very nice young fella. We went through a packet of 20 fags before the day was through. It was a very hot day. After many stops we arrived at our destination at 4.30. One Jerry car had to be left and destroyed on the way and various others towed. There was a crate of C rations in the back of one of the lorries; the boys left these behind and told us to help ourselves. We took several tins of ham and eggs and breakfasts. The latter contain 4 biscuits, a tablet of cereal, sweets, a small package coffee extract and sugar. They dropped us on the Frankfurt autobahn. Talked to an M.P. asked him if he could put us on anything heading west. Told us we had just missed lorry to Frankfurt. He stopped 2 lorries full of prisoners heading for airfield at Erfart. The driver had already passed his destination by 30 kilometres (lucky for us) and he continued a further 30 before he found his mistake. He made many more wrong turnings before we arrived and as we were 50 men cramped in a truck, tempers got very frayed. Even though on our way home after 3 years of hell, hunger, fatigue and weariness, getting thrown about on the gharry made us absolutely cheesed off. We got dished out with a breakfast B ration which is a package containing small tin egg and bacon, 4 biscuits, coffee extract, 4 cigs, toilet paper, fruit bar and chewing gum. We ate this and felt much better and drank cold coffee and cold cocoa having a terrific thirst. I undressed and slept like a log on bare bed boards.

SAT MAY 12

Good mess hall here. Plates, knives, forks, spoons. Eggs (scrambled) tomatoes and porridge breakfast. Dinner, spuds, chops, peas, fruit. Met up with a lot of boys on our kommando, Dave, Jimmie, Bernard, but they went to airfield in morning. We had to stand by in afternoon

but we were unlucky as there was no more planes. Dinner at night was
a terrific meal. 3 hunks of pork, potatoes, beans, tomatoes, bread and
butter, stewed apples and thick cocoa. Make the Jerries sick if they
could see the stuff that gets thrown away. I had a lie on my bed after it.
Made brew in record time of 5 minutes at night.

WEEKLY SUMMARY 5ᵀᴴ – 12ᵀᴴ

Week opened with usual rumours and doubts. Things began to stir up
a little on Monday when we saw the German army in retreat and in
evening when it was decided to march to Chemnitz. Tuesday brought
our fears and doubts to an end when we crossed the Russian's path,
then came the long weary march to Chemnitz which was brought to
a hilarious close by the Yank Jeep and brandy. The inaction of this was
relieved by issue of Red X parcels. Thursday made arrangements to
move by convoy instead of waiting for official move on Friday, travelled
130 miles by convoy and were picked up by official PW gharries and
deposited at the cur centre at Erfurt. Expected to move Saturday. Got
on well with the Yanks they being very generous and ingenious. Their
efficiency and keenness surprised me. Nice to be on the last stage of
journey home. Good to be able to say it won't be long now and mean it.

SUN MAY 13

Had breakfast at 7.30 and were told to parade for immediate move.
Travelled to airfield and was on the plane and away in five minutes. Yank
efficiency. K rations on the kite types B and D. Quite a smooth trip,
just a few bumps. The ploughed fields looked beautiful and straight
from the air. Landed in Brussels, tea and sandwich, 5 fags all ready at
the airport, after which gharries took us straight to the camp. Were
immediately disinfested with some sort of powder and filled in various
forms. Had a first rate dinner. Hunted the locality for a barbers without

success, had 3 beers and found the clothing store where we changed our tramps clothing for RAF blues. So many blokes came in during the day that cookhouse couldn't provide another meal, so we had to dig out the Jerry brot sandwiches that we had put up for such an emergency. Had free biscuits, tea and cigs at Y.M.C.A. (we were dished out with 20 fags and chocolate on arrival) went to bed at 9.30. Weather sweltering.

BACK TO ENGLAND

MON MAY 14

Paraded immediately after breakfast and gharries took us to airport 20 kilometres away. The city is simply a mass of flags. Everybody waved at us en passant. About ½ hours wait on airfield before we got on C27 again, RAF pilot this time. Cooler today and windy. More bumpy than yesterday (scenic railway), 2 blokes sick. Ran into cloud over channel and rode above it. It cleared up over the Thames estuary and we saw the nice quiet green of England's pastureland as a contrast to the neat ploughed land of Germany and Belgium. On landing we were conveyed to a big hanger where tables and chairs were set out. We were squirted with powder, after which we got good cake, Swiss roll and tea and 10 cigs. What a change to here women speaking English. A WAAF shook hands and welcomed us home on arrival. We were then conveyed to Baker Street Station and went by train to Aylesbury where we got a tasty meal of eggs and mash, bread and butter, I went two helpings. On the gharry again to Waterloo station where we had to wait from 8 – 10.30. Still couldn't get hair cut, so had a rest and a meal at Y.M.C.A. for 11^d. Changed trains at Basingstoke, had sandwiches and tea at buffet.

TUES MAY 15

1.30 a.m. set off for Cosford where we arrived weary and tired in the half-light 6 a.m. Immediately transported to a hangar where our particulars, for railway warrant, were taken and I sent off telegram.

Then breakfast after which shower and change into hospital blue.
2 hours pause during which I had shave and haircut, though I could
have done with a sleep. On with the routine at 11 a.m. filled in
interrogation forms and collected new RAF kit. Break for dinner, then
off again. Filled in pay forms, gave in foreign currency, recovered pay
in advance, filled in identification papers, were photographed and
filled in various other forms relating to captivity etc. X ray, medical
and malnutrition card B-13. Was in a proper daze at the finish, having
travelled 24 hours and been questioned etc. 12 hours without any sleep.
The service was good, food good and organisation splendid. If we
had to go just around the block we were taken by lorry. Collected our
month's ration of chocolate and fags at reduced prices in evening. Had
nice supper of bread and cheese, cake and cocoa and then to bed in
between sheets in pyjamas. What a well earned rest. Going to be hectic
tomorrow, must be ready for it.

Wed May 16

Up for breakfast at 7 a.m. Fried liver in onion sauce. Excellent. Received
our railway warrants and passes. Lorry took us to Cosford station where
we got a train to Wolverhampton. Peter stayed to see Heyes. I caught
10.23 to Crewe. Then I caught the 1.50 to Preston where there was
an immediate connection to Burnley. Changed at Blackburn to get
through to Bank Top. Good job I did for Mrs. Heyes had a taxi waiting
to take me home. What a great feeling to see the folks again. Alice
turned up from work at about 6.30. She's much fatter, I'm only about
5 lbs heavier than she. Talked into early hours, listened to a few of my
records. Collapsed into bed 12.30 and passed out. Great to be home.

Thurs May 17

Saw Aunt Jane early morning, she hadn't changed a bit. Aunty then
came for morning, made good coffee for Mum and self. Went in

evening to see Uncle Dick and had ½ hour with Auntie Janey. Returned to find Uncle Tom and Auntie Minnie and Allan waiting for me. Allan changed a lot.

FRI MAY 18

Went down to office and had hectic 1 ½ hour. Mobbed by girls. Talk to Mr. Harvey and Mr. Hirst. Saw Anne on the counter and she had to get a stool to get at me. As nice as ever. In evening went to Aunty Ruth's with Dad and had a short chain smoking session together with a cup of Horlicks and chocolate bar from Florence. Picked Dad up at church saw the choirmen and then proceeded to Aunt Sally's where Frank had just arrived for week's holiday. Had cake and tea.

SAT MAY 19

Harold arrived early morning 8.30 and so I got up. Went to Aunty Janey's bought her some flowers and also took some home. Cost me 8/- altogether. Went to football match with Harold and Frank, calling for Uncle Tom. Saw Mr. Chadwick at match and much back slapping and hand shaking ensued. Burnley won 5-1. In evening the family and myself went to Mrs. Tattersalls, where daughters Florence and Martha together with the latter's chap assembled. Talked all evening and had splendid supper.

WEEKLY SUMMARY 13TH – 19TH

At last things began to move at the required speed. Two air trips in 2 days took us to Blighty where typical Blighty weather (cloudy) made us feel at home from the start. From then onwards no effort was spared to get us home without delay. We were thankful for a good night's rest at Cosford before going home. The great day did at last arrive. What a wonderful relief and how grand to see everybody again not looking much the worse for wear. What a great feeling to see so many people genuinely pleased to see you. Can't help thinking of the not so distant bad old days and comparing them with my present good fortune.

SUN MAY 20

Went to church in morning with Alice and took communion. Was very much affected by it. Attempted, with little success, to write letters in afternoon. Played billiards with Harold in evening, made 25 break. Had some records on. Sounded grand after all this time.

MON MAY 21

Set out in afternoon with Mary Pollard, Alice and Harold. Bus to Higherford, went walk in direction of Colne and then the rains came so caught the bus back home. Had records on till tea time. Went walk with Harold in evening – quite pleasant. Harold goes back tomorrow early.

TUES MAY 22

Wrote letters to Pete and Bill in morning. Frank came in afternoon. Weather not promising so went to Roxy saw Edward G. in "Armst The Woman". Not bad. Played billiards in evening. I won both games. Then we had an excellent gramophone recital. Beety's 7th and many of my choice records.

WED MAY 23

Up betimes, washed, shaved etc. and a hearty breakfast. Went to Duke Bar Branch saw Leonard, Ms. Dickinson, miss Collinge of the old firm and had a good chin wag. Managed to buy some decent fags on way home, saw Billie and Ethel Heys in their shop. Went over to see

Chadwicks in afternoon; they weren't in so had tea with Whalleys. Met mother in centre at 7 p.m. and went to POW RA meeting where we had tea and cakes and I got £2-2-0 gift. On way home rested in Thursby gardens.

MAY 24 THURSDAY

Had a morning in for a change. In afternoon went Auntie Alice's and saw a great change in her; she must have lost 5 stones having had 2 seizures. Uncle Ike was the same as ever. I helped him to water the plants and collected the eggs. Had a good tea, talk etc. and then proceeded to Evelyn's in the evening. Susan was in bed but had talk with Evelyn and Auntie Annie who doesn't look much older, and of course had a good supper. They had been expecting me tomorrow and had made apple pies etc.

MAY 25 FRI

Went to Mrs. Smiths in morning, had a drink of wine and reminisced about Rev. T. Smith. In afternoon went to Aunty Alice Ann's and had a jolly evening with her and Philip. Returned home tired out.

MAY 26 SAT

Went to town early morning and sent telegram to Pete. Harry Swire conveyed me to office where I talked with various people till 12.30. Jack Parkinson was quite sanguine about the future of us returning blokes and he introduced me to the new girls who are more than somewhat. Was weighed at chemists have gained about 8lbs since arrival. Went to Chadwick's in afternoon with Harold. Had tea.

WEEKLY SUMMARY 20TH – 26TH

Hectic week of visiting. Grand to see everybody but how tired one gets. Apart from getting tired easily, I feel a lot better.

SUN MAY 27

Had breakfast in bed for first time and had quiet morning. Had bath after dinner. Made tea for mother, Harold and self in afternoon. Went to Wilkinson's in the evening and had a very enjoyable time. Lots of fun. Barbara, Rosa and Connie Hamer were there.

MONDAY MAY 28

Went to Bradford by bus to see Peter. He looked well. Only Pat and Joan were home. Listened to some records in afternoon and also went a walk in afternoon. In the evening Joan, Pete and I went to cinema "Dragon Seed" – rather boring. Pat put lot of Stan Holloway records on when we got back, also had a few classics.

TUESDAY MAY 29

Went with Peter to the dentist in the morning. Pat put records on for us in afternoon. Difficulty with buses going home; Shipley – Bradford – Halifax – Hebden Bridge – Todmorden – Burnley; had to change at every place.

WED MAY 30

Went to see Phyllis at Oak Lea in morning. Caught 11.37 to Blackburn and Met Cecil there. Had nice dinner at the Sharples's and went nice walk with Cecil in afternoon. Played soldiers with Derek (10) and Margaret (14) at night and staged a big war with aircraft, tanks, artillery, horseman etc. Afterwards we played bagatelle, after which the youngsters went to bed. Talked till midnight with Mr. and Mrs.

THURS MAY 31

Up at 7 a.m. and went to Accrington office with Cecil. Stayed there a short time and then continued to Burnley. Went and saw Alice before her music exam. Mr. Birtwell came down at 11.30 and gave us communion. Alice failed Advanced Senior with a few marks. Went to Auntie Janey's for tea; took her to Odeon at night to see Rachel Field's "And Now Tomorrow" Loretta Young and Allan Ladd. Not bad. Had supper at Aunty Janey's and ate more than somewhat.

JUNE 1 FRIDAY

Had quiet morning, listened to my recording of Mozart's Violin Concerto. Very good indeed. Met Aunty Alice Ann with Mother in afternoon and went to Mrs. Astin's for tea. Quite nice. Saw Phyllis and Frank. Did not get home very late. Dad played some Chopin.

JUNE 2 SATURDAY

Quiet morning. Practised piano a bit. Harold came in afternoon. Went to Uncle Tom's for tea. After tea Dad, Tom, Harold and I went for walk in Towneley Park and Thanet Lee Wood. Beautiful.

WEEKLY SUMMARY

Can't get over this sudden contrast. People here living quietly on as though nothing had happened, whereas in Germany everything was confusion, chaos, disaster and destruction, the people not knowing what to do nor where to go. Don't know how I am going to settle down to office life, it seems such a meaningless existence. Weather – showers every day.

June 3 Sunday

Rained practically all day. Went to Aunty Sally's for tea and had quite a good evening. Put a few of Frank's records on.

June 4 Monday

Peter came over in the morning. Took him over Nelson golf links in afternoon. Very blustery weather. We took Alice and Mary to Odeon at night. Edward G. Robinson and Joan Bennett in "The Woman in the Window". Very good indeed. Came back home over the park.

June 5 Tuesday

Rained all day till evening when Peter had to go back. Had records on and looked at books etc. Wrote letters at night.

June 6 Wednesday

Wrote letters in afternoon. Went to Auntie Jen's at night. Uncle Dick was greatly interested in my yarns. Harold came over for 48 hours in the evening.

June 7 Thursday

Managed a short walk in the morning with Harold. In afternoon we took the bus to Colne and walked over to Higherford via Barrowford locks. Very nice; there were a few showers but we managed to dodge them. Went to Aunty Janey's for supper.

June 8 Friday

Another unsettled day. Went to Roxy with Harold. Vicki Baum's "Hotel
Berlin". Very good. Very nice evening so we went walk round Fence,
got a lift from a district nurse up Greenhead Lane.

June 9 Saturday

After dinner took bus to Bury via Rawtenstall. Met Harold at Bury
where we took the train to Manchester. Went round two book shops,
I bought two of H. Williamson's books and Harold bought Priestley's
new book. Went to the "Tatler" news cinema where there was a good
programme. Arrived home at about 10 p.m.

WEEKLY SUMMARY

Nothing seems the same. I am unable to analyse my emotions at all.
I should be feeling on the crest of the wave, full of joy and unbounded
relief at having finished with that living death in Germany. But I don't
and cannot explain, even to myself, why. Is it reaction after those last
months of tension and nervous excitement. My capacity for enjoyment
seems to be at a low ebb. Films, books, country, music; all fail to make
the impression they used to do and I fully expected to have a keener
appreciation of all these things after those long barren years. The
shadow of that past still looms over me, perhaps time will make the
shadows fade, for until it does, true enjoyment cannot be mine.

June 10 Sunday

Another not very promising day, but managed a walk down garden
before tea.

June 11 Monday

Weather still very unsettled. Went with Mother to Aunt Annie's for tea. Susan not quite as shy as hitherto. Went to Aunt Alice's after tea, she seemed a little better. Uncle Ike has some wonderful flowers.

June 12 Tuesday

Saw Fred Smith about my teeth – nothing required doing but we had a long and amusing talk. Looked at a lot of old letters in the afternoon. Read part of "Howard's End" at night.

June 13 Wed

Went to Duke Bar office in morning and had a long chat with Mr. Dickinson. Went to Clitheroe with Aunty Janey in afternoon. Very windy and not much sun but had a good time; went up to the castle visited the park and had tea at a nice café. Had supper at No. 8.

June 14 Thurs

Had hair cut and went to Head Office. Saw Mr. Pilkington for first time. Had long chat with various of my acquaintances and returned home at 5.30. Took Alice to Odeon at night. "Wilson". Quite an effective film.

June 15 Fri

Rained practically all morning. Wrote letters in afternoon.

SATURDAY JUNE 16

Harold unable to come over today. Went down to Duke Bar office in morning. A quiet day.

SUNDAY JUNE 17

Harold came over for the day. Went for a walk and read at the garden.

MONDAY JUNE 18

Went to Aunty Janey's for tea. Went to see Major Milnes the Nat. Lib. Candidate in evening to get him to sign my voting form, but he was unable to do so due to being a candidate. Had a 20 minute talk with him and put forward a few questions which stumped him more than somewhat.

TUESDAY JUNE 19

Sent telegram to Peter. Went to Welfare Office to get my voting form signed. I got a buckshee officer to sign it as there was a long queue up there. Went to Head office, Mr. Hirst took me to the Burnley re-settlement centre where I got a few pamphlets. Changed into civvies in afternoon. First time for nearly 5 years. Felt queer. Went walk in afternoon and up to garden with Alice and Mary at night.

WED JUNE 20

Went to Shipley to see Peter. Played table tennis in evening at Aspinall's office, enjoyed it very much.

Afterwards went to Bingley and had a drink of beer. Returned to no. 36 and Mr Squires created an awkward situation by coming in drunk and in a troublesome mood. Pity for Mrs. Squires and Pat, they've had to put up with it for a long time apparently.

THURS JUNE 21

Peter returned to Burnley with me in the evening.

FRI JUNE 22

Took Peter nice walk down Barden along Pendle water and back along canal bank. Took him to Towneley in afternoon and had a look at the picture gallery. Went to Palace at night. Tod Slaughter in "Jekyll and Hyde". Positive disgrace to the profession. Robert Louis Stevenson would turn in his grave.

SATURDAY JUNE 24

Read in the garden in afternoon and went for walk round Heasandford River at night.

SUMMARY

Peter and myself came to the conclusions as to why life does not seem what it should. In Chemnitz we had so much to look forward to, we had a goal to reach (ie. freedom) and it always looked touch and go whether we would ever reach it. Now we have reached it the savour seems to have gone out of everything, for not only has the excitement gone out of our lives but also the goal has been passed and we await a new one to give us a future to look forward to.

MONDAY JUNE 25

Visited Queens Park and watched the boating in Thompson's park, don't yet feel fit enough to do any rowing myself. Went to Aunty Janey's for tea and listened to a play on the wireless at night.

TUESDAY JUNE 26

Went to Duke Bar office and had a chat with Leonard. Went to Nelson in afternoon with Harold and walked back along river through Brierfield woods. Somebody was shooting at rabbits and a couple of shots whistled very close by us.

WED JUNE 27

Walked to Newchurch with Harold and visited Mrs. Dawson's. She had just returned from holiday at Fleetwood. Harold wasn't very well at night.

THURS JUNE 28

Very dull threatening day. Went to Savoy in afternoon. "American Romance" Brian Donlevy. Quite good. We went walk round Nelson golf links at night.

FRI JUNE 29

Harold and I went to Colne on the bus and walked over Catlow Bottoms to Haggate. Rained a bit but quite a good walk. At night went to Abel Street School to hear Burke the Labour candidate speak.

SAT JUNE 30

Was going to the cricket match but the weather turned out very bad. Listened to "The Planets" on the gramophone in afternoon.

SUMMARY OF WEEK

Still feel in a very muddled state of mind. The thought of working at the BBS (Burnley Building Society) for the rest of my life seems futile and appalling. What other course is left open to me requires more concentration than I can, at the moment, apply.

SUNDAY JULY 1

Weather again not promising. Read up at the garden in afternoon. Went for walk with Harold at night.

MONDAY JULY 2

Went with Harold to the Empire in the afternoon. "Arsenic and Old Lace". Absolute scream. In the evening went long walk round Roggerham and through Hag Wood along Heasandford river. Very pleasant.

TUESDAY JULY 3

Saw Leonard at Duke Bar office in the morning. Meant to go to Whalley with Harold in afternoon but bus was full so went to Shore and walked down by the Organ Rocks and the wood to Todmorden where we caught a bus back home. Went to Major Milne's meeting at Mechanics with Alice and Harold. Much fun and heckling. Grammar School master attempting to ask a question was shouted down by Milne aided by his mike.

WEDNESDAY JULY 4

Depressing day. Had a read at the garden in afternoon. Saw Harold off at night, his leave having finished.

THURSDAY JULY 5

Voted for Mr. Burke (Soc) in the General Election. Had tea with Leonard Dewhurst at his house and went with him to the Bowling Club at night.

FRIDAY JULY 6

Haven't been feeling well for two or three days and awoke this morning again feeling very much unrefreshed.

SATURDAY JULY 7

Alice, Dad and Mother set off on their holiday to Morecambe. Went to the office and tackled Mr. Hirst about my post war position. He tried to be reassuring but wasn't very concrete. Returned home and made the dinner (fried chops, garden peas, potatoes), Harold coming over at 1.40 p.m. Went to garden in afternoon and had talk with Jack Ashton. Had a walk at night and listened to Yehudi Menuhin play Beethoven's violin concerto on the wireless.

SUNDAY JULY 8

Made dinner again – fried chops, scollops, potatoes and peas. Spent most of the day in the garden reading, it being too close to walk far.

MONDAY JULY 9

Travelled to Morecambe to stay with the folks. Train crowded with
day trippers going to Blackpool. Arrived Morecambe 12.30 p.m. In
afternoon went with Alice, Mary and Norah to hear the military band.
In evening went to play "Grouse in June" – very good. After show I
took Mary on the Dodgems – just the job.

TUES JULY 10

In morning went with girls on motor boat. Went to Lancaster in
afternoon with Mother, Dad and the girls and looked round the castle.
In evening had a few drinks with Mr. Clarke, had a long walk on the
front and a good talk.

WED JULY 11

Went up to Morecambe Head; it rained a little. Raining in afternoon,
so went to Tower cinema. Cronin's "Keys of the Kingdom". Very good.
Caught the 6.40 train back. Change at Lancaster, usual congestion at
Preston. Arrived home 10.30. Auntie Leu and Uncle Dick came up to
see me.

END OF LEAVE –
BACK TO COSFORD

THURS JULY 12

End of my leave. Arranged by phone to meet Peter at Wolverhampton. Packed my kit and caught the 12.12 to Wolverhampton. Didn't realise I had put on my civvy tie till I was on the station. Met Peter in Wolverhampton and proceeded to Cosford. Saw a lot of our old kregie friends, Bernard, Jimmie. Had a few drinks in sergeant's mess at night.

FRI JULY 13

Preliminary medical in morning. I had to have another X-ray. Few drinks in Sergeant's mess, then went to camp cinema (excellent place) and saw Chas Boyer and Irene Dunne in "Together Again". Very amusing.

SAT JULY 14

Missed breakfast in morning. Full medical Board in afternoon. All under 36 release group and having done over 12 months POW service get their release. I am 32 group. The M.O. was dissatisfied with my physical condition so I am being sent to the Medical Rehabilitation Unit to recuperate. Damned nuisance. Peter got through alright. One of the MO's examining the body was a woman of about 25, but I missed her. The eye specialist gave me a thorough examination as I told him of the spots and lines that have been appearing in front of my vision for some years. He assured me that nothing was fundamentally wrong. Thank God for that. Peter took Bernard and myself to see Jim Heyes. We went to his club, an excellent place, and had a talk and a few drinks. Had supper at Jim's home and just caught the last bus 10.55; thought we had missed the last train but there was another at 11.20.

SUNDAY JULY 15

Went to Jim Heyes again with Peter and Bernard. Missed the last bus again and had to walk to the station; missed our train and had to wait for the 12.40 a.m.

MONDAY JULY 16

Reported to the M.R.H. in the morning. After a wait of two hours saw M.O. in afternoon. He tested my muscular reaction and graded me IIID which means I will be here for 3 weeks, till I get up to V grade. Went to camp cinema at night. "Laura". Quite good. Peter and Bernard went home today.

TUESDAY JULY 17

Went round workshops in morning and took a walk, swimming, and short walk in afternoon. Grand baths. Went walk round countryside with Jock Hey and Jack Topping in evening. Very nice country.

WEDNESDAY JULY 18

P.T. in the morning, medicine balls etc. and a pet talk on the course. Played touch rugby in afternoon after which we went for a swim. In the evening Jock Hey and myself went to Wolves and saw a play "Acacia Avenue". Amusing. Had a plaice and chips supper after the show.

;A drink, then off back to the camp. Most of the chaps and a lot of the girls get into a terrible drunken condition.

THURSDAY JULY 19

P.T. and game of basketball in the morning. P.T. and a spot of cricket in the afternoon till the rains came. Did a lot of vaulting at P.T. and had a go with the bat at cricket. Every muscle in my body aches just now.

FRI JULY 20

Basketball and swimming in the morning. Collected my pass in the afternoon and travelled home. Changed at Wolves, Stoke and Manchester. Arrived home 10 p.m. 7 hours travelling.

SAT JULY 21

Harold came in afternoon. Listened to the "Prom" and went to Tivoli with Alice. "Christmas Holiday" Very poor film. Deanna Durbin – gone off.

SUN JULY 22

Rained most of the morning. Had to travel back by the 3.32 from Central Station. Met one of my cronies in Manchester. Arrived Wolves 9.45. Had a drink and a good supper. Arrived Cosford 11.30. Terrible amount of loose women, drinking and walking the streets of Wolves.

MON JULY 23

P.T. etc. in morning. Cinema in afternoon. Went pleasant walk to Albrighton with Jock Hey. Met Les Bruce there and had a few drinks.

Tues July 24

P.T. and games in morning. Trip to Owens' manufacturers in afternoon. Saw all the processes of making steel life boats, aeroplane parts, refrigerators etc. Had a nice tea at Owens' expense and had a look round a prefabricated house. Good idea but not very good outside appearance. Went to Queensberry Club at night in Birmingham. Played table tennis, watched dancing, had a few drinks.

Wed July 25

Saw M.O.in morning and got moved up to IVD. Had two games of basketball. Watched football match in afternoon. P.T.I's beat kreigies 4-3. Cinema at night. "Practically Fours" Fred Murray and Claudette Colbert. Very good.

Thurs July 26

P.T. in the morning, swimming in the afternoon. Went to camp cinema in the evening. Laurence Olivier and Joan Fontaine in "Rebecca". Seen it before but still good.

Fri July 27

General Election results. Socialists returned with huge majority Stremmons. P.T. vaulting etc. and games basketball in morning. Saw Ben Vickery, Tom Williams and Ted Ransom. Went to Jim Hayes' in evening. Went to his club, played snooker and drank. Stayed the night at their house.

SAT JULY 28

Jim had gone to office when I got up. Had good breakfast, chatted a
while with Joan and then departed. Walked to station and just caught
a train 11.30 a.m. Had a sleep in the afternoon and went into Wolves
again at night, the empty barrack nearly driving me nuts. Went to
Grand Theatre where the rep. company enacted "Michael and Mary"
A.A. Milnes. Very good. Had supper at a restaurant, a drink and then
caught 10.40 back to camp. Wolves full of bad types. Fearfully browned
off today.

SUN JULY 29

Stayed in bed till 10.30. Walked to Albrighton with Tom Tyler and
John Philby and then took train to Wolves. Had meal at Lyon's
and afterwards went to Odeon. "Captain Fury". Had a few drinks and
returned to camp.

MON JULY 30

P.T. in morning. Cinema in afternoon. Spent evening in Sergeant's mess
reading and drinking.

TUES JULY 31

P.T. and game of hockey. Swimming in afternoon. Went to camp cinema
at night. "Love Story". Some good piano music in it.

WED AUG 1

P.T. and games. Wrote letters at night.

THURS AUG 2

Medical Interview in the morning. Moved up into VB. Had a long pleasant walk in the sunshine. Swimming in the afternoon. Went walk with Jock Hey to Wolverhampton. Had a drink then went to the Grand Theatre and saw an excellently acted play, "Missing Believed Married". Had a good supper at the Central restaurant, a walk, then back to camp.

FRI AUG 3

Swimming in morning. Sun bathing in afternoon. Beautiful day, just like Italian weather. Went to camp cinema at night. "Man in Half Moon Street".

SAT AUG 4

Set off for home 8.20 arriving there at 4.20 having long waits at Wolves and Manchester. Went up to garden with Harold at night. Very hot again today.

SUN AUG 5

Had a good walk over the golf links finishing up at the garden at night.

MON AUG 6

In the afternoon went to Padiham on the bus, walked to Sabden, by-passed Higham and came over the fields to the bottom of Barden. Had tea at Auntie Janie's with Harold and Alice.

TUES AUG 7

Rained all morning. Set off by 3.48 train; had a meal at Crewe, arrived in Wolves 8.30 p.m. but had to wander round till 9.40.

WED AUG 8

Back to the old routine. P.T. in morning. Went to inter unit Sports meeting in afternoon. Mile race very exciting. 4 M.R.H. won easily with the P.T. school second, officer cadet school came in a bad last. Bless 'em. Went to camp cinema at night. "Man in the Iron Mask".

THURS AUG 9

Russia declares war on Japan. Much speculation on the new atomic bomb. I think it probable that they will invent something to destroy the world eventually. I have a terrible cold. Did P.T. in morning but dodged off in the afternoon. Wrote letters and went to bed early.

FRI AUG 10

Should have gone swimming but cold too bad. Had medical after break and was discharged as fit; have to report to Squadron office on Monday morning. Weather wonderful today. In the evening I walked to Albrighton and arrived back in time for supper and the cinema.

SAT AUG 11

Failed to arise for breakfast but managed dinner in good time. Sunbathed and read Shaw's "St. Joan" in the afternoon. Went to Wolves in the evening and saw the rep. company perform Ian Hay's "Little Ladyship" at the Grand Theatre. Had a good supper at the Central restaurant, a walk round, and then back to camp.

SUN AUG 12

Managed to get up for breakfast. In afternoon went to Wolves with Philby and Tyler. Had a snack at Lyons' and then went to the Odeon and saw an amusing film. Had supper at Central restaurant and then returned to camp.

MON AUG 13

Went the rounds with a clearance chit in the morning. Transferred to hut in 106 P.R.C. in afternoon. Went to Albrighton at night with Jimmie Hamilton whom I saw for the first time this afternoon. We had a good yarn and a few drinks.

TUES AUG 14

Interviewed by the medical president in the morning and filled in a lot of forms etc. Interviewed by a welfare officer and decided to go to a resettlement camp. Went out with Jimmie to Albrighton in evening. Rather merry when we returned.

WED AUG 15

Japanese surrender announced 12 p.m. last night, bonfires were made during the night, the platform for the C.O. being burnt. I slept through all the revellings. Went to Hednesford and collected my civilian suit. Not bad. Pay parade in afternoon. Went to Penn to see Jim Hayes and wife. Big crowd and loudspeakers, lights, bonfires etc in Wolverhampton.

THURS AUG 16

Had my release medical in morning. Went with Reggie Harmer into
Wolves at night and went to cinema, "They were Sisters". Very good.
Couldn't get a drink anywhere when we came out. Much revelling,
dancing, fireworks in the centre. Two girls picked us up and eventually
saw us off at the station in the customary manner.

HOME ON LEAVE

Fri Aug 17

Get off for home. Arrived Manchester 11 a.m. and put my kit in the left luggage office. Had a good walk round and went to a cinema. Bing Crosby in "Over the Waves". Caught the 8.05 train and arrived home 10.30.

Sat Aug 18

Did not get up very early. Harold came in the afternoon. Had records on in the evening.

SUMMARY

Am gravely troubled about the future. In a quandary as to whether to go back to the B.B.S. or to try something new and more satisfying. Will have to make a decision shortly.

Sun Aug 19

Went walk round Heasandford in afternoon with Harold. Granville, Evelyn and Susan were in when we returned. Harold and I played cricket with Susan and later took her on the children's playground down Barden. Had records on later.

MON AUG 20

Went to see Aunty Janie and Aunty Sally and late afternoon took mother up to Uncle Ike's, Aunty Alice wasn't in.

TUES AUG 21

Was going to go to Old Trafford to see the Test Match but it was raining all morning so I stayed in. Went to Odeon in afternoon. Noel Coward's "Blythe Spirit". Very amusing and exceedingly well acted.

WED AUG 22

Caught the 8.40 to Manchester the day being fine. Went first to the Albert Hall where I asked John Barbirolli (not knowing then that it was he) where I could get a ticket for the concert at night. He directed me to Halle booking office where I obtained one. I then went to Old Trafford for the last day of the Test. 4 wickets fell before lunch, the Aussie's requiring 5 runs to avert an innings defeat with 3 wickets to fall. Cristofani put England in a tricky position by scoring a brilliant century. By quick scoring England managed to pull off the victory, scoring 141 for 3. Hatton 29 and Robertson 37. Played nice correct cricket and Edrich, 45 not out, quickly knocked up the required runs, Hammond being rather subdued. I managed to get to the concert just in time. Oberon overture. "Song of Summer", Delius, beautiful, Piano Concerto A minor (Schumann) soloist Iso Elinson who was capable without giving the work full justice, Siegfried Idyll and Francesca de Rimini, Tchaikovsky. Very good on the whole.

THURS AUG 23

Practised the piano at which I am not gifted. Went the Roxy with Frank who is on holiday. "To Have and Have Not". Humphrey Bogart. Story by E. Hemmingway. Very good.

FRI AUG 24

Rained more than somewhat today. Went with Frank to Aunty Alice Ann's where Philip told a lot of his far-fetched yarns.

SAT AUG 25

In afternoon I went to Bury to meet Harold. Walked over Radcliffe and had tea at Harold's landlady's. Her daughter Elsie is blind. After tea we took a pleasant walk by the reservoir catching the bus in Bury at 8.30.

SUN AUG 26

Nice day again. In afternoon Harold and I went to Aunty Sally's and went a walk up Carr Road, Weckly and Brierfield Woods. After tea mother and Dad turned up with the bad news that Alice had had a bicycle accident when going to Rimmington and had been taken to Reedyford hospital. I took Mother to the hospital. Alice looked very dazed having broken her collar bone and having head injuries. She half seemed to recognise us which is a good sign.

MON AUG 27

Took Aunty Janey up to Aunty Annie's in the afternoon. I went down to Aunty Alice's in the evening; her improvement from the stroke is very slow.

TUES AUG 28

Rang up the hospital, Alice's condition satisfactory. Went walk round golf links with Frank.

WED AUG 29

Went to the office and had interviews with Mr. Hirst, Mr. Harvey and Jack Parkinson. They seem quite anxious to have me back but I couldn't get anything definite about salary. Mr. Hirst talked about London office about which I cannot arouse any enthusiasm. I am still in a quandary as to what to do for the best. Went to Reedyford. Alice improving.

THURS AUG 30

Went to the office and had a talk with J.P. about the forthcoming training scheme for the Building Society's Institute.

FRIDAY AUG 31

Went to Empire at night. "Music For Millions" with Jose Ituebe. Very good.

SAT SEPT 1

Went to Oldham to meet Peter outside the rugby ground as prearranged. He didn't turn up so I went on to the ground just before the kick-off. Bradford North won easily 22-0. Kitchen and Battew were outstanding. I didn't spot Peter after the game so I went on the station where he turned up; he had missed a connection at Rochdale arriving at the ground at 3.45. we went into Oldham and had a meal, after which we caught a train to Rochdale where we had a wait of an hour for a

train. We went into Rochdale and had a few drinks. I had to change
again at Todmorden.

SUN SEPT 2

Went to hospital with Harold. Alice not eating much but looks a little
better. We walked back home along the canal bank.

MON SEPT 3

Went up to garden in the morning.

TUES SEPT 4

Bernard Scholfield came over from Todmorden at dinner time. I took
him a walk round by Runklehurst and Heasandford before he caught
the bus back to Todmorden. He is going to the Resettlement camp at
Scarborough tomorrow.

WED SEPT 5

In uniform I managed to buy some cigarettes; the first I have been able
to buy for a fortnight.

THURS SEPT 6

In the morning went to Elgin Mufy Company for a hospital
recommend. In afternoon set off with Uncle Dick to get Alice's bike.
Buses were full at Barden top so we walked up to Harpers where we got
a bus to Barley. We set off on the Downham Road and soon got a bus
which took us almost to the house. We had to wheel the bike all the
way back stopping for tea at Nutter's, Barley. It was a beautiful day and
I enjoyed the walk. Had supper at Aunt Jannie's

FRI SEPT 7

Did some weeding in the garden in the morning. Went into town and bought some books. Listened to the Prom at night. Beety's violin concerto. Had my first piano lesson.

SAT SEPT 8

Went to Bradford. Missed the 9.55 a.m. to Halifax so had to catch the Hebden Bridge bus. Had dinner at the Squires' where I made the acquaintance of Wendy Squires who accompanied us to the rugby match. Wigan defeated Bradford North 17-8. Wigan too lively and keen for Northern. Had to change buses at Bradford, Halifax, Hebden Bridge and Todmorden. Arrived home 10.30 p.m.

SUN SEPT 9

Went with Harold to hospital. Alice much better now sitting up. Walked back on canal bank.

MON SEPT 10

Practised piano in morning. Went into town in afternoon bought some books.

TUES SEPT 11

Went up to the garden in the morning. Practised piano in afternoon.

WED SEPT 12

Garden in morning. Went to Reedyford with Mother to see Alice who is recovering nicely.

THURS SEPT 13

Went to the Food Office for ration cards and managed to bag 40 fags, having to go to six shops for them. Went to Uncle Tom's for tea.

FRI SEPT 14

Garden in the morning. Went to the office in the afternoon and had talks with various of the staff.

SAT SEPT 15

Went to Halifax in the afternoon. Had a long wait at Hebden Bridge due to bus queues and so missed Peter at Halifax. I saw him as soon as I got on Halifax rugby ground. Halifax defeated Barrow 10-2. We had a meal in Halifax and a drink after which we returned to our various homes. Peter is going to work in Bristol on Tuesday.

SUN SEPT 16

Went to Reedyford with Harold in afternoon. Alice seemed a lot better. We walked back home.

MON SEPT 17

In the afternoon I went with Harold, who is on leave, to Roughlea first taking bus to Higherford. Very nice walk, weather brightening up later on.

TUES SEPT 18

Harold and I took bus to Harle Syke and went through the country to Nelson coming home over golf links.

WED SEPT 19

In morning went walk round Runklehurst. Weather deteriorating. Practised piano 2 hours in afternoon.

THURS SEPT 20

Harry came up in the morning. Surprise. Went walk round Extwistle Hall in afternoon with Harold. We went to the Odeon at night. Chas Laughton in "Suspect". Very good.

FRI SEPT 21

Bus to Summit and walked on the moorland road towards Bacup and cut over the moors to Burnley Road and caught bus at Towneley.

SAT SEPT 22

Showers all day. Went to the football match, Burnley vs Bury. Burnley were defeated 3-2 after leading 2-1 at half time. Gardner played very well at outside right.

SUN SEPT 23

Horrible day raining on and off all day. Stayed and practised, listened to wireless.

MON SEPT 24

Not a very promising day but risked a walk from Colne to Higherford and picked a lot of blackberries. Kept fine whilst we were out. We went to Aunty Janie's for supper.

TUES SEPT 25

Intended to go to Clitheroe with Harold and Aunty Janey but we missed the bus and took the bus to Todmorden instead. Went in the park and museum. A cake, sandwich and cup of tea cost us $1/3_d$ a piece. Had supper at Aunty Janey's.

WED SEPT 26

Harold and I went to Chadwick's as arranged. Harry soon turned up and we listened to records and chatted. A good tea then more records and talk.

THURS SEPT 27

In the morning I met Harry in the centre and we went to the office where we were supplied with tea at 10.45 and OXO at 12. Had to collect a ration card at the food office. Rained most of the day so Harry, Harold and myself went to the Odeon and saw "Way to the Stars" – Air Force picture. Not bad. Practised piano in evening.

FRI SEPT 28

Went to Duke Bar office in the morning and saw Leonard and Mr. Dickinson. Harry came in later. Went walk with Harold in the afternoon round Worsthorne. Met Harry in town at night intending to see Joe and Fred Davis but they do not perform till week on Monday. We went to variety show at the Palace instead.

SAT SEPT 29

Intended to go to Keighley to see rugby match but Mother was not well at dinnertime, so I stayed in till Harold arrived at 1.40; we went walk along river to Brierfield and back along canal bank.

SUN SEPT 30

Went to Harry's in afternoon; Mary was over on weekend. The three of us went to the empire where the Municipal orchestra were playing. Not very satisfying. Louis Kenter soloist was brilliant and Joan Creso was quite good.

MON OCT 1

Harry came in afternoon. We played bowls on Queen's Park and got plenty of advice from old stagers. Listened to a few records after tea, then we went to the Grand where there were two poor pictures showing.

TUES OCT 2

Practised piano in the afternoon and had a lesson in the evening. Had supper at Aunty Janey's – a good do.

WED OCT 3

Went to office with Harry who had interview with Mr. Hirst whilst I chatted with Marjorie and Anne. We went to Towneley in the afternoon and had a game of bowls. I practised piano in the evening.

Thurs Oct 4

Went to Preston with Harry. Visited the art gallery and the park and then went to Victoria Hospital where Mary showed us round the various departments. Mary came out with us in the evening. We dined at the New Vic and went to the empire to see "The Alibi". After the show we went back to the hospital where Mary made us toast and coffee. Left Preston 9.08 arrived Burnley 10.30.

Fri Oct 5

Met Harry in the afternoon. Intended to go swimming but school children were in the baths, so we listened to some records at Beattie's.

Sat Oct 6

Alice's birthday. Went to reserve match and saw Burnley defeated by Manchester United reserves 3-2. Johnny Hanlon who was at IVB was playing for United. Tea at Harry's. Mary, Harry and myself went to Pentridge at night. "Constant Nymph", Charles Boyer, Joan Fontaine. Very good.

Sun Oct 7

Went walk round golf links with Harold in afternoon. Very nice weather just now. Went down to bus station with Harold in the evening.

Mon Oct 8

In the morning had a haircut and went up to the garden. Played bowls on Queen's Park with Harry in the afternoon. Saw Joe and Fred Davis give snooker and billiards exhibition at the mechanics. Very clever.

Tues Oct 9

Went to the garden and helped Dad move the chrysants from garden to greenhouse. Good work done. Went to mixed bathing at central baths with Harry. Did a length straight off and did a bit of diving. Enjoyed it very much. Had coffee and biscuits at the Lubeck after. Practised piano in the evening.

Wed Oct 10

Raining all morning. Wrote letter and practised in afternoon. Went to Aunty Janey's for supper.

Thurs Oct 11

Went into town for ration cards. Practised piano for 2½ hours in the afternoon. Rained most of the day.

Fri Oct 12

Went to the Odeon in the afternoon. Not bad. "Tomorrow the World" Fredrick March. Alice got up for short time. Had piano lesson at night.

Sat Oct 13

Harold came in the afternoon and we went to the football match Burnley making a goalless draw with Preston North End.

Sun Oct 14

Went for short walk with Harold in the morning, and took Alice out for a short while before dinner. Went a walk round by Runklehurst and

Heasandford in the afternoon. Beautiful weather for this time of the year.

Mon Oct 15

Took Alice short walk in morning and afternoon, practised piano in the evening.

Tues Oct 16

Short walk with Alice before dinner. Bernard Scholfield came in the afternoon full of enthusiasm about his teacher's course. Took him walk round Runklehurst to the centre via Queen's Park. We had coffee and a sandwich at the Lubeck after which Bernard caught bus back home. Spent evening practising piano with moderate success.

Wed Oct 17

Short walk with Alice in morning. Went walk down Robinson Lane and along the river in the afternoon. Went to Aunty Janey's for supper. Sausage, apple sauce and mashed potatoes. Lovely grub.

Thurs Oct 18

Had walk in afternoon – Crescent, King's Causeway, golf links, Harle Syke. Went with Dad to the Odeon. "Henry V" Laurence Olivier. Acting excellent.

Fri Oct 19

Practised in the afternoon and had bath at night.

SAT OCT 20

Went to Duke Bar office in the morning and had a talk with Mr. Dickinson. Went walk with Harold in the afternoon. Alice, Harold and myself spent the evening with Florence and Mary at Tattersall's. Very nice supper. Mr. & Mrs. Jones came to our house at night.

SUN OCT 21

Good spell of weather broke today. Rained all afternoon. Practised piano. Went down to Aunty Janey's at night.

MON OCT 22

Morning of inactivity. Practised in afternoon, then took shoes for repair, bought shirt and tie, ordered records at Beattie's. Writing at night.

TUES OCT 23

Rained most of the day. Went with Alice to Batley's.

WED OCT 24

Went to North Street baths in the evening with Uncle Dick who showed me the correct strokes. Had supper at Aunty Leu's afterwards.

THURS OCT 25

Weather been terrible all week. Rainy and windy. Went to Aunty Janey's for supper.

FRI OCT 26

Went into town, called at Refuge Assurance Company. Saw George
Sutton who has been a prisoner in Japan. He looks pretty seedy. Went
to the Roxy to see "Magnificent Obsession". Not bad. Collected my
repaired shoes, bought some plaice for supper, and a painting book for
Susan's birthday.

SAT OCT 27

Went to Evelyn's with Granville in the car and gave Susan her present.
I went to football match in afternoon. Burnley 1 Blackburn Rovers 4.
A terrible game.

SUN OCT 28

Weather not very nice but went walk with Harold in the afternoon.
Had some records on at night. Beethoven's 4th Symphony.

MON OCT 29

Practised in the afternoon. Wrote letters at night. Rained all day.

TUES OCT 30

Went down to Aunty Janey's in the morning and had dinner with Alice.
Went walk in afternoon and saw John Wadsworth an old schoolmate.
Called in at home where the Bishop called and talked to Alice and
myself. Went down to Aunty's for tea and wrote letters.

WED OCT 31

Collected Alice at Aunty Janey's and took her to Thompson's Park where we had tea and cakes. Had tea at home and practised.

THURS NOV 1

Alice came home today; went walk in afternoon.

FRI NOV 2

Went walk over to Brunshaw and dropped in on Granville and Evelyn and had tea with them. After tea we took Susan to the Empire to see "Thunderhead", quite a good film.

SAT NOV 3

Went to Halifax to see the Yorkshire League Cup final between Bradford North and Wakefield Town. Had arranged to meet Peter but missed him at the bus station. Bumped into Mrs. Squires in the passage behind the stand – what a fortunate coincidence – she guided me to Peter and Mr. Squires. We all went back to their home in Bradford where we had a good tea. Norah was there. I managed to get home at 10.30.

SUN NOV 4

Went walk with Alice in the morning and with Harold in the afternoon.

MON NOV 5

Went to Florence's marriage with Jimmy Wolfe an American soldier – he seems quite a nice bloke. We had tea at the Sunday School. Quite a large party of us and we had fun and games.

TUES NOV 6

Went to Aunty Janey's for supper having practised and had a walk in afternoon.

WED NOV 7

Had walk with Alice down Robinson Lane in the afternoon. Piano lesson at night.

THURS NOV 8

Went into town in the morning for ration cards and collected my Pathetique Sonata records at Beattie's. Paul Eardly visited us late afternoon.

FRI NOV 9

Went into town with Alice in the afternoon.

SAT NOV 10

Went to Swinton to see Lancashire (17) vs Yorkshire (16) rugby league match. Really excellent game. Spent the evening in Manchester. Saw Bette Davis in "The Great Lie". Took train two hours to get back.

NOV 11 SUNDAY

Nice day but cold. Went walk with Alice in the afternoon and then longer one with Harold.

Nov 12 Monday

Went walk round by Rookin's farm with Alice in the afternoon.

Nov 13 Tuesday

I have got a rotten bad cold.

Nov 14 Wed

I am getting more than somewhat restless due to this waiting game for the resettlement camp. Had I known that I would have had to wait so long I would not have applied for it.

Nov 15 Thurs

Went with Alice to Elgin and took her a walk round Glen View. Went Aunty Janey's for supper; meat pie, boiled onions and green peas.

Nov 16 Fri

I am now nicely immersed in cold.

Nov 17 Sat

Harold came in the afternoon and I went for walk with him. Last night I saw "Picture of Dorian Grey". Gruesome but good.

Nov 18 Sun

Did little of any moment all day. Harold went back at night.

Nov 19 Mon

Stayed in most of the day due to my cold which is slightly worse.

Nov 20 Tues

Went down to Aunty Janey's for dinner and tea, Alice is staying with her for a few days.

Nov 21 Wed

Went into town in the afternoon then went up to Chadwick's and was amazed to hear Harry has been working at the office for a fortnight. I was under the impression that he had gone back to his station and he was under the impression that I had gone to my resettlement camp. He did not come in till 8 p.m. as he had been working overtime. Had a good talk.

Nov 22 Thurs

Wrote to the RAF cancelling the resettlement course and asking for my release. I've been waiting 3 months for this damned course. Took Alice for a walk in the afternoon.

Fri Nov 23

Went into Head Office and saw Mr. Hirst who has recently been appointed secretary in Mr. Harvey's retirement. I offered to come to work at the office next week but he told me to wait and see if my release came through next week. Went with Harry to see "Barrett's of Wimpole Street" at the Savoy in the evening.

SAT NOV 24

Went to Joan Hartley's 21st birthday party at the Café Royal in the evening. What a feed. There were ten girls and three men, Harry and an RAF chap comprising the other two. We all went to the variety show at the Palace at night. After the show eight of us had tea and cake at Gwen's house.

SUN NOV 25

Harry came to tea. I played the piano but not very well.

MON NOV 26

Took Alice to Barley and after a walk we had tea at Nutter's. Very nice day.

TUES NOV 27

Went for a walk round Worsthorne with Harry in the afternoon. We called on Betty whom I have not seen since my return. She has a child but her husband was killed over in Holland. We had tea at Chadwick's and then went to the Empire to see "Song to Remember" with Paul Muni. "Life of Chopin". Very good.

WED NOV 28

In the morning, Alice, Aunty Janey and I went to Clitheroe; had dinner there and went a nice walk through the park in the afternoon. Lovely day for this time of the year. Returned home for tea.

Thurs Nov 29

In the afternoon I went over to Accrington to see Cecil Sharples. Had a good talk. They are however pretty straight at the office.

Fri Nov 30

Went to Head Office again and arranged to go to Head Office on Monday. Went with Alice to Empire in the afternoon. A film worth seeing, or rather hearing again.

Sat Dec 1

Went to meet Harold at Radcliffe. I had my dinner in Bury. Met Harold and we then proceeded to Manchester where we heard a piano recital given by Hegwig Stein at the Houldsworth Hall. We had tea at Woolworth's and then went to a News Cinema. Travelled back home via Whitefield, Bury and Rawtenstall. Arrived home about 10 p.m.

Sun Dec 2

Mary came to tea. I saw Harold off on the bus at night.

Mon Dec 3

My first day at the office for nearly 5½ years. Got a steady job checking bonus calculations on shares. Office closes at 6 p.m. on Mondays. Played table tennis after work, a lot of the girls play. I found myself left with five of them at the finish. I played very well considering my lack of practise.

TUES DEC 4

Still doing the bonus calculations. Half day closing. Terrible day. Windy and raining. Practised piano in afternoon. Wrote letter in the evening.

WED DEC 5

Same job. Worked overtime till 7 o'clock then played table tennis. Have to go to Cosford tomorrow for my discharge so packed a few belongings.

BACK TO COSFORD
FOR DISCHARGE

THURS DEC 6

Arrived Manchester 12 a.m. and had dinner at a services club. Arrived Cosford at about 6.30 p.m. and found that I had got next bed but one to Dobson of IVB. Received small slip of paper with which to report to Squadron office on Friday morning. Had a Guinness for supper and then went to camp cinema.

FRI DEC 7

Reported to Squadron office and received large sheet of paper requiring three signatures, Disposal Board, release Medical and Release Section. Obtained these in the morning and told to report to squadron office for clearance chit in the morning. Went into Wolverhampton at night and visited Joan and Jim Hayes. Jim did not come in till late but I had a good talk with them. Young Peter is a fine baby.

SAT DEC 8

Reported at Squadron office and told to report again Monday morning. What a bind. Went to Tettenhall in the afternoon and saw Wolves beat Nuneaton 12-9, Rugby Union. Not a bad game; Wolves backs quite good. Had tea in Wolves and then went to the Hayes'. Went to the club with Jim and played snooker most of the night. Won a bob. Knocked quite a bit of beer back but was not affected. Stayed night at Jim's slept on mattress in front of fire.

SUN DEC 9

Made the fire before Jim and Joan got up. Jim and myself took young Peter to get his photograph taken. Jim supported him with a cushion whilst I made him laugh. We all went to Joan's parents in the afternoon. On our return Jim and myself went to the club and had a couple of drinks. Returned to camp at 11 p.m.

MON DEC 10

Reported Squadron office and for the rest of the day a party of us were escorted round the camp getting cleared from all departments. Stores, pay office, medical etc. etc. Went to camp cinema at night.

TUES DEC 11

Off to Hednesford to get my release. Very efficient. Like going through a sausage machine. Follow the green arrows and eventually you come out a free man.

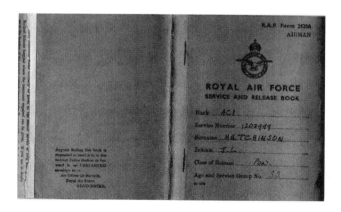

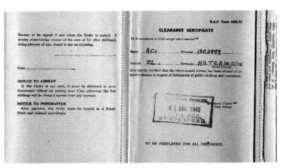

RETURN TO CIVILIAN LIFE

TUES DEC 11

Caught train at Stafford for home and got into same compartment as 3 WAAFS and 2 RAF all discharged today. One of the WAAFS was going to Nelson and was quite good looking; however I broke my journey at Manchester and had tea there. Went to Halle booking office and asked for a ticket for the concert, I got a 10/- ticket free of charge. Concert was very good especially Schubert's 9th and Bax's "Island of Than". The donor of my ticket (a doctor) came to speak to me at the interval. Train took 2¾ hours to get from Manchester to Burnley.

WED DEC 12

Went to food office in the morning and got my ration books etc. Called in the office in the afternoon and made arrangements for starting tomorrow.

THURS DEC 13

Started work, Ken Boys, Dick Lupton and Tom Parker are back and we form a new department "ex. serviceman's" section. We are doing the year end work, ledger balancing, calculating bonus and interest on share accounts etc. Worked overtime at night. Played table tennis after work.

FRI DEC 14

Work as usual. Monotonous, but we have fun between times. Quite a lot of the girls play table tennis in the evening now.

SAT DEC 15

After work went shopping with Harry. Harry came to our house in the evening and Florence also. We played billiards, I made 27 break.

SUN DEC 16

Went to work. Dick Lupton went to work with some mistletoe. Anne Mophet and Lilian Newton caught me unawares with it. Played table tennis. Margaret Oates refused to be caught by Dick.

TUES DEC 18

Worked overtime in the afternoon. Had tea at Redmans new café with Harry and then went to Harry's house., afterwards going to the Pentridge with Harry and Mr. and Mrs. Chadwick. "The Thin Man Comes Home" Will Powell and Myrna Loy.

WED DEC 19

Calculating accrued interest all day, overtime at night, then table tennis.

THURS DEC 20

Accrued interest again.

Fri Dec 21

Calculating interest arrears on mortgages for a change. Bit more interesting. Stomach in a bad way.

Sat Dec 22

Dick Lupton gives me his ticket for the dance at Belvedere club on Monday. After work Dick and myself took charge of some mistletoe belonging to Eileen Dillon. Caught Eileen, Margaret Oates, Marjorie Thornton and A.N. other. I don't know all the girls names yet. Listened to a record at Beattie's and bought it. Harold home on leave.

Sun Dec 23

Have a cold. Didn't go out except for short walk in the morning. Stomach terrible every morning.

Mon Dec 24

I was putting decorations up and I banged a nail through the gas pipe. Harold turned gas off at the main and I went to Blaylock's plumbers. None of the men were in and it looked like a bad job, but a sailor, Jack Blaylock, happened to be home on leave and volunteered to do the job. Did.

Met eight of the office girls outside the Wellington and proceeded to Belvedere club. Mr. Hirst was there, Bob Spencer, Tom Parker, Clifford Armstrong. I had many willing tutors at dancing and had a very enjoyable evening. In a mistletoe dance Eileen and myself were caught five times. Finished the evening with Margaret Oates and managed the St. Bernard waltz quite well. Took her home and her father met us half way.

TUES DEC 25

Stomach still in wretched condition, seems to have a pocket of air which makes me heave every morning. Didn't do the Xmas dinner real justice. Alice and myself went to Tattersall's for tea. We played games etc. Quite enjoyable.

WED DEC 26

Harold accompanied me to Halifax where we met Peter as arranged. Went to rugger match, Huddersfield beating Halifax 12-7. Good game. Huddersfield backs excelling. Fiddes scored a fine try running about half the length of the field. Couldn't get any eats in Halifax so returned home. Listened to "Messiah".

TUES DEC 27

Back to work. Much leg pulling about Monday. Played table tennis after overtime.

FRI DEC 28

Allocated bank credits in the morning. Finished work about 8.30 and had one game of table tennis.

SAT DEC 29

Was in the office all day from 8.45 a.m. to 12 p.m. having 2 (½ hour) breaks for dinner and tea and ¼ hour for supper. At night worked on adding machine, capitalising and taking out deposit ledgers. Home by taxi.

SUN DEC 30

Office at 1 p.m. – 12 p.m. Machining again. Had a bath at 1 a.m.

MON DEC 31

Office 1 p.m. – 5.15 p.m. Machining – extracting ledgers. Evening off. Played piano.

EPILOGUE

After his ordeals my Father returned to work at the Burnley Building Society eventually becoming Insurance Manager for the Society based at the Burnley office.

He met my future mother at work in December 1945 and they were married on April 1st 1950. They lived in Burnley all their lives where my sisters, Catherine and Helen, and I, were brought up.

April 1st 1950

Honeymoon to Scarborough

BUILDING SOCIETY COLLEAGUES WED

Two members of the staff of the Burnley Building Society were married at St. Peter's Church, Burnley, on Saturday.

The bridegroom was Mr. James L. Hutchinson, son of Mr. and Mrs. E. Hutchinson, of 295, Colne-road, Burnley, and his bride was Miss Margaret Oates, daughter of Mr. and Mrs. J. W. Oates, of 342, Brunshaw-road, Burnley.

Given away by her father, the bride was gowned in white figured satin and lace, with an embroidered veil held in place by a coronet of orange blossom. Her bouquet was of pink carnations.

She was attended by her cousin, Miss Irene Oates, who wore a dress of apple green silk covered with net and a headdress to match, and carried a bouquet of red carnations and white lilac.

Mr. Harry Chadwick (friend of the bridegroom) was best man and Messrs. Frank Tattersall (cousin of the bridegroom) and Smith Stanworth (cousin of the bride) were groomsmen.

The ceremony was performed by the Rev. S. Birtwell, Vicar of St. Luke's Church, Brierfield, and the bridegroom's father, Mr. E. Hutchinson, played the organ.

After a reception at the Sparrow Hawk Hotel, Burnley, the couple left for the honeymoon at Scarborough.

They are to live at 74, Morse-street, Burnley.

Included in the presents were two from the staff of the Burnley Building Society.

Dad wrote an article for the News Chronicle in September 1950, in which he recounts his respect and gratitude to one of his captors- Feldwebel Siebert.

NEWS CHRONICLE, Wednesday, September 27, 1950.

The Good Enemy

ORDINARY HEROES

IT was September, 1944. I was a prisoner of war in Germany, a member of a working party at Nieder-wiese, our work being the up-keep and repairing of the railway lines. The work was hard, the guards were glum, the civilian bosses were arrogant. The atmosphere was hostile and depressing.

A month of this and we were transferred to form a working party at Chemnitz, a big railway centre in S.E. Germany. It was here that we made the acquaintance of Feldwebel Siebert, who was in charge of the party.

I liked him from the start. On our first parade he looked at each man with a slight smile and a twinkle in his eye. I felt instinctively that here was a man of character, understanding and humour.

My first impression remains, for he did all in his power to make our position more bearable. He usually had a few words for us after the evening parades, his humour and paternal manner easing any bitterness that had grown with the years of captivity.

The raids

There were times when he lost his temper, but they were usually occasions when privileges he had gained for us were abused, or when S.S. men were present. The worst rage I saw him in was when there had been a case of food pilfering among the prisoners, and it was ironical to be reminded in such a strong manner of our duty to fellow countrymen.

Sunday was our day off from work and apart from the rest, there was little of interest to do. To relieve our boredom, the Feldwebel sometimes brought his projector to the camp and showed us some beautiful slides of his holidays, giving us a commentary with the interpreter's help.

Early in 1945 the raids came to S.E. Germany and, after Leipzig and Dresden, Chemnitz received its most devastating raid on the night of March 5. It left the city completely in flames. Herr Siebert marched us to safety in a wood on the outskirts. On April 14 he received orders to evacuate us to Marien-berg as the Americans were very near. Instead he marched us into the city and hid us in a cellar for the day.

We last saw him on April 15, some three weeks before our liberation. The Americans had been shelling the city for almost a week, and Feldwebel Siebert announced his intention to get through to the American lines and inform them of our position.

Whether he was arrested by the S.S. for desertion or whether he got through to the Americans I don't know, but he could wish for no greater compliment than that all his prisoners wished him well as much for his sake as their own.

J. L. HUTCHINSON, 24, Morse-street, Burnley.

Dad was invited to the local premiere of the film "The Great Escape" and featured along with fellow POWs in a news article printed in September 1963.

My father sadly passed away whilst walking with his life-long friend, Peter Squires, with whom he had shared so many hardships during their time as POWs. They were on their way to watch me play football at the local council pitches in Towneley Park but never arrived, Peter told me that Dad asked him to pause a moment as if he was going to tie a shoe lace, he collapsed to the floor suffering a severe and fatal heart attack.

JRNLEY EXPRESS AND NEWS, SEPTEMBER 25, 1963.

'THE GREAT ESCAPE' – THEY WERE THERE

DURING the last war, many thousands of British prison-ers passed through German POW camps, a few of those prisoners—some from Stalag Luft III, were at the Odeon cinema, Burnley, on Monday for the local premiere of 'The Great Escape," the film story of the largest and most effective mass breakout of POW's in military history—the escape from Stalag Luft III.

The Mayor and Mayoress of Burnley (Ald. and Mrs J. Lord) were among the ex-POW's who were guests of the cinema's manager, Mr Roland Jones, at a reception before the film was shown.

And what did the men who were actually in the camp think about the film? Apart from a small amount of Hollywood glamour, some were amazed at the way the appearance of atmos-phere of the camp had been re-created.

PICTURE shows the ex-POW's with the Mayor and Mayoress, and the manager of the cinema. From left, back row, Messrs E. Bellis, A. Thornton, G. Horn, J. A. Witherspool, R. Ashworth, W. Sharpe, R. Carter. Seated: Mr Roland Jones (manager), Mr P. Davity, the Mayoress, the Mayor, Mr J. A. A. Cakebread, Mr J. L. Hutchinson. Front row: Messrs T. C. Clucas, L. A. Bone and W. Marshall.

A FILM THAT WILL REVIVE MEMORIES

TWENTY-THREE ex - prisoners of war, 16 of whom were imprisoned in Stalag Luft III, will go to the Odeon Cinema, Burnley, on Monday to see "The Great Escape," the film of the mass outbreak from the notorious prison camp.

Mr L. Jones, manager of the Odeon, has traced the men through Mrs Alice Heap, of Huf-ling-lane, who, during the war, as secretary of the Burnley and district Prisoners of War Rela-tives Association, was responsible for tracing prisoners and bring-ing news of them to their families. Mrs Heap is also being invited to see the film.

The men who have been invited are: Messrs Will Marshall, Richard Ashworth, Robert Atkin-son, Phillip Bates, Edward Bellis, David Bentley, Lawrence Arthur Bone, Denis Leonard Brewer, George Stanley Burnett, John Alfred Cakebread, Ronald Carter, Frank Richard Chadwick, Thomas Clucas, George Horne, James Leslie Hutchinson, Anthony Brian Kidson, Roland Phillips, Walter Sharp, Richard George Shaw, Alan Thornton, Kenneth Wood-cock, Jack Wotherspoon and James Rawson.

Collapsed while walking

A MAN who spent the whole of his working life with the Burnley Building Society has died suddenly.

Mr James Leslie Hutchinson, from Cliviger, was out walking with a friend when he collapsed and died on Saturday. He was 68.

Mr Hutchinson, a Burnley man born and bred, attended St Andrew's Junior School and then Burnley Grammar School. At the age of 17 he started work as a counter clerk at the Burnley Building Society and worked his way up the ladder of success until he became manager of the insurance department.

The only break in his employment came in 1940 when he became a radio officer with the RAF, stationed in Cyprus and North Africa during World War II. In 1942 he was captured by the enemy and held in prisoner of war camps in Italy and Germany.

It was on his return to the Burnley Building Society in 1945 that he met his future wife Margaret, whom he married in 1950.

On his retirement in 1980, Mr Hutchinson, a keen gardener, devoted more of his time to his hobbies, which included walking and classical music. A nature and animal lover, he was a treasurer of Burnley Horticultural Society, which he joined in 1953.

He also joined the Burnley Probus Club, where he acted as treasurer for four years and was a keen Burnley FC supporter, rarely missing a Turf Moor match.

He leaves a wife, daughters Catherine and Helen, and a son, Richard, who have been receiving letters from from all over the country from Mr Hutchinson's many friends and workmates.

The funeral is today at 3.30 p.m. at Burnley Crematorium and donations can be made to the Burnley Hospice Appeal.

Having transcribed my father's diaries I am in awe of the resilience he showed to come through these ordeals at an age when the majority of us would have been enjoying our formative years broadening our horizons, our circle of friends, and living normal lives. His time was spent mostly in squalid conditions with fellow servicemen, low on sustenance, with doubt, fear and uncertainty ever present.

During his imprisonment in Germany he was put to hard physical labour repairing the damage caused by the RAF for whom he was serving, and who were close to finishing his life during the constant bombing raids close-by. This hardship and deprivation did, however, provide a goal to aim for – release, which, when it arrived, left a huge void upon return to civilian life when he and some of his fellow prisoners found it difficult to find ambition and direction in their newfound freedom.

I hope you have found these factual accounts interesting and thought provoking, being my own father's records I found them both fascinating and at the same time alarming. My intention is now to donate the original diaries to the Royal Air Force Museum at Cosford, were I hope they will remain as a permanent record.

Richard Hutchinson

CONTACTS FROM THE WAR YEARS

Fellow Servicemen

Peter Squires	36 Kendall Avenue, Moorhead, Shipley, Yorks.
Bill H. Gardner	'Southways', Irnham Road, Minehead, Somerset.
Willie McNeish	39 Aspley Street, Glasgow, W1
Jock C. Hay	'Ellingowan', 30 Back Hilton Road, Aberdeen, Scotland.
Jim Hayes	61 Belmont Road, Penn, Wolverhampton.
Bernard Scholfiled	22 Stoney Royd Lane, Todmorden.
Alan Docker	Springbank, Carlton Road, Carlisle, Cumberland.
F. Tattersall	70 Haydn Road, Chaddesden, Derby.
Leslie J. Jordan	12 Blackpool Road, Preston.
Albert Brown	17 Wycliffe Road, Shipley, Yorks.
G.B. McCorry	97 Costons Lane, Greenford.
Stan Phipps	346 High Street, Cheltenham, Gloucestershire.
Ben H. Vickery	178 Holbrook Lane, Holbrooks, Coventry.
H.J. Clark	5 Wilton Drive, Glasgow, W1
T. Byrne	18 Taine Street, Hill Top, West Bromwich, Staffs.

Durban South Africa

Mr. & Mrs. J. S. Parr	11 Park Lodge Gardens, Berea, Durban, Natal, S.A.

Cyprus

Aliki A Crispi	5 Kimon Street, Printing Office, Nicosia, Cyprus.
Rebecca Savridon	6 Artemis Street, Nicosia, Cyprus.
Loulla Economides	4 Stassickrates Street, Nicosia, Cyprus.
Sophulla I. Charalambides ("Spitfire")	8 Aristotle Street, Nicosia, Cyprus.

Germany

Feldwebel Siebert	Unknown

FOOD PARCEL CONTENTS

Canadian

4oz Chai	14	5oz Prunes	6
½lb Sugar	12	8oz Soap	4
Klim	20 lb	12oz Bully	9
1lb Butter	17	10oz Meat Roll	10
Biscuits	16 lb	4oz Cheese	6
5½oz Chocolate	10	8oz Salmon	8
1lb Marmalade	15	3oz Sardines	6
Raisins	8	8oz Salt & Pepper	1

New Zealand

4oz Chai	14	Prunes	6
Malted Milk	10	Rabbit	14
Jam	10	Lamb & Peas	11
1lb Honey	15	10oz Cheese	14
1lb Butter	17	Peas 1lb 5ozs	11
Chocolate	10		

England No.18 North Row

2oz Chai	8	Sultanas	9
4oz Sugar	7	Soap	4
Nestles Milk	12	3oz Cheese	5
Cocoa	10	Paste	4
4oz Chocolate	9	Custard	4
Sweets	3	Beef & Dumplings	11

Apple Jelly	8	Bacon	12
½lb Marge	8	Bluns	6
Biscuits	12	Meat Roll	6

English 15 Bermondsey

2oz Chai	8	Soap	4
4oz Sugar	7	Apple Pud	12
Nestle Milk	12	Creamed Rice	9
4oz Chocolate	9	Beef & Veg	10
½lb Syrup	9	Bacon	12
½lb Marge	8	Tomatoes	5
Biscuits	12	Meat Gal	6
3oz Cheese	5		

English 16 Birmingham

8oz Chai	8	1lb Meat & Veg	10
4oz Sugar	7	½lb Pork Sausages	9
Nestle Milk	12	Tomatoes	5
4oz Chocolate	9	Meat Roll	10
½lb Syrup	9	3oz Cheese	5
½lb Marge	8	Cocoa	10
Biscuits	12	Soap	4
Fig Pud	14	Yorkshire Pud	8

English 15 Carnarvon

2oz Chai	8	1lb Palethorpes M&V	9
4oz Sugar	7	½lb Walls Meat Roll	6
Nestles Milk	12	Bacon	12
4oz Chocolate	9	Tomatoes	5
10oz Jam	8	Cheese	5
½lb Marge	8	Sultanas	10

| Biscuits | 12 | Chicken & Ham Paste | 2 |
| Soap | 4 | | |

English 16 Southall

Chai	8	1lb meat Veg & Rice	10
Sugar	7	Aston's Meat Roll	7
Milk	12	Jam Pudding	12
Choc	9	Pascall's Sweets	3
12oz Raspberry Jam	11	Cheese	5
Marge	8	Chicken & Ham Paste	3
Biscuits	12	Bacon	12
Soap	4	Tomatoes	5

English 18 Hitchin

Chai	8	Blackcurrant Puree	5
Sugar	7	Soap	4
Milk	12	Marmite Cubes(6)	4
Choc	9	Pascall's Sweets	3
Marge	8	Salmon	8
Biscuits	12	Muscatells	8
Harris' Meat Roll	10	Moi Mixed Veg	5
Marmalade	13	8oz Steak & Veg	5
Cheese	5	Custard Powder	3

English 17 London

Chai	8	Cheese	5
Sugar	7	Soap	4
Milk	12	Bacon	12
Choc	9	Tomatoes	5
Marge	8	Pascall's Sweets	3
Biscuits	12	Treacle Pud	13

Harris' Meat Roll	10	Irish Stew	7
Marmalade	13	Crab Paste	4
Ovaltine	8		

English 18 North Row

Chai	8	Mustard	5
Sugar	7	Soap	4
Milk	12	Sardine Paste	4
Choc	9	Pascall's Sweets	3
Marge	8	Bacon	12
Biscuits	12	Raisins	9
Harris' Meat Roll	10	Tomatoes	5
Grapefruit Marmalade	11	Beef & Tomato Pud	14
Cheese	5	Cocoa	10

Dumfries Scotch

Chai	8	Cheese	5
Sugar	7	Soap	4
Milk	12	Prawn Paste	4
Choc	9	1lb Sausages	15
Marge	8	Prunes	6
Biscuits	14	Diced Carrots	5
Harris' Meat Roll	9	1lb Beef & Veg	10
Lemon Curd	9		

X-mas Parcel

Chai	8	½lb Confectionary Sweets	9
Sugar (3 blocks)	10	1lb Cake	16
Milk ½ Tin	6	1lb Pudding	15
Choc	9	1lb Tomato Pud	12
¼lb Butter	11	1lb Mac & Braised Steak	12

| ½lb Choc Biscuits | 13 | Marmalade | 12 |
| Cheese | 5 | | |

Paddington 15

Chai	8	Cheese	5
Sugar	7	Soap	4
Milk	12	Salmon Paste	4
Choc	9	Carlton Pud	13
Marge	8	Beef & Tomato Pud	14
Biscuits	12	Tomatoes	5
Harris' Roll	10	Bacon	12
Marton's Marmalade	13		

Southall 17

Chai	8	Cheese	5
Sugar	7	Soap	4
Milk	12	Prunes	5
Choc	9	Pascall's Sweets	3
Marge	8	Macs Veg	5
Parton Biscuits	10	Palethorpes M&V	9
½lb Walls Meat Roll	6	Salmon	8
Morton's Marmalade	12	Cocoa	10
Yeastex	3		

North Row 15

Chai	8	Cheese	5
Sugar	7	Soap	4
Milk	12	Morton's Apple Pud	12
Choc	9	Meat & Rice	10
Marge	8	Salmon	8
Biscuits	12	Cocoa	10

Morton's Beef roll	8	Beans in Tomato	8
Marmalade	13		

Perth 16

Chai	8	Cheese	5
Sugar	7	Soap	4
Milk	12	6oz marmalade Pud	7
Choc	9	1 lb Beef & Carrots	10
Marge	8	Whole Carrots	6
½lb Healthy Life Biscs	12	Bacon	12
Harris' Meat Roll	9	Tin Oats	8
Bramble Jelly	11	Sweets	3
Bournvita	8		

Lea Green 15

Chai 2oz	8	Cheese	5
Sugar 4oz	7	Soap	4
Milk 14oz	12	Sultana Pud	14
Choc 4oz	9	Beef Casserole	10
Marge 8oz	8	Mixed Veg	5
Biscuits 8oz	12	Bacon	12
Lusty's Gal 10oz	10	Creamed Rice	9
Syrup 8oz	9		

Paddington 14

Chai	8	M&V 1lb	10
Sugar	7	Bramble Jelly	11
Milk	12	Cheese	5
Choc	9	Soap	4
Biscuits	12	Apple Pud	13
Marge	8	Pilchards 15oz	14

| Galantine | 8 | Egg Flakes 2oz | 5 |
| Tomatoes (½ size) | 4 | | |

Northampton 16

Chai	8	Syrup	9
Sugar	7	Cheese	5
Milk	12	Soap	4
Choc	9	Apple Pud	13
Biscuits	12	Egg Flakes	5
Marge	8	Tomatoes	5
Meat Roll	8	Bacon	12
Cocoa	10	Steak & Tomato Pud	14

Invalid Milk Parcel

2 tins Nestles	24	2oz Chocolate	4
½lb Horlicks	10	2 tins Cheese	
10			
Benger's Food	8	Bemax	6
Allenburn's Diet	10	2 Creamolas	10
4½oz Ovaltine	8	Creamed Rice	9
Ovaltine Tablets	5	Lemon Curd	9
Chivers Jelly	4	Egg Flakes	5

GLOSSARY

Kamsin	Hot South Westerly Wind from the Sahara.
Gharry	Horse drawn carriage, (but in this account Army transport vehicle).
Treacled	Walked slowly without purpose.
Scilly	Soup made from grain cereals.
Tiffin	Snack or light meal.
Klim	Dried milk.
Magasin	Storehouse.
Schlagel	Bucket elevators/conveyors.
Jinnbo	Tool used for setting rail lines.
Bensine	Petrol.
Feldwebel	"Field Usher" – non-commisioned officer.
Arbeit	Work or labour.
Kregies	Family of fellow prisoners.
Lager/lageret	Storehouse.